Learning and Teaching Across Cultures in
Higher Education

D1202299

Also by David Palfreyman

LEARNER AUTONOMY ACROSS CULTURES: Language Teaching Perspectives
(*editor with Richard Smith*)

Learning and Teaching Across Cultures in Higher Education

Edited by

David Palfreyman
Assistant Professor, Centre for Teaching and Learning
Zayed University, Dubai

and

Dawn Lorraine McBride
Assistant Professor, Faculty of Education
University of Lethbridge, Canada

Selection and editorial matter © David Palfreyman and
Dawn Lorraine McBride 2007
Chapters © the authors 2007

All rights reserved. No reproduction, copy or transmission of this
publication may be made without written permission.

No paragraph of this publication may be reproduced, copied or transmitted
save with written permission or in accordance with the provisions of the
Copyright, Designs and Patents Act 1988, or under the terms of any licence
permitting limited copying issued by the Copyright Licensing Agency, 90
Tottenham Court Road, London W1T 4LP.

Any person who does any unauthorized act in relation to this publication
may be liable to criminal prosecution and civil claims for damages.

The authors have asserted their rights to be identified as
the authors of this work in accordance with the Copyright,
Designs and Patents Act 1988.

First published 2007 by
PALGRAVE MACMILLAN
Houndmills, Basingstoke, Hampshire RG21 6XS and
175 Fifth Avenue, New York, N.Y. 10010
Companies and representatives throughout the world.

PALGRAVE MACMILLAN is the global academic imprint of the Palgrave
Macmillan division of St. Martin's Press, LLC and of Palgrave Macmillan Ltd.
Macmillan® is a registered trademark in the United States, United Kingdom
and other countries. Palgrave is a registered trademark in the European
Union and other countries.

ISBN-13: 978–0–230–54283–9 hardback
ISBN-10: 0–230–54283–2 hardback

This book is printed on paper suitable for recycling and made from fully
managed and sustained forest sources. Logging, pulping and manufacturing
processes are expected to conform to the environmental regulations of
the country of origin.

A catalogue record for this book is available from the British Library.

Library of Congress Cataloging-in-Publication Data

Learning and teaching across cultures in higher education / edited by
David Palfreyman and Dawn Lorraine McBride.
    p. cm.
Includes bibliographical references and index.
ISBN 0–230–54283–2 (alk. paper)
    1. Multicultural education. 2. Education, Higher—Cross-cultural
studies. 3. College teaching—Cross-cultural studies. I. Palfreyman,
David, 1964– II. McBride, Dawn Lorraine.

LC1099.L419 2007
378.1'2—dc22   2007023312

10 9 8 7 6 5 4 3 2
16 15 14 13 12 11 10 09 08

Printed and bound in Great Britain by
CPI Antony Rowe, Chippenham and Eastbourne

Contents

Part 2   Practice

List of Figures

List of Tables

Notes on the Editors and Contributors

David Palfreyman works at the Centre for Teaching and Learning at Zayed University, Dubai. His background is in second language education. Before going to Dubai he worked with educators in Turkey and in the UK and taught also in Italy and Spain. His current research interests include the contributions of sociocultural context to university learning, and in particular, how learners' family and peer groups contextualize learning. He is the editor, with Richard C. Smith, of *Learner Autonomy Across Cultures*, also published by Palgrave Macmillan.

Dawn Lorraine McBride is in private practice as a psychologist, but also teaches as an Assistant Professor at the University of Lethbridge, Canada, specializing in cross-cultural issues relating to counselling and teaching. She formerly taught in the United Arab Emirates.

Gerhard Apfelthaler is Professor and Chair of the Department of International Management at Fachhochschule Joanneum, a leading university of applied sciences in Graz, Austria. Professor Apfelthaler has enjoyed careers as a diplomat in Austria's foreign commercial service, as an educator and administrator in higher education and as a private consultant. He has written several books on international market entry and cross-cultural management.

Natalia Yevgenyevna Collings is an Assistant Professor at Central Michigan University, USA. A Russian national, while working in Russia she specialized in English and Russian languages and literature, worked as an elementary schoolteacher and as an interpreter for a university. In the last seven years she has led large groups of students from the United States to Russia in the summers and has taught courses in Russian language and culture.

Johannes C. Cronjé is a Professor of Computer-integrated Education at the University of Pretoria, South Africa, following an early career as a schoolteacher and then seven years teaching business communication at the Pretoria Technikon. He has travelled extensively as guest lecturer, keynote speaker, and guest researcher and professor at universities in the USA, the Netherlands, Finland, Norway, Ethiopia, Botswana, Mozambique, Namibia and Sudan.

Garth Davies is an Assistant Professor at Simon Fraser University, Canada. He received his Ph.D. from Rutgers University in the USA. His primary interests lie in the development of research methods and the application of statistical analyses to a range of substantive issues, including perceptions of and experiences with social boundaries.

Catherine Doherty is a Lecturer in Socio-Cultural Studies at Queensland University of Technology. She trained initially as a sociologist, then as a primary teacher. She now works in teacher education after twenty years of teaching in adult literacy, migrant English and tertiary preparation programmes, working with indigenous students, international students and students with disabilities. Her current research interest is in how cultural identities get constructed through educational practices, both online and face-to-face.

Susana Eisenchlas is a Senior Lecturer in Linguistics at Griffith University in Australia. An Argentinian, she migrated to Australia in 1988 after living in Israel and Japan. She teaches in intercultural communication, gender and language, and language-teaching methodologies. She has also been a member of the Spanish studies programme and taught Spanish for fourteen years.

Silvina Ituarte is an Assistant Professor at California State University, East Bay, USA. An Argentinian by birth, with an MA in social ecology and a Ph.D. in criminology, she has settled in the USA where she has taught for the past ten years; she has also taught in China.

Kuni Jenkins is Professor at Te Whare Wananga o Awanuiarangi, a tertiary college of Maori students in the Bay of Plenty, New Zealand. She is a Ngati Porou woman committed to the field of Maori education. For nearly two decades she was a primary schoolteacher in predominantly Maori schools; and working with Maori girls boarding schools, she joined with Alison Jones in researching how the desire for learning exists in tension with the process of 'being taught' and 'being the teacher'.

Alison Jones is Professor of Education at the University of Auckland, New Zealand and a scholar in critical studies in education, seeing pedagogy as necessarily a form of political struggle and influenced also by the field of psychoanalysis and education. Her educational career is motivated by her identity as a Pakeha (i.e. a White, non-indigenous, New Zealander) and its implicit relationship to Maori people.

Eija Källström is Assistant Head of Department of Business, Media, and Technology at Arcada Polytechnic in Helsinki, Finland. She has many years of experience in teaching in higher education. Her teaching and research area is ICT in International Business.

Regitze Kristensen is Head of Development and Internationalization at Tietgen Business College, Odense, Denmark. She has taught for many years in higher education, and has been the international project manager of many international projects in the field of new teaching methods and internationalization.

Catherine Manathunga is a Lecturer in Higher Education at the University of Queensland, Australia. She provides academic professional development programmes for supervisors and research students and has taught for thirteen years in several universities in Brisbane, Australia, in the disciplines of history, politics and education.

Irene C. L. Ng is a Senior Lecturer in Marketing, Director for the Centre for Service Research, and Head of Postgraduate Studies at the School of Business and Economics, University of Exeter, UK. She is currently also the Group Vice Chairman of the SA Tourism group with regional offices in Singapore, Malaysia and China. She has taught on Executive and MBA programmes worldwide and is also a marketing advisor to several international firms in Singapore, Malaysia, South Africa, Australia and the UK.

Niall Palfreyman is a Professor in Mathematics in the Department of Biotechnology and Bioinformatics at Weihenstephan University of Applied Sciences in Freising, Germany. His current post follows eighteen years of problem-solving, learning and teaching in the computer industry in England, Germany and America. He is interested in human communication – in particular group problem-solving communication in design teams and in education.

Ulf Schuetze is an Assistant Professor in the Department of Germanic and Slavic Studies at the University of Victoria, Canada. He has studied or taught at seven universities in four countries on three continents, specializing in second language acquisition.

Parlo Singh is Head of School in the School of Education and Professional Studies, Griffith University, Australia. She migrated to Australia from India as a child with her parents in the early 1960s and Punjabi is her first or home language. Parlo worked as a primary school-teacher for five years before completing a Ph.D. in the sociology of education. She has published widely in the area of cultural identity, equity and schooling.

Lois Smith is Co-ordinator of the Project for Enhancement of Learning and Teaching at the University of Wollongong in Dubai. She trained as an English Language teacher and enjoyed teaching a wide cultural mix of students in various institutions in the UAE. She joined her current institution five years ago, moving during that period from teaching English to coordinating and facilitating educational development for faculty, and learning development for students. She has taught in monocultural, government institutions, and currently works in a multicultural environment with a mix of students and faculty from all over the world.

Julie Ann Svenkerud is an Associate Professor at Buskerud University College in Norway. She is the head of the English language programme including teacher education. Her field of interest, pursued through extensive teaching experience in higher education, is cross-cultural communication.

Susan Trevaskes is an Australian Research Council Fellow in the School of Languages and Linguistics, Griffith University, Australia. Her main research interest is in the area of Chinese criminal justice and she is currently writing a book on state responses to serious and violent crime in China. She and Susana Eisenchlas have co-edited (with Anthony Liddicoat) *Australian Perspectives on Internationalising Education* (2003) and she has co-authored a number of book chapters and journal articles in the area of teaching intercultural communication.

A Note on Terminology

Due to the range of backgrounds of the contributors to this book, a variety of terms are used to refer to roles in education. The following terms are used interchangeably to refer to those teaching in tertiary education: *educator, faculty, instructor, lecturer, professor, teacher* and *tutor*. The terms *student* and *learner* are used to refer to those intended to benefit from this teaching.

Transcription Conventions

. . .	pause
[. . .]	omitted material
[ ]	added material
( )	non-verbal material
italics	translated material

Introduction: Learning and Teaching Across Cultures in Higher Education

David Palfreyman

Cultural issues in teaching and learning are becoming increasingly significant in universities and colleges. Higher education in many countries has recently seen an increased focus on issues of teaching and learning, balancing the traditional emphasis on the research role of universities and colleges. Teaching and Learning Centres have mushroomed, supporting a scholarship of teaching and learning (Boyer, 1990; Richlin, 2001) exploring issues such as teaching approaches, learning orientations and strategies, e-learning, assessment, curriculum planning, ethics, skills and employability, broadening participation, and student research. At the same time the growing pace of globalization is highlighting a cultural dimension in all these areas: when students or educators, materials, methods or understandings of subject matter move into new settings, contact zones are created in which cultural factors become more salient, providing new challenges and new resources for teaching and learning.

Responding to this cultural dimension of higher education requires university and college educators to engage in relatively new teaching practices in which they may not have expertise or training. For example, a teacher in a multicultural university or college classroom may need to promote intercultural awareness, use comparative perspectives in presenting material, reconsider 'universals' in university learning and teaching, acknowledge and use local knowledges and locally appropriate methodologies, or promote the development of an 'ethnographic imagination' (Willis, 2001). It is these areas of practice that are the focus of this book.

The developments mentioned above remain relatively under-represented in the literature on teaching and learning in higher education. The majority of the available works in the field draw on practice and research in English-speaking countries (e.g. Ouellett, 2005; Carroll and Ryan, 2005), in settings which are (treated as) culturally homogeneous and basically Western. One well-known exception is the literature on the Chinese Learner (e.g., Watkins & Biggs, 1996), which has studied in depth a particular cultural group; another is the sizeable literature on Teaching English as a Second Language, which has tackled cultural issues in a range of contexts, but in relation to language rather than content teaching. The scholarship of content teaching and learning therefore remains without a serious attempt to view practice and research through a cultural lens across a range of contexts.

Learning and Teaching Across Cultures in Higher Education is intended for anyone who has an interest in intercultural aspects of learning and teaching in higher education. Raising awareness of other cultures (or your own) may be an objective of your course; or you may have noticed issues in your courses (whether in students, in materials or in yourself) which you suspect may be 'cultural' in some sense (i.e., involve patterns of values, thought and behaviours). You may be interested in setting up intercultural contacts (either face-to-face or using computer-mediated communication) between students and others; or you may be engaging with issues of the modern global context such as internationalization of curriculum, global flows of students and educators, cultural diversity and more inclusive admission policies. This book contains theoretical rationale, resources and examples to assist you in understanding and tackling such situations.

In this book we aim to inform the work of university and college educators internationally, by drawing together and developing approaches for a scholarship of teaching and learning across cultures. We present issues and practice relating to higher education in cross-cultural settings, and through the scope and the development of the book we aim to make connections between diverse perspectives. First in line with the concept of the scholarship of teaching and learning, we aim to link research and practice. Second, we recognize that higher education in general involves the teaching of particular disciplines, and we discuss cultural issues across a variety of these (including cultural studies, business/management, and mathematics). Third, we consider different aspects of education, including learning orientations, e-learning, distance education, and assessment. Fourth, in the spirit of globalization we bring together work from different geographical regions: Africa, Asia, Australasia, Europe and North America. Finally, we aim to raise awareness of the different types of intercultural situations that exist in modern times: thus we include contributions written both by cultural 'insiders' and by 'outsiders' to the settings described; and situations where culture forms part of the course *context* as well as situations where it is part of the course *content.*

The literature

The scholarship of teaching and learning (SoTL) is a relatively new discipline, which has emerged from professional practice. For this reason some of those working in SoTL bring from other disciplines theories and research about how learning and teaching work; but there are also many academics who come to SoTL from the practical concerns of their teaching, and who are raising issues, developing strategies and seeking concepts in order to understand, plan and evaluate their practice in a deeper and more systematic way. This is especially true of intercultural SoTL. The literature in anthropology and cultural studies offers subtle and complex models of culture, although as Ng (this volume) points out, these models do not feed easily into practice; at the same time, there is a range of pragmatic understandings of culture which have grown out of practice in education and also in business. Since the contributors to this book include practicing educators in a range of disciplines, both types of model will be found here, but there is a need for the two approaches to temper each other: objective research and reflection on underlying cultural theory can help to ensure that practitioner models are not based on narrow conceptions or ethnocentric stereotyping (e.g., Jones & Jenkins, Manathunga, this volume), while practical concerns and experiential data from practitioners 'in the field' can help to provide a grounding for more theoretical models (e.g., Smith, this volume).

Individual chapters in this book define and present culture in various ways, but they share a broad conception of culture as 'the shared patterns of behavior and associated meanings that people learn and participate in within the groups to which they belong' (Whitten & Hunter, 1992, p. 3). Culture is therefore seen as linked to underlying patterns and 'ways of knowing' (Belenky et al., 1986; Niall Palfreyman, this volume), rather than necessarily to specific behaviours or objects. Although nationality is a convenient way to label differences between groups (especially in large-scale studies such as those of Hofstede, 2001), at a finer level of detail there exist various (sub)cultures within one country, or across countries (Holliday, 2005): in tertiary teaching and learning one can talk about the 'culture' of a particular discipline (Becher, 1993; Hativa & Marincovich, 1995; Ng, Niall Palfreyman, this volume), or of an institution (e.g., Cronjé; Kristensen et al., this volume; Wright, 1994). Furthermore, the 'shared' nature of culture does not mean that everybody in a group thinks or behaves in the same way: different people use the resources of their culture(s) in different ways in different contexts (Cowan, 1990; Kağıtçibaşı, 1998).

The work of Hofstede (1986; 2001) is drawn on by a number of authors in this book (Apfelthaler et al.; Cronjé; Smith), who explain Hofstede's contribution in relation to their own work. In terms of his findings, a given nationality may be placed at a certain point along each of five dimensions, for example being 'more individualist' or 'more collectivist' in its orientation. The work of Triandis (1995) and Nisbett (2003, cited by Ng, this volume) similarly tries to abstract general values held by individuals in particular (national) cultural groups. The positive aspect of Hofstede's work in particular is that it offers an economical typology of cultures, based on a large body of quantitative data. Reservations regarding the application of this research centre around the issue of essentialization (Kubota, 2001; Doherty & Singh, Jones & Jenkins, Manathunga, this volume), whereby differences between cultures are oversimplified and national groups treated as monolithic. Broadly speaking, the concept of culture remains useful in practice, and research supports our intuitions that generalizations can be made about social groups; however, these generalizations should always be scrutinized, and not applied inappropriately in dealing with learners (Holliday et al., 2004).

The process of becoming part of a culture is referred to as *socialization*. Children the world over are socialized into their primary community, but adulthood and tertiary education bring particular kinds of secondary socialization into the culture of academia and perhaps of other national groups. This may be a smooth process of increasing participation in a new community (Lave & Wenger, 1991), but may also involve some false turns, alienation and periods of 'going through the motions' (Airey & Linder, 2006; Collings; Ng, this volume). The process of entering a new culture highlights issues of *identity* and difference (Manathunga, this volume), as the learner in effect adds a new persona to his/her previous identity. Work on intercultural situations has developed the concept of *intercultural competence* (Byram, 1997; Eisenchlas & Trevaskes, this volume; Hinkel, 2001; Schuetze, this volume,). This refers not simply to participating in a particular second culture, but to transferable skills of relating to other cultures and mediating between them and one's own culture.

Moving from intercultural learning to intercultural teaching, we can characterize tertiary educators as managers of intercultural transition. Often the transition in question is students' transition into the culture of academic study or of a particular discipline (Biggs (1999) for example, plays down the significance of ethnic culture in favour of a focus on the transition to tertiary learning); sometimes educators may enter the world of their students to some extent, becoming intercultural learners themselves. Nowadays this may well take place in the context of a virtual community using Computer-Mediated Communication (CMC) and Information and Communication Technology (ICT) (Cronjé; Kristensen et al.; Schuetze, this volume).

The concept of negotiation of meaning between teacher and student, between student and material and between students underlies the educational approach known as constructivism (Bruner, 1990; Cronjé; Smith; Niall Palfreyman, this volume), which sees learning as 'a dynamic process in which learners construct new ideas or concepts on their current/past knowledge and in response to the instructional situation' (UNESCO, 2006). The view of learning as negotiation resonates with the dialectic between explicit and implicit knowledge discussed by Kristensen et al., and Niall Palfreyman (this volume). It also has a special significance for education in intercultural contexts which, as the chapters in Part 2 of this book illustrate, involve efforts to mediate between disparate cultures. The aim of many of the contributors to this book is to stimulate a dialogue between worldviews in order to find some common ground: a 'fusion of horizons' (Gadamer, 1975, p. 273) which makes the cultural world both of the teacher and of the learner mutually more accessible and comprehensible. Cultural dialogue and negotiation may involve various aspects of tertiary learning, including course content, the way it is presented, and also methods of teaching and relating to students. Anthropological studies of education (e.g., Kimball, 1978; Spindler, 1997) can illuminate local 'cultures of learning' (Cortazzi & Jin, 1996), which in turn can inform the development of *appropriate methodology* (Holliday, 1994) for a particular context. For an educator in an unfamiliar setting, openness, flexibility and an 'ethnographic imagination' (Willis, 2000) are essential in this process, as illustrated in Cronjé's chapter (this volume).

Critical Theory has highlighted the links between culture and *power* (Rose, 1996). Power relationships are in any case a key issue in higher education settings (e.g. Bourdieu and Passeron, 1965; Manathunga, this volume), and the power differential between different cultural groups and their respective values should not be ignored. Bernstein (1973) defines curriculum (sometimes treated as a purely rational concept) as 'what counts as valid knowledge' (p. 85) in a particular educational setting, making it clear that it is educators and institutions that tend to establish the ground rules for content and process of education. Educators who are also members of a more powerful cultural group (be it globally or in the local setting) may well impose roles, values, activities and interpretations on students and in the process stifle the kind of learning that they wish to promote (Jones & Jenkins, Manathunga, Smith, this volume). One response to this has been work with Indigenous communities on bringing Indigenous knowledge into the classroom (Teasdale & Ma Rhea, 2000; Jones, this volume). The Funds of Knowledge movement (Moll et al., 1992) has similarly tried to raise educators' awareness of the knowledge possessed by students' community, with an aim to bringing this knowledge into the curriculum – an approach taken also by Eisenchlas and Trevaskes (this volume). Ultimately, however, there may be limits to this process, and Jones and Jenkins' chapter in particular alerts us to the pitfalls of over-optimistic attempts to promote intercultural dialogue.

How this book is organized to help the reader

Building on the cross-cultural and intercultural perspectives referred to for example in Apfelthaler et al. (this volume), in this book we aim to promote a *transcultural* awareness of teaching and learning. This can be defined as a sensitivity to general, underlying factors and approaches, as independent as possible of any single culture, which helps us to decide appropriate goals and methods in diverse cultural and intercultural contexts, without imposing stereotyped interpretations or 'ready-made' solutions. The book is organized into two sections: Part 1, *Issues*, includes reports of research on teaching and learning in cross-cultural settings, and discusses issues and concepts emerging from this research that are relevant to other situations of cultural contact; Part 2, *Practice*, consists of reports of courses and programmes involving cross-cultural work, and examines what we can learn from these.

The book thus includes a range of data and concepts relating to specific cross-cultural contexts around the world; and we aim to help the reader to apply insights from these other contexts in understanding and interacting with her/his own cross-cultural context. We do this by providing with each chapter the following:

- *Background information.* Each chapter includes sufficient background information about the context studied to help you identify common issues with your own context, as well as differences, and understand how the concepts and findings described might be relevant to your own context.

- *Resources list*. Following each chapter the author provides a short list of useful resources for educators interested in looking further into the topic of their chapter.
- *Reflection questions*. Each chapter is followed by reflection questions which will help you to draw out the transcultural implications of the ideas discussed in the chapter, and to relate the content of each chapter to your own context. These questions can be used for individual reflection or for discussion.

Part 1
Issues

Preface to Part 1: Issues in Multicultural Tertiary Education

David Palfreyman

The first section of *Learning and Teaching Across Cultures in Higher Education* presents studies which explore constructs and issues related to cross-cultural education. The authors in this part of the book draw on concepts from the literature on culture and education to analyse data gathered from particular learner groups and teaching contexts, with the aim of understanding these groups and contexts in a deeper and more principled way. The chapters in Part 1 are sequenced to move broadly from learner focus to teaching focus; they apply concepts drawn from empirical as well as theoretical literature, from psychological models through sociological interpretations to more political/critical perspectives, illuminating the relation of culture to attitudes, social identity and power relationships in teaching and learning situations.

The first chapter, Apfelthaler et al.'s 'Cross-cultural Differences in Learning and Education' reports on a large-scale EU-funded attitude survey of almost 3,000 students across two Western European and two South-East Asian countries. The authors review major streams of literature relating to learners' attitudes and approaches to learning, and highlight some key concepts including learning styles (Kolb, 1976), Deep and Surface learning (Marton and Saljö, 1976) and cultural typologies (Hofstede, 2001). They examine some 'stereotypes, myths and realities' relating to these groups of students, and identify factors which distinguish European from Asian students, as well as ones apparently unrelated to this geographical distinction. They also consider the role of gender and institutional culture in the results, and offer some recommendations for teaching in response to their findings.

The next chapter, Irene Ng's 'Teaching Business Studies to Far East Students in the UK', studies a group of students who have been the focus of a number of studies of learning orientation: students from cultures with Confucian roots (including China, Japan and Korea). Ng's contribution is particularly interesting because she herself grew up in a Confucian culture, and is also thoroughly integrated into the culture of Western business practice. She draws skilfully on her own understanding of these two cultures and of her experience of mediating between them, as she analyses interview data from students who are engaged (not always wholeheartedly) in a similar cultural journey. She discusses ways in which students attempt to adopt what they see as valued ways of thinking and knowing, while often maintaining a sceptical distance in order to deal with perceived dissonance between the two cultures.

In 'Cultural Learning in the Absence of Culture?', Collings examines another situation of cultural transition: US students who are learning Russian as a second language, and the irregular nature of their engagement with Russian culture and with classroom culture. Collings draws on the work of Bakhtin and Vygotsky (reading these Russian authors, incidentally, as a cultural insider) to unpick what it means to be a student or a learner, deepening our understanding of how students engage (or not) with classroom culture and also with the wider cultural world which the teacher may try to bring into the classroom. Like Ng's students, the US students found ways of distancing themselves from aspects of the cultural curriculum that they felt unready for, although after the course ended some of them engaged with Russian culture as a result of experiences outside the classroom. Collings' chapter, although on one level about Russian culture, also gives us insight into the cultures of classrooms and how learning ebbs and flows in ways only partly related to teaching.

Ituarte and Davies's chapter, 'Perception of "Self" and "Other"', also uses data from the US, looking at the diversity of cultural background among local university students, how this affects the students' perceptions of each other's cultural groups, and the implications of this for their learning. She presents data from a survey in two US universities, and draws conclusions about social boundaries and their impact. This chapter prefigures themes discussed in the chapters by Eisenchlas and Trevaskes and by Jones and Jenkins (this volume).

In contrast to the large-scale student population studies of the preceding chapters, in 'Intercultural Postgraduate Supervision' Manathunga explores the often intense and close relationships between doctoral supervisors and their students. She reviews thought-provoking concepts from postcolonial cultural theory: contact zones, transculturation and unhomeliness; and uses these to analyse the experience of a number of supervisors and their students in Australia. Using interview data from both sides of the supervisory encounter and from contrasting cultural backgrounds, Manathunga explores not only issues of cultural transition, but also the dimensions of identity and power. In particular, she reveals how supervisors may perceive and behave in ways likely to empower or disempower doctoral students who are themselves becoming academics. By learning about students' backgrounds, socializing them into Western academic norms and scaffolding their efforts to develop as scholars, the supervisors play a key role in students' development, but the process can also involve ambivalence and discomfort on both sides.

Singh and Doherty's chapter 'Mobile Students, Flexible Identities and Liquid Modernity' presents a stimulating discussion of concepts in cultural studies which help to understand the dynamics of intercultural contact at a societal and personal level. The authors discuss the identities which Western institutions set up for students from East Asia, and how these identities are taken up and/or challenged by students themselves. These identities are formed in the context of representations about particular cultural groups (including stereotypes), of global economic patterns, and of students' personal strategies for shaping their 'own' life. Singh and Doherty present interview data to show how students negotiate these cultural spaces, and suggest ways in which Australian and other universities could respond more effectively to this complex situation. It is interesting to compare this exploration of students' identity with Ng's insider perspective on similar issues.

Jones and Jenkins conclude Part 1 with a critical perspective on a concept that underlies many of the other chapters in this book: intercultural dialogue. In 'Cross-cultural Engagement in Higher Education Classrooms', they examine the idea that higher education can promote intercultural understanding through dialogue, and point out that this ideal (even as it is enacted in 'critical pedagogy') may be linked to a desire by more powerful cultural groups to consolidate their own position, rather than a real wish to engage with and learn from another culture. The authors are educators in New Zealand, where an indigenous Maori minority maintains traditions alongside a White majority. In this context, the authors challenge the idea that contact between cultural groups is the best or only way to promote mutual understanding. Having experimented with segregated groups of students, they propose a methodology whereby the two cultural groups, instead of 'facing each other', instead 'stand side by side' to consider different perspectives on their shared past. They suggest that intercultural teaching take into account three elements: *reflexivity*, whereby students and teachers consider their own position and motivations; acceptance of some 'inevitable *ignorance*' about the cultural Other; and *knowledge* developed through mutually respectful exploration of shared issues.

1
Cross-cultural Differences in Learning and Education: Stereotypes, Myths and Realities

Gerhard Apfelthaler, Katrin Hansen, Stephan Keuchel, Christa Mueller, Martin Neubauer, Siow Heng Ong and Nirundon Tapachai[1]

Despite the fact that both learning styles and cross-cultural differences have been important research topics for decades, surprisingly little work has been done on comparisons of learning behaviour across cultures and its impact for teachers working in culturally mixed settings. This chapter is based on a research project funded by the European Union seeking to provide fresh knowledge on cross-national differences in attitudes towards learning of students from selected countries. It reports on the results from Austria, Germany, Singapore and Thailand and outlines some of the implications for teaching in higher education.

Introduction

This chapter reports on the outcomes of a two-year research project conducted by researchers at universities in Austria, Germany, Singapore and Thailand. It will start by providing insight into the motivation for this project, which is mainly rooted in the dramatic increase of international student flows. Next, it will present a short summary of extant learning styles research related to this project. Then, the methodology of the research project is described and the results presented. In the discussion of the results, some implications for teaching in higher education are outlined.

Context

The context of the research underlying this chapter is not rooted in one country only, it is cross-national. In the worldwide pursuit of global competitiveness, higher education is becoming ever more important for countries, West and East, North and South, as is evidenced by growing enrolment in institutions of higher education worldwide. In addition, not only is higher education as such becoming more important, but international student flows[2] have also increased steadily and sometimes dramatically over the past decades. According to recent estimates (Bohm et. al., 2004), the number of students pursuing a university degree outside their home country will increase from about 2.1 million in 2003 to approximately 5.8 million by 2020, with demand for places in English-speaking destination countries forecast to rise from about 1 million currently to about 2.6 million places in 2020.

As a result, lecture halls and seminar rooms worldwide are increasingly becoming culturally diverse. This carries the potential for serious challenges for students, professors and administrators in higher education. Surprisingly enough and somewhat disappointingly, to date researchers have by and large neglected the potential link between learning styles and culture.

Thirty years ago Kolb (1976) introduced to the world of education the idea of learning styles, which may vary according to personality, life experiences, and the purpose of learning. Only a few years later Lawrence (1979) published his famous book *People Types, Tiger Stripes* which was based on work by Isabel Myers Briggs (Myers and McCaulley, 1985). With this publication Lawrence turned educators' attention to the fact that people can differ significantly in their learning behaviour on a much broader scale than can be immediately perceived in a classroom. In the three decades since, a plethora of research on learning styles has emerged and learning style research has become quite popular for researchers in the past two decades. And yet, there was and still is very little to turn to when it comes to the question of how students in different cultures study and learn.

Taking up the challenge to advance this topic was the motivation for a team of faculty members at FH Joanneum University of Applied Sciences (Graz, Austria). They formed a team of researchers with Singapore Management University (Singapore), Kasetsart University (Bangkok, Thailand) and FH Gelsenkirchen (Germany) to start a two-year long research project on national differences in studying and learning behaviour of students, generously supported by the European Union. The basic premise for the research (following Hofstede, 1986) was that the cultural differences between the countries involved in the project would have a clear influence on the way students interact with professors, with other students and with their learning environment in general. The results of our research are reported in this chapter.

Literature review

Based on sometimes painful experiences of differences in learning behaviour, many educators have pursued a deeper understanding of a complex problem (e.g., Coffield et al., 2004). An initial review of the existing literature showed that there are three major streams in learning styles research. The first stream, including Kolb (1976) or work on the Learning Styles Questionnaire (LSQ) by Honey and Mumford (1992), sees variance in learning styles as based in differences in personality, life experiences, and the purpose of learning. This stream is strongly influenced by Kolb's four basic learning styles. In this model, students are either *accommodators* who favour concrete experience and active experimentation (good at carrying out plans), *divergers* who prefer concrete experience and reflective observation (good imaginative ability), *convergers* who are good at abstract conceptualization and active experimentation (good problem solvers and decision makers), or *assimilators* who like abstract conceptualization and reflective observation (good at inductive reasoning).

The second stream of research revolves around the idea of Deep and Surface learning, terms originally introduced by Marton and Saljö (1976), and further developed by Entwistle and Ramsden (1983) and Biggs (1987) among others. One of the most important characteristics of this stream is that Deep or Surface learning are not attributes of individuals, but rather sets of behaviours shown by individuals in reaction to a specific learning environment; this means that when the learning environment changes, the learning style can change. In contrast, in Kolb's (1976) view, learning styles are more or less constant traits of individuals. While Surface learning is cognitively oriented, focuses on memorization, is extrinsically motivated by the fear of failure, and is directed strictly towards the task at hand, Deep learning tries to create meaning and to understand the coherent whole, derives from intrinsic motivation, and relates previous knowledge to new knowledge. For example, Surface learning implies clearer descriptions of rules and responsibilities for group work than Deep learning, which involves creating a working environment to fit the learners' own preferences and procedures. In addition to the Deep and Surface approaches, Biggs (1987), Ramsden (1988) and Entwistle (1992) identify a third approach to learning, the Strategic (or Achieving) approach. Unlike Deep or Surface learning, Strategic learning aims to obtain the highest possible grades or other rewards by identifying assessment criteria and then applying appropriate and well-organized study methods. Widely used survey instruments in this stream of research include the Experiences of Teaching and Learning Questionnaire (ETLQ) by Entwistle (1992); the Learning and Studying Questionnaire (LSQ) by Honey and Mumford (1992); the Study Process Questionnaire (SPQ) by Biggs et al. (2001); the Revised Approaches to Studying Inventory (RASI) by Entwistle and Tait (1994); the Approaches to Study Skills Inventories for Students (ASSIST) by Tait, Entwistle and McCune (1998), and several others.

Outside of these two streams of learning styles research exists a rather mixed bag of models which are of less impact than the ones already described. Nevertheless, surveying the literature on the topic it becomes clear that even the two dominant approaches have very rarely been used in cross-national comparisons. Some studies (e.g., Kember & Gow, 1990; Richardson, 1994; Volet et al., 1994; R. M. Smith, 2001) have attempted either to validate instruments in different populations (such as different nationalities or different levels of education) or to compare different populations using these instruments, but by and large there is still no consistent body of literature on the topic, thus warranting new empirical research.

Cultures, according to Hofstede (2001), vary mainly along five dimensions: *power distance, uncertainty avoidance, masculinity, long-term orientation,* and *individualism.* The more recent GLOBE study (House et al., 2004) shows a large overlap with Hofstede's original research. The GLOBE constructs are *power distance, uncertainty avoidance, collectivism I* (institutional) and *collectivism II* (in-group collectivism), *humane orientation, assertiveness, gender egalitarianism, future orientation,* and *performance orientation.* Six of these dimensions resemble Hofstede's dimensions, but have been modified based on a critical discussion of Hofstede's concepts and results.

No matter what the dimensions, when cultures (or countries, as units of analysis) show different scores on these dimensions, this is bound to have implications for learning styles insofar as cultural patterns in a learning environment ultimately reflect the cultural patterns in the wider society. This has led to the formulation of the hypotheses for this research.

Hypotheses

Based on a thorough survey of the literature and a careful assessment of the immediate usability of expected results for professors and teachers, we tested the hypotheses that *students in the participating countries*

(Austria, Germany, Singapore, Thailand) show different attitudes towards the following aspects of education:

1. working in groups
2. interaction with professors
3. teaching methods
4. students' own role in the education process
5. the physical teaching environment.

Method

Although learning styles models and learning styles inventories abound, and the literature above was taken into account in planning this study, a conscious decision was made not to use directly any of the existing survey instruments and thus not to follow strictly any of the existing streams of literature. The main reasons for this decision were:

1. Questions about the applicability of constructs or survey instruments in other countries or in a cross-cultural setting (e.g., Richardson, 1994) arose as the vast majority of research on learning styles originates from only a few countries (e.g., Australia, Hong Kong, and the UK).
2. Existing studies involving Asian countries are inconclusive or even contradictory. Whilst some authors identify the Asian learner in general as surface and rote learners, others challenge this view (e.g., Watkins & Reghi, 1991).
3. Many learning style inventories show psychometric weaknesses. Coffield et. al. (2004) state that only three of the thirteen instruments they reviewed came near to satisfying their criteria for reliability and validity.
4. Most of the models we reviewed seemed difficult to translate into practical recommendations for improving learning environments and teaching. We aimed for an inventory that would yield practical results.

As a consequence, a new questionnaire had to be developed. The development was based on three core understandings: a workable definition of learning styles, a shared understanding of the concept of cross-cultural differences, and the concept of attitudes.

The first core element refers to learning styles. In the context of this project we used one of the most popular broad definitions of learning style as given by Smith (1982) who defines learning style as 'the individual's characteristic ways of processing information, feeling, and behaving in learning situations' (p. 24). Price (1983) adds that when people learn, they perceive, think, and interact with instructors, methods and environments; they develop tendencies and preferences that accompany learning. This development brings about one's learning style, a characteristic way of learning which might or might not lead to performance. Smith's and Price's definitions served as a basis for the development of questionnaire items.

The second core element refers to culture, cross-cultural comparisons and intercultural interactions. 'Cross-cultural' here applies to research across borders, which can be seen in many dimensions such as geographical or ethnic borders among others. This research focuses on the observation of individuals from different cultures, on observations of different cultural groups (Lenartowicz and Roth, 1999), or on comparisons of one to another (Avruch & Black, 1991). The focus is on cultural differences and similarities, finding out that certain aspects of learning will differ while others might be uniform between different countries (Weinert, 2004). 'Intercultural', on the other hand, focuses on *interaction* between people descending from different cultures or between people coping with a different ('strange') culture (Adler and Bartholomew, 1992; Barmeyer & Bolten, 1998; Lenartowicz & Roth, 1999).

The third core element of the questionnaire development is rooted in the work of Ajzen (1993) who distinguishes three components of attitudes: cognition as expression of beliefs, affect as expression of feelings, and conation as expression of intentions. A major guiding principle for the development of our own survey instrument was Ajzen's view that 'given that the three components reflect the same underlying attitude, they should correlate to some degree with each other. Yet, to the extent that the distinction between cognitive, affective, and conative response categories is of psychological significance, measures of the three components should not be completely redundant' (p. 43).

We combined these core concepts in the design of our questionnaire instrument, using the concept of learning style as a description of the attitudes of a typical individual in a culture towards aspects of learning, thus facilitating cross-cultural comparisons of learning and studying. After a thorough review of the literature, the new instrument was designed in several collaborative face-to-face and virtual work sessions among the multicultural research team, resulting in a collection of a total of 92 items on students' attitudes to group work, interaction with professors, teaching methods, the individual's role in the educational process and the physical learning environment (e.g., 'Students deeply understand topics only when the topic can be discussed in class' or 'I never criticize my professor'). Based on Ajzen's (1993) three components of attitudes, each research question/construct generated three items spread throughout the questionnaire, to elicit the cognitive, affective and conative elements of attitudes respectively, for example:

9. Cheating in exams should be strictly prohibited.
28. I feel bad if I cheat in exams.
73. I never cheat in exams.

These items were supplemented with nine demographic questions. After the first draft, the questionnaire was critiqued and improved by outside experts, translated and back-translated, as well as pre-tested on student populations in Austria, Germany, Singapore and Thailand.

After slight final modifications the new instrument was administered to approximately 432 business students in Austria, 629 business students in Germany, 601 business students in Singapore and 1164 business students in Thailand. Forty seven per cent of the respondents were female; 30 per cent of the students were studying the first year at an institution of higher education, and 70 per cent belonged to an advanced level. Students mainly came from an undergraduate level, studying for a degree related to business administration. It is important to note that data collection in the four countries was restricted to certain regions for reasons of accessibility and convenience: Vienna, Graz and Innsbruck as university hubs in Austria, the Ruhr region in Germany with a high number of universities compared to the rest of the country, and Bangkok in Thailand. In the German-speaking countries, both traditional universities and universities of applied sciences (cf. Palfreyman in this book) were included in the sample.

Results

Statistical analysis (including frequency analysis, factor analysis, univariate variance analysis, Levene test) of the data revealed attitudes to learning for 23 different aspects of learning to be significantly different between nationalities. See Table 1.1 for the most significant findings.

From Table 1.1 it can be seen that the divide does not always run between Asian countries on the one side and European countries on the

Table 1.1: Largest differences in attitudes towards learning

Aspect of learning	Country with maximum agreement (1 = strongest agreement)	Country with maximum disagreement (5 = strongest disagreement)	Mean	Austria	Germany	Singapore	Thailand
1. Criticism not allowed (degree to which students think it is not acceptable to criticize their professor)	Singapore	Austria	3.02	4.64	3.59	2.23	2.90
2. Preferred gender homogeneity of study groups (degree to which students prefer to work in groups of the same gender, e. g. study groups, presentations, etc.)	Singapore	Austria	3.36	4.05	3.84	2.69	3.20
3. Cheating allowed (degree to which academic dishonesty is accepted, e. g. cheating in exams; plagiarism, etc.)	Thailand	Austria	2.11	2.41	2.32	1.97	1.96
4. Professor's responsibility for student's success (degree to which students think that their professors are responsible for their own success or failure; e. g. receiving a bad grade may be interpreted as a failure to instruct students properly)	Thailand	Singapore	3.08	3.42	3.26	3.49	2.63
5. Learning not beyond the required scope (degree to which students' are unwilling to pursue learning beyond the required scope of a class; e. g. students refuse to engage in further reading)	Thailand	Singapore	3.28	3.30	3.29	3.80	3.00
6. Memorizing (degree to which students have a preference for memorization of content, e. g. the memorization of passages from textbooks)	Thailand	Austria	3.34	3.88	3.42	3.12	3.32
7. National homogeneity of work groups (degree to which students accept / prefer national homogeneity in groups, e. g. study groups, presentations, etc)	Thailand	Germany	3.20	3.63	3.65	3.08	2.86
8. Non-equal Interaction (degree to which students see themselves as different in status to their professors)	Thailand	Singapore	2.55	2.78	2.77	2.90	2.22
9. Group study preferred (degree to which students' prefer to study in groups)	Thailand	Germany	2.35	2.55	2.65	2.26	2.15

Note: (5-point Likert scale: 1 = strongest agreement, 5 = strongest disagreement; n = 2400; all differences significant at .001 level).

other. Based on this observation, separate analysis of the differences of students' attitudes between the two subgroups of Asia (Singapore and Thailand) and Europe (Austria and Germany) was conducted. This analysis confirmed that the dividing line throughout all the aspects covered in our research concerns every country and does not allow us to speak of 'Asian' or 'European' learners. In fact, out of a total of 23 aspects of learning only the first seven listed in Table 1.2 showed significant differences between Asia as a whole and Europe as a whole. At the same time, a number of clear Intra-Asian and Intra-European differences were identified.

It can be seen from Table 1.1 and Table 1.2 that Asian and European students hold different attitudes to certain issues; e.g., on the basis of our results it is fair to assume that European students, by and large, do not shy from criticizing professors. In addition, our results also point to intra-Asian differences concerning this question: students from Thailand are more likely to criticize their professors than students from Singapore. The stereotype of the Asian learner as highlighted by Biggs' work (Myers & McCaulley, 1985) therefore is both confirmed and challenged – on the one hand Asians are different from Europeans; on the other hand it is not correct to assume that all Asians hold the same attitudes towards learning. The explanation for these intra-continental differences can lie in a variety of factors, including the fact that the analysed national cultures differ significantly, and/or the fact that there are distinct educational cultures which are manifest in the institutional frameworks.

In order to control for other variables which could distort the effect of national culture on behaviour, we ran a separate analysis in which we took a closer look at the influence of gender and institutional factors. First, we split the samples into male and female populations. T-tests of the data revealed significant, but rather small differences between male and female students within and across nationalities for a number of selected items. As Table 1.3 shows, it can be assumed that very little of the variance in the data can be explained through gender (blank cells indicate no significant difference).

As can be seen from Table 1.3, the most apparent gender differences in our data can be found in Germany, followed by Austria, and by far the fewest in Singapore. For example, German female students prefer professors who show empathy, they are stricter against cheating, prefer written exams more strongly than their male colleagues, and are stricter when it comes to keeping deadlines. It is interesting to compare this with the four countries' ranks on Hofstede's (2001) masculinity index,

Table 1.2: Inter-continental and intra-continental differences in attitudes towards learning

Dimensions with significant differences between Europe and Asia	1. Criticism not allowed (degree to which students think it is acceptable to criticize their professor) 2. Preferred gender homogeneity of work groups (degree to which students prefer to work in groups of the same gender) 3. National homogeneity of work groups (degree to which students accept / prefer national homogeneity in groups) 4. Cheating allowed (degree to which academic dishonesty is accepted) 5. Relevance of job prospects (degree to which students choose programmes / courses on the basis of job prospects) 6. Group study preferred (degree to which students' prefer to study in groups) 7. Use and importance of technology (degree to which students prefer professors who use multimedia technology in the classroom)
Dimensions with significant differences within (surveyed) Asian countries	1. Professor's responsibility for student's success (degree to which students think that their professors are responsible for their own success or failure) 2. Learning not beyond the required scope (degree to which students' are unwilling to pursue learning beyond the required scope of a class) 3. Criticism not allowed (degree to which students think it is acceptable to criticize their professor) 4. Non-equal interaction (degree to which students see themselves as different in status to their professors) 5. Preferred gender homogeneity of work groups (degree to which students prefer to work in groups of the same gender) 6. Empathy and students' suggestions (degree to which students prefer professors who show empathy and accept students' suggestions) 7. Preference for written exams (degree to which students prefer to have assessments in the form of written exams)
Dimensions with significant differences between (surveyed) European countries	1. Cheating allowed (degree to which academic dishonesty is accepted) 2. Memorizing (degree to which students have a preference for memorization of content)

Table 1.3: Differences in attitudes towards learning by gender

Factor	Austria (female/male)	Germany (female/male)	Singapore (female/male)	Thailand (female/male)
1. Consistency and intensity of effort (degree to which students have a preference for consistency and intensity of effort)	—	2.2 / 2.1	—	—
2. National homogeneity of work groups (degree to which students accept / prefer national homogeneity in groups)	—	3.6 / 3.8	—	—
3. Empathy and students' suggestions (degree to which students prefer professors who show empathy and accept students' suggestions)	1.8 / 1.7	—	—	—
4. Cheating allowed (degree to which academic dishonesty is accepted)	—	2.7 / 2.4	—	—
5. Seating arrangement (addresses students' preference for specific types of seating arrangement)	—	2.4 / 2.6	—	2.4 / 2.6
6. In-class discussion for better understanding (degree to which students' prefer to have in-class discussions on the course content)	—	—	—	2.3 / 2.4
7. Learning not beyond the required scope (degree to which students' are unwilling to pursue learning beyond the required scope of a class)	—	—	—	2.9 / 3.0
8. Non-equal Interaction (degree to which students see themselves as different in status to their professors)	—	—	—	2.2 / 2.3
9. Preference for written exams (degree to which students prefer to have assessments in the form of written exams)	3.0 / 2.7	2.7 / 2.4	—	—
10. Applicability of study (degree to which application of study content is important to and enjoyable for students)	1.5 / 1.3	—	—	1.7 / 1.6
11. Professors as experts (degree to which students expect their professors to be recognized experts in their area of teaching)	—	—	1.7 / 1.6	—
12. Grading based not only on exam (degree to which students' accept / prefer that grading in a course is based on one exam only)	2.0 / 1.8	—	—	—
13. Keeping of deadlines (degree to which students consider and accept deadlines as binding)	2.3 / 2.1	2.6 / 2.4	—	—

Note: (5-point Likert scale: 1 = strongest agreement, 5 = strongest disagreement; n = 2400 all differences significant at .001 level).

which is much higher for Austria and Germany than for Singapore or Thailand (i.e., in the first two countries males in particular place more emphasis on ego-goals such as achievement rather than social goals such as rapport). The only gender-related difference to report from Singapore concerns the demand of 'expert professors' – male students there show a slightly stronger agreement.

Next, a closer look was taken at the influence which the type of institution has on the differences in attitudes towards learning. This was especially warranted as there are two distinct university tracks in Austria and Germany – traditional universities with a stronger emphasis on academic disciplines and a stronger orientation towards theory, and the so-called universities of applied sciences which have a stronger orientation towards the needs of specific industries and which are more applied in their teaching. As Table 1.4 shows, running t-tests we were able to find several small, but nevertheless statistically significant differences in the attitudes towards learning among students in these different types of universities.

In overview, the results in Table 1.4 show that students in Austrian universities of applied sciences are more open to different abilities of student peers and to exams other than written ones. They seem to be more active in class (criticism, discussion) and more demanding or used to higher standards related to professor's expertise, seating arrangement and use of technology. Job prospects are more relevant to them than to their peers from traditional universities. Especially in the case of Austria these observations may be rooted in the fact that Austrian universities of applied sciences have rather strict entry requirements and tend to attract students who are more competitive, whilst entry into traditional universities is completely open to all students regardless of their merit or aspirations. This may well have created an atmosphere in which challenge and performance are valued. To a lesser extent, the same holds true for Germany. However, in this case the reasons may be rooted solely in the fact that German universities of applied sciences have a stronger application and industry orientation. The reason of merit-based admission does not apply for Germany as the German system still has stronger entry restrictions in the traditional university track.

Austrian students appear to be indifferent about the issue of job prospects (i.e., they are not more or less relevant than other motivations for study such as interest, parents' preference, etc.), while students in Germany, Singapore and Thailand seem to take job prospects into consideration, with Thailand and Singapore scoring highest of the surveyed countries. Furthermore, students from all surveyed countries agree that

Table 1.4: Differences in attitudes towards learning by type of university

Aspect of learning	Germany		Austria	
	University	University of Applied Sciences	University	University of Applied Sciences
1. Relevance of job prospects (degree to which students choose programmes / courses on the basis of job prospects)	—	—	2.4	2.2
2. Initiative, excellence in classroom (degree to which students' initiative and excelling in the classroom is accepted / preferred / pursued)	3.0	2.7	—	—
3. In-class discussion for better understanding (degree to which students' prefer to have in-class discussions on the course content)	3.5	2.3	2.3	1.9
4. Non-equal interaction (degree to which students see themselves as different in status to their professors)	—	—	2.7	2.8
5. Professors as experts (degree to which students expect their professors to be recognized experts in their area of teaching)	—	—	2.1	1.6
6. Criticism not allowed (degree to which students think it is not acceptable to criticize their professor)	—	—	3.4	3.7
7. Written exam (degree to which students prefer to have assessments in the form of written exams)	—	—	2.7	3.0
8. Grading based not only on exam (degree to which students' prefer that grading in a course is based on one exam only)	2.1	2.0	—	—
9. Personal space in classroom (degree to which students seek personal space in the classroom)	2.4	2.2	—	—
10. Seating arrangement (addresses students' preference for specific types of seating arrangement)	—	—	2.5	2.1
11. Use and Importance of technology (degree to which students prefer the use of multimedia technology in the classroom)	—	—	2.2	2.0
12. Homogeneity of ability of student peers (degree to which students' tolerate / seek being in groups of students with different levels of ability)	—	—	2.5	2.7

Note: (5-point Likert scale: 1 = strongest agreement, 5 = strongest disagreement; n = 2400; all reported figures significant at .001 level).

interactive arrangements are conducive to learning: differences between the surveyed countries are minimal. While students from Thailand and Germany seem undecided about who bears dominant responsibility in student success, students from Austria and Singapore disagree that the professor has a responsibility in student success.

Discussion

Most of our results show some apparent links to relevant findings from the literature on cross-cultural differences, especially to those by Hofstede (2001) and the GLOBE project (House et al., 2004). For instance, several aspects of the attitudes towards learning from our results seem to be related to differences in power and status. Most evidently, students in Thailand perceive themselves as not being equal to their professors, which is in alignment with the relatively high scores on Hofstede's and GLOBE's Power Distance dimensions for Thailand. The scores on the 'Criticism not Allowed' and 'Cheating not Allowed' items can be related to the same dimensions by Hofstede or GLOBE, on which both Singapore and Thailand show relatively high values. Even the 'Memorizing' item might fit into that pattern of explanation, as the acceptance of memorization may be interpreted as an expression of showing respect and obedience towards professors. Thailand's somewhat extreme position on the 'Professor's Responsibility for Student Success' item is remarkable along the same lines. The strong belief in status differences in Thailand apparently has created a feeling of dependence on professors, which in return establishes a certain responsibility for professors towards their students – students expect the professor to watch out over them and make sure they succeed. With one of the lowest power distance scores Austrians, on the other hand, don't share the view that being critical of their professors should be avoided or even disapproved of.

When it comes to the individualism–collectivism dimension, which is also known from both the Hofstede and the GLOBE studies, links can be established between our results and these studies which confirm many of Hofstede's (1986) predictions for studying behaviour in this dimension. Students from countries with a collectivistic orientation also show a more positive attitude towards working in groups. In addition, they prefer study groups to be somewhat homogeneous which again points into the direction of collectivism. Even the responses to the item 'professors can be criticized by students' can be interpreted through this dimension in a meaningful way: in collectivistic cultures, formal harmony is a key value which needs to be maintained at all cost. This implies that professors must not be criticized by their students. In return, in collectivistic cultures, students expect their professors to take responsibility for their success or failure, an assumption our data confirms for Thailand.

It proved to be more difficult to identify clear patterns in linking the differences emerging from our data to the concept of uncertainty avoidance, i.e., the degree to which individuals try to avoid risk, uncertainty and ambiguity, and strive for security and certainty. Students from Singapore and Thailand have relatively lower values on this dimension in the Hofstede and GLOBE studies compared to Austrian or German students and are therefore assumed to be more risk-taking, innovative, and less conservative or obedient to rules in their behaviour. This might explain why they are more willing to embrace new technology in the classroom. Other potential links between uncertainty avoidance and the results of the study, however, are rather weak. For instance, it was expected that students from cultures with high uncertainty avoidance would be looking for security which is better provided by traditional classroom seating. With interactive seating they might feel uncomfortably exposed. The results only partially (in the case of Singapore) support this expectation. The same is true for initiative and excellence; it might be expected that only students from cultures with low uncertainty avoidance such as Singapore would value these traits, but this was not confirmed by the data. Other expectations, such as that students from uncertainty avoiding cultures like Austria or Germany would feel more comfortable with the precise memorization and retrieval of texts could not be confirmed by our data.

Taking a look at questions of masculinity and gender egalitarianism it is remarkable that gender homogeneity is clearly more strongly preferred by Singaporean students than by Austrian or German students. Looking at masculinity scores this would have been the expectation for the more masculine countries, such as Austria. One possible explanation, however, may be rooted in the fact that Singapore scores higher on gender egalitarianism than Austria or Germany. As a result, the importance of gender diversity which Austrians and German students feel might not be relevant in the Singapore context. Another explanation may be that Austrians' and Germans' preference for groups which are diverse in gender is not necessarily an expression of gender equality, but quite to the contrary – as we can only make assumptions of the roles of female students in work groups – as an expression of gender inequality. As Hofstede's (1986) masculinity dimensions also carries the facet of relationship orientation vs. task orientation, we may even use it to explain the fact that cheating seems to be a much more commonly acknowledged practice in Austria than in other cultures. The common assumption in a masculine, achievement-oriented, competitive society which values challenge and advancement may be that whatever leads to results should be allowed, including not playing by the rules. The same holds true for the question of criticizing a professor. Only in more 'feminine' societies (such as Singapore and Thailand in this sample) which value relationships and harmony over tasks and achievements would criticizing professors not be acceptable behaviour. Students in 'feminine' societies normally show more modest behaviour (Hofstede). Equally, the fact that students in Thailand see professors as being responsible for their own success or failure may be interpreted as a consequence of stronger relationship orientation than in masculine societies.

Recommendations

Based on the results outlined above and the interpretation within the wider context of national culture it is possible to make recommendations on a large number of diverse topics such as group work vs. individual work, oral vs. written exams, professors as experts, criticism vs. respect, memorization vs. application and many more. For example, based on our research, it appears that students from Austria, Germany, Singapore or Thailand are all willing to work in gender diverse groups. Nevertheless, teachers should be aware that while Germany and Austria have preferences for gender diverse groups, Thai and Singaporean students are somewhat neutral about it. When putting together study or project groups, teachers should therefore avoid having gender homogeneous groups in Austria or Germany, while these would be more likely to be tolerated by Thai or Singaporean students. Another recommendation based on our research is that when instructing students from Thailand, Singapore or Germany, professors need to be aware that students might show less genuine interest in the subject of study as they are propelled by extrinsic motivations. It might therefore be necessary for the instructor 'to go the extra mile' in order to make them enthusiastic and have them actively participate in class. What can be done, for example, is to highlight how relevant a class topic is towards the goal of landing a good job after graduation. More recommendations, by country, include the following:

For Austrian students it is not that important that professors are experts within their field. A possible explanation is offered by

Hofstede's (1986; 2001) Power Distance Index (PDI) dimension. The extremely low Power Distance index points into the direction of a less status-oriented and less hierarchically structured society which actually has a disbelief in authority, even if it is expert authority.

Another finding concerns academic honesty. If instructors are dealing with students from Austria, they are well advised to find modes of assessment which leave less room for dishonesty. Austrians generally show a more lenient attitude towards plagiarism or cheating on exams. Therefore, for instance, professors should make sure to find modes of assessment that prevent such behaviour. This type of behaviour may be explained by both moderately high Uncertainty Avoidance (UAI) which makes Austrians attempt to reduce the risk of inferior grades and a very high score on Masculinity (MAS) which induces Austrians to be very competitive, even at the expense of honesty and ethical behaviour.

German students feel free to criticize professors. There seems to be a clear link to Hofstede's (1986; 2001) Power Distance (PDI) dimension. In Germany, with a moderately low score on the PDI, there is less of a hierarchical relationship between professors and students and it is therefore allowed and common for students to criticize their professors. Students may be even expected (by fellow students and professors) to challenge the views of professors in the classroom. Would students refrain from critical contributions to in-class discussions they might be considered too timid, as lacking interest in the class, or even as less capable. German students also have a much stronger preference for written exams and dislike exams or a mix of different types of assessment. This fact may be explained through a combination of Germany's low PDI and medium Uncertainty Avoidance (UAI) scores. First, on the grounds of low PDI, knowledge is considered a matter that needs to be handled in a way that leaves little room for subjective interpretations as in the case of oral exams. And secondly, written exams also cater to the apparent need of Germans for greater certainty and security as evidenced by Germany's medium score on UAI. Instructors teaching in Germany need to respect this by adapting their grading policy so that grading is mainly based on written forms of assessment such as mid-term and end-term exams, written reports or written case study assignments.

A combination of several dimensions – low Uncertainty Avoidance (UAI), high Power Distance (PDI) and medium Masculinity (MAS) makes students in Singapore very competitive. Students are more risk-taking and subscribe to values such as challenge and advancement, and are therefore taking a very pro-active approach to their own education. They like to participate in discussions with their professors, don't mind to be worked hard and also engage in studying beyond the required scope of classes. When professors are used to more timid and deferential behaviour in students, they may feel challenged, maybe even criticized. They need to prepare themselves for such situations by being well-prepared, by always being one step ahead of the students, and by setting a demanding pace and depth in their courses. In no way must instructors interpret Singaporean students' behaviour as rude or inappropriate. Quite to the contrary, the high Power Distance (PDI) renders the pro-active behaviour of Singaporean students an act of respect and appreciation of the professor.

Due to lower Individualism (IDV) scores, students from Thailand feel less comfortable with anything which requires them to stand out as individuals. Instructors are therefore advised to rethink their didactic approach and make it possible for students to work more in group contexts (e. g. group projects as opposed to individual assignments). Our findings also show that students from Thailand strive for better understanding through consistency and intensity of effort. This means that Thai students are usually well prepared when coming to class. Instructors teaching in Thailand therefore always have to make sure that they are equally well prepared in class. One potential explanation could be a higher score on the Power Distance (PDI) dimension. As professors generally deserve the respect of students, they will do everything not to let the professor down. At the same time, however, we found that among Thai students one of the strongest motivations to study a specific subject is job prospects. That means that they are extrinsically motivated and therefore may show less of an interest in the content presented to them during the course of their study programme. Instructors need to address this issue by choosing an approach that makes the link between their course and future job opportunities very explicit. Again, this may be related to Thailand's score on the Power Distance (PDI) dimension.

A large number of recommendations based on the results of our research have been compiled into a handbook.[3] Through the use of our results, students and professors alike will be able to adjust their behaviour to a culturally foreign environment. At the same time, a number of new, interesting questions have been unearthed. One of the most important insights has been that the idea of one 'Asian learner', especially the 'Asian rote learner' has to be discarded as has been suggested by other authors (e.g., Kember & Gow, 1991 or Watkins & Reghi, 1991). We not only identified clear differences between Singaporean and Thai students as well as between Austrian and German students, but we also found some striking similarities between Asian and European students. In some cases Asian students unexpectedly scored even higher than European students in some aspects of learning (e.g., in the case of 'not learning beyond the required scope' where students from Singapore were wrongly expected to be less willing to engage in additional learning than Austrians or Germans). More insight into these observations can be expected through an extension of our study into other countries.[4] One potential explanation for some of the counter-intuitive results including the similarities between Asian and European countries could be globalization of teaching practices. Although there is widespread criticism of the didactic model of the US business school which fosters dialogue, interaction and criticism (Saner & Yiu, 1994) its global influence can't be ignored. Assuming that the US influence has been more readily accepted in some Asian countries, this would even explain the higher scores of Asian students – reflecting higher individualism and competitiveness.

Based on the differences identified for different types of universities (traditional vs. applied), we also recommend a closer look at the influence of factors in the internal and external environment of institutions of higher education. As learning (or teaching) styles are not necessarily only properties of the individual, but rather emerge out of an interaction between learner and the learning environment, it is important to look beyond the narrow view of individual attitudes. Richardson (1994) found evidence that learning styles 'vary systematically from one culture to another' (p. 449), but at the same time his analysis does not attribute undesirable approaches to learning to personal characteristics of individuals, but instead to students' 'attempts to cope with counterproductive institutional practices that are likely to show systematic cultural variation' (p. 464). We find it therefore important for future work to include multiple concepts of culture besides national culture, such as organizational and company culture.

From a methodological perspective it has to be admitted that our original hope, to identify a set of a few selected patterns or factors – learning styles – in our data which would enable us to classify learners from different countries into a typology has not materialized. Instead we identified a larger number of meaningful attitudes towards learning with significant differences between countries. The results will be more meaningful once additional countries are integrated in the survey. In addition, further research must include more representative samples from various regions of countries and it also has to account for different subjects of studying, different types of institution, teachers and their style of teaching which all can have an impact of students' approaches to learning.

Reflection questions

1. Look at Table 1.1. From your perspective, how would you respond to the nine items which showed significant differences between countries?
2. Based on question 1, where do you see the greatest need for adaptation of your own teaching style when moving into a culture which holds attitudes in contrast to your own?
3. Think about the studying behaviour of students in your context. In your view, what influences their behaviour most – national culture, institutional culture or personality traits?
4. If you have teaching experience in both the Western and the Asian parts of the world, would you endorse the stereotype of the 'Asian rote learner'?

Notes

1. In alphabetical order.
2. Student flows in this context refers to students pursuing a degree outside their home country. It does not include short- and medium-term foreign student exchanges.
3. Available from the authors upon request.
4. Projects in such diverse countries as Argentina, Colombia, France, India, Mexico and Peru are already under way.

Resources

Gordon, L. (1993). *People types and tiger stripes*. Gainesville, FL: Center for Applications of Psychological Type.
 Classic book on differences in learning styles. A must-read for all interested academics.
Hofstede, G. (1986). Cultural differences in teaching and learning. *International Journal of Intercultural Relations, 10*, 310–20.
 An article on how the dimensions of Power Distance, Individualism/Collectivism, Uncertainty Avoidance and Masculinity/Femininity relate to teaching and learning.
http://eu-india.fh-joanneum.at and http://eu-alfa.fh-joanneum.at
 Websites on follow-up projects involving universities in Argentina, Austria, Colombia, France, Germany, India, Mexico and Peru. Includes a complete

documentation of the project, including reports, presentations, further links and contact information.

www.communicon.info/

The website accompanying the research project at the heart of this chapter. The website provides a complete documentation of the project, including reports, presentations and further links.

www.ed.ac.uk/etl/

A very informative website on a project titled 'Enhancing Teaching-Learning Environments in Undergraduate Courses' at the University of Edinburgh. A number of articles on state of the art research in learning styles is available from this site.

2
Teaching Business Studies to Far East Students in the UK

Irene C. L. Ng

This chapter offers insights into the challenges students from the Far East face on courses in the UK. In addition, it investigates students' perceptions of the value of the business education obtained in the UK, and of the applicability of that education in the students' home countries. The results show that Far Eastern students employ thinking strategies that are different from Western students; they face dissonance in studying ethics and corporate social responsibility, which they consider as a 'Western logic'; they have difficulties in understanding Western-based epistemology; and they look on a UK education more as a signalling/certification tool than as a valuable learning experience. The study concludes with suggestions on how some of the issues raised could be addressed.

Introduction

This qualitative study endeavours to bring insights into two issues. First, to understand the teaching and learning difficulties faced when Far East students come to the UK for education, and second to understand how students perceive the value of the business education obtained and its perceived applicability in the students' home countries. The chapter reviews the differences in typical Western[1] and Eastern thought processes, and how these create a learning/teaching gap. It then follows on to discuss cultural issues that surface in learning business, particularly as business as an academic subject is of Western origin and is also valued precisely because of that. Eastern and Western business styles are also discussed.

Following on from the literature review, the chapter presents its methodology and findings. Four major issues are presented that pose a learning/teaching challenge in the delivery of business education. The chapter concludes with a discussion of the findings and how instructors could manage the challenges faced in teaching a multicultural and multinational classroom.

Context

Business education in the UK has become immensely popular amongst Far East[2] students. The UK Higher Education Statistics Agency reported a 6.1 per cent increase in overseas students for 2004/05, to a total of 318,400, with business and administration being the most popular subjects and accounting for 27 per cent of total overseas students doing higher education in the UK. After the EU, China is the number one contributor of students, with Malaysia, Singapore, Japan, Hong Kong and Taiwan within the top ten list (Higher Education Statistics Agency, 2006). This phenomenon is not restricted to the UK: in Canada, out of 70,000 foreign students enrolled in Canadian universities, almost five out of every ten were from Asia, and China accounted for almost 44 per cent of these Asian students (University Enrolment, 2005).

The IDP forecasts growth in higher education worldwide from around 100 million places in 2000 to 260 million in 2025, of which seven million will be international students going overseas or taking courses from overseas (Daniel, 2004). Far East students, particularly from China, are amongst the highest in numbers. The reasons are both economic and cultural. Nine years after the financial crisis of 1997, Asian economies are enjoying a comeback and many East Asians have embraced capitalism with a passion. Making money is now the order of the day and business seems to be the vehicle towards wealth and prosperity. With increased economic activity, the demand for business skills has increased and so have the salaries of graduates. This situation is even more pronounced in China, where the last two decades of economic liberalization have brought in immense investments, to the extent that there has been a critical shortage of employees trained in management (Lau & Roffey, 2002). This has resulted in high numbers of Chinese students studying overseas, as well as a proliferation of management education and executive training programmes being made available within China (McGugan, 1995). The drive to acquire business skills, information and strategies has also pushed the number of MBAs awarded globally to record numbers (Ng, 2006).

Another reason for an increased interest in education is cultural: Confucian philosophy and East Asian upbringing place tremendous value on education. Even in the United States, where 5.5 per cent of the population was Asian in 1995, Asians accounted for 40 per cent of the students in the University of California, a testimony that education is part of an 'investment culture of Asians' (de Bono, 1996, p. 56), and that the pursuit of education is expected of young people, rather than something they could choose not to engage in. With higher student mobility, higher education institutions worldwide have to cope with increased diversity in the classroom, and educators are faced with the issue of multiculturalism.

Literature review

Multiculturalism is the buzz-word of this age, where calls for greater acceptance and tolerance are made in every context, be it in politics, business, economics or education. As Trotman (2002) puts it, 'multiculturalism tries to restore a sense of wholeness in a postmodern era that fragments human life and thought' (p. ix). Hence, multiculturalism emphasizes mutual respect and tolerance of each other's cultures.

In Asia, multicultural life began long before the word was coined. Malaysia, Singapore and indeed, the whole of South-East Asia has been a collection of multicultural societies since trade began in the third century, as travellers from various origins stayed on in their host countries and eventually made them their own (Stuart-Fox, 2003). The coordination and management of multiculturalism, borne out of necessity, has been embedded in the lifestyles, beliefs, actions and growth of such societies. A Chinese in Malaysia speaks an average of three languages, and exhibits a mix of nationalistic, ethnic, religious and acculturated characteristics in their everyday lives. However, since multiculturalism in these societies is a tacit practice, there has been little research or documentation until lately as to what has worked and what has not. Although studied by anthropologists, the anthropological account of culture is so complex that it does not sufficiently inform the study of multiculturalism for the purpose of action, policies or thought within a multicultural society (cf. Turner, 1994). Clearly, multiculturalism is not merely a study of cultures but also one that has a *purpose*, i.e., as Turner puts it, 'a conception of culture as empowerment for collective action, self production and struggle' (p. 424).

Nowhere is this truer than in multicultural education. Research on multicultural education focuses on ethnic identities and cultural pluralism with the aim of either reducing prejudice and discrimination in the classroom to promote a shared culture (i.e., 'melting pot' perspective, cf. McNergney and Herbert, 2001), or promoting core human values ('global' perspective, cf. Ameny-Dixon, 2004). The former view has its origins in the USA, where smaller cultures are expected to give up their identities to assimilate into a shared American macroculture (Bennett, 2003). The latter view seeks to dispel the idea of having only one way of thinking and one way of life, and strives instead to promote respect and appreciation of various cultures by increasing cultural competency (Green, 1989; Gollnick & Chinn, 2002), i.e., a concept of a cultural mosaic rather than a melting pot (McNaught, 1988). Clearly the melting pot perspective may not be applicable in an institution of higher education where the diversity of cultures arises from having students from all over the world, rather than cultures within a country. Such students do not wish to give up their cultural identities as they may have no wish to stay on after their studies and indeed, most would choose to return to their home countries after acquiring their foreign degree. Even the global perspective of multicultural education does not provide sufficient answers, particularly when students come from vastly different educational systems and societies, have dissimilar values and subscribe to different philosophies, with much of it tacitly embedded in language, lifestyles and social networks. In other words, with today's instructors faced with both a multicultural and a multinational classroom, lessons from existing scholarship in multicultural education seem inadequate to assist instructors in delivering a better education experience.

The differences in learning styles may be more pronounced in the case of Far East students, particularly those with Confucian backgrounds. Far East cultures are generally considered to have different approaches to philosophy, knowledge and debate, and to exhibit different habits of mind. Despite some reservations (e.g., Ortner, 2003), Nisbett's (2003) review of numerous research papers in experimental psychology demonstrates that the Western Aristotelian-based attitude is based in the need to control others and the world through the creation of mental models by categorizing objects and events to answer the questions of 'why?' and 'who is right?'. This attitude focuses on attempting to obtain underlying principles through debate, and is linked to thinking that education is good in its own right. In contrast, the Eastern, Confucian-based attitude is not concerned with control of others or the environment, but is rather concerned with self-control. Debate is discouraged as leading to discord, and there is often a willingness to concede merit in the other person's point of view. There is not really an interest in 'why?' or 'who is right?' but rather in answering more pragmatic 'how' questions. Education, in this regard is valued for the practical consequences of action. A compilation of the differences between 'Western' and 'Eastern' habits of mind arising from this attitude is presented in Table 2.1.

Table 2.1: 'Western' and 'Eastern' habits of mind

Key elements where thought processes may differ	'Western' thought process	'Eastern' thought process
Patterns of attention and perception	Attending to objects and classifications	Attending to environments and relationships
Basic assumptions about the nature of the world	World consists of separate objects	World consists of seamless substances
Controllability of the environment	Environment can be changed and controlled	Environment needs adjusting to
Tacit assumptions about stability and change	Assumes stability	Assumes change
Preferred patterns of explanation of events	Focuses on the specific and on objects	Focuses on the broader context and environment
Use of formal logic	Formal logic central to understanding of events	Formal logic set aside to attain desirable conclusions
Use of dialectical approaches	Hegelian approach with confrontation between thesis and antithesis leading to new synthesis and superior answer	Confucian approach seeking the Middle Way allowing for the correctness of the other's viewpoint

Source: (Nisbett, 2003: 44–5; 171).

Admittedly, there are differences between Asian countries, as well as gender differences which interact with culture (just as it is similarly flawed to consider Westerners as a homogenous group). Yet broad differences exist, and it is not surprising that a learning/teaching gap may exist when Far East students study in the UK.

Cultural characteristics also influence the structure of communities. Tsang (1998), referring to an earlier work by Hwang (1987), observes that 'many Chinese have lived in encapsulated communities that are hierarchically organized, with major economic and other resources controlled by a few power figures who could arbitrarily allocate resources' (p. 65). Hence, cultural issues have had a tremendous influence on structural, political and economic organization in Eastern societies; in other words, the Eastern habit is not merely cultural but also structural, allowing for the culture to be expressed. Against this backdrop, one of the aims of this study is to investigate the issues that arise when Far East students from such environments study in a Western environment such as the UK.

Multicultural education literature often avoids the role of the subject discipline in the understanding of multicultural learning. Since disciplines can also be viewed as cultures (Becher, 1993), the understanding of multicultural education should also take into account the subject matter being taught. In the case of business education for example, it is commonly acknowledged that the practice of business worldwide is by no means homogeneous. The Internet site www.worldbiz.com provides reports on business practices, customs and protocol, cross-cultural communication, negotiating, and etiquette when doing business in more than 120 countries. Academic literature has also acknowledged that, particularly in Asia, there are stark differences in the way business is being structured or carried out (e.g., Yau et. al., 2000). The Western view of business is basically selfish, opportunistic and instrumental, conforming to the philosophy of the market economy. In Milton Friedman's widely-quoted words, 'The social responsibility of business is to increase its profits' (Friedman, 1970). Good business is still perceived in the West to be hard-headed, aggressive and a 'lean and mean profit machine' through instructions such as 'The Lean Six-Stigma', a popular business methodology aimed at giving companies a competitive edge in a global marketplace (Sterman, 2005). Despite the rise of 'soft capitalism' i.e. 'the rhetoric of new cultures of work and organisations, claiming self-motivation, self-actualization and emotions of belonging and sharing as the motivation for enhancing productivity and commitment to the organisation' (cf. Heelas, 2002;

Heikkinen, 2004, p. 492), the firm's historical role in economic theory is price-guided (rather than management-guided) and serves the market for the benefit of shareholders. There is very little room for negotiation within such a philosophy for 'softer' issues. Yet, soft issues exist, for it is difficult to imagine that the function of an individual within a modern organization is fully and homogeneously logical, rational, self-interested and instrumental. In fact, a scathing critique by Ghoshal (2005) suggests that business schools have condoned pessimistic assumptions of the human person within the firm, denying the ethical and moral responsibilities in business theories, and are in part responsible for corporate failures such as Enron's.

In contrast, Eastern business styles and organization are formed through the understanding of human interactions. Long before the current structure of economic societies and the organization of businesses, trade in Asia (as also in Europe) was already flourishing. Trade routes between China and the rest of Asia were the conduits for immigration, commerce, political maneuvering and cultural understanding, and the period between the mid-fifteenth to the mid-seventeenth century has been called the 'age of commerce' in Southeast Asia (Reid, 1988). Despite its long history, the knowledge of how and why commerce was so successful as it was is largely tacit, and East Asians have never explicitly understood, or documented, how they have made it work. To this day, many East Asian companies are still loosely structured, with very little sense of accountability, and with strong kinship biases. For example, Korean chaebols (conglomerates) that are responsible for the country's industrialization and increased standard of living over the last 40 years started as family businesses and are still family-managed to this day. A study conducted in 1978 found that out of 2,797 executives of large Korean enterprises, some 12 per cent were directly related to the founders by blood or marriage (Kim & Kim, 1989) and another study found that 31 per cent of top executives were family members, 40 per cent recruited from outside and 29 per cent promoted from within the firm (Lee & Yoo, 1987). One could argue that the rise of soft capitalism such as that described above in the West is born out of the need to generate trust, which is hard to come by in a pure capitalistic society (Thrift, 1997). Eastern communities rely on nepotism and kinship to generate that trust, as well as to reap the benefits of such trust – albeit in a manner that is less acceptable to modern Western sensibilities.

The Chinese are also generally considered to be a communal society whose lives tend to revolve around relationships (Nisbett, 2003).

Simmons and Munch (1996) emphasize that 'almost no other culture gives such high importance to maintaining interpersonal relationships . . . They socialize while eating and drinking, but a major goal of this socialization is relationship-building'. Nisbett (2003) also states that the Chinese tend to detect relationships more readily from events than Westerners and the achievement of harmony in relationships is the chief goal of Chinese social life. The building of relationships is the lifeblood of the Chinese community, with roots extending into politics, business and society (Luo, 1997).

In the eyes of today's Western world, many East Asian organizations are opaque and the legal systems in such economies immature (In praise of rules, 2001). Asia's embrace of today's Western-style capitalism is therefore seen as another pragmatic step towards better trade relations with the rest of the world, and an opportunity to learn the Western rules, through which investment and capital can then flow freely. Paradoxically, while Western business research is trying to learn the 'softer' skills of business, East Asian businesses are learning to be leaner and meaner. Or are they? While East Asian economies are learning the formal, transparent and explicit rules of business organization, such rules rest on a foundation of social, cultural and ethical habits that are too often taken for granted. Hence, while Ghoshal (2005) may charge that current business education propagates 'ideologically inspired amoral theories' (p. 76) that free students from moral responsibilities, such responsibilities may already be embedded within the Asian social and cultural habit.

The above suggests that students who study business in the UK may, on one hand, have difficulties in learning due to cultural differences, and on the other, learn business in the Western context only to return to an environment that they are ill-equipped to manage. Western business education is amoral, and it avoids contextualizing its knowledge as far as possible, so that the knowledge can be imparted to multiple persons and applicable in various contexts. However, curriculum development in business education often implicitly assumes that the business context is within a Western-style domain, with its corresponding legal and socio-economic framework. With management theories and techniques originally developed in the West, this means that business educators need to be aware of a possibility of 'pedagogical imperialism' in their efforts to educate the Far East student. On the other hand, Western-style business organization is what the majority of today's business world subscribes to, and the appeal of Western education is in part because of this, as well as the belief that Western-style organization of business is fairer, given its rules of corporate governance, transparency and social responsibilities. Even businesses in Asia, despite the Eastern style, are changing, as testified by the recent incident of Hyundai where the Chairman's effort to ensure the succession of his son to chairman-ship of the company has created a furore (Hyundai Apologises, 2006). Yet tensions between Eastern and Western styles exist, and researchers have acknowledged that, particularly in China, local political, philo-sophical and cultural characteristics may result in different ways of organizing economic activity (Boisot & Child, 1996).

With globalization as an economic, cultural, and social homogenizing force (Crawford, 2000), there is a necessity to investigate the value of business education in the Western context to Far East students. This study therefore aims to gain insights into the following questions:

- What are the manifestations of culture that result in teaching/learning difficulties for Far East students in the UK?
- How do Far East students perceive the value of a Western-based business education?

Researcher position

It is often acknowledged that the research process includes the position of the researcher (Sikes & Goodson, 2003). Hence, it is important to locate my position with respect to the research I am conducting so that the reader may understand the study from the perspective of my background, with the potential insights and biases that it brings.

As a female Malaysian Chinese, I was educated in Malaysia but com-pleted my first degree in Singapore, in Physics. Being part of an entrepreneurial Chinese family, I started my working life in the family business environment immediately after graduation, and spent eleven years in senior management of large companies based in Malaysia. I decided then to embark on my doctoral studies in Marketing as I believed that there would be value in my business experience that could be brought into research and teaching. I found that I enjoyed research and the spirit of enquiry, and moved into a lectureship position in a business school in the UK.

I soon found out that, unlike many UK academics of Far East descent who have studied entirely in the UK, I came into the country very much wearing 'Far East lenses' (cf. Brookfield, 1995), without much acculturation. This, I felt, helped me to empathize with Far East students. Yet, after three years in the UK and being immersed in contemporary academic practice, the 'Western lens' has also been somewhat acquired. Having come to the UK and into academia late in life has helped keep both lenses separate and allowed me to see the strengths and weaknesses of both cultures in terms of the teaching and learning experiences. My aim in this study is to improve the school's understanding of students' learning experiences as well as to employ my cultural background, business experience and academic sensitivity to study a phenomenon that clearly embodies all three dimensions.

Methodology

Data was collected through notes taken on critical incidents (Tripp, 1993), in-depth student interviews and a focus group interview. Observations were obtained through interaction and conversations with postgraduate students from Taiwan (three students), China (two students), Thailand (three students) and Singapore (one student), in a business school of a UK university, where some 60 per cent of the student population are from the Far East. The conversations and interactions were many, since I was directly responsible for postgraduate students at the school, as part of my administrative duties. As such, I had first-hand encounters with problems, issues and discussions pertaining to the postgraduate student community within the school. Other observational and anecdotal data was also collected from minutes of meetings, comments from module instructors teaching postgraduate Far East students and discussions with colleagues on teaching issues.

Soliciting opinions and thoughts from Far East students through interviews was difficult. Two particular difficulties are noted. First, social desirability (i.e., the inclination to respond in a manner that is socially desirable, rather than expressing one's true feelings) has a particularly strong influence on Far East students. Hence, many conversations started with students reporting how they thought they should feel, rather than how they actually felt. Only after obtaining much data over time and gaining some measure of trust did the actual feelings slowly materialize. Second, some Far East students were keener to understand why I was asking the question than to give an honest answer. The belief was that there was a right answer to the question, and they wanted to be helpful. Third, many Far East students were often reluctant to say anything negative about any situation: to get the data, questions had to be triangulated so that answers clearly showed any negative feelings without informants' explicitly saying so. Three categories of insights are presented below.

Results

Thinking and communication strategies

Observations from teaching Far East students both in the Far East and in the UK, as well as in-depth student interviews, suggest that the degree of risk aversion, particularly an aversion to appearing 'wrong', is high amongst such students. As such, Eastern students are not generally participative in class discussion. However, being in the UK seems to give students the perception that their thoughts may be allowed a little more freedom. Some admit that they 'dare to speak out' a little more in the UK than they would do otherwise. The multicultural environment seems to allow for less inhibition, much as anonymity in an online chat room makes the chatter less inhibited. Students also admitted that learning how to speak out helps them 'be distinctive'. One student claimed that 'Employers will see a difference between you and other employees because it shows that you have a mind of your own'. Thus, students find that those who speak out more are rewarded with a growing confidence, although they acknowledge that they would act differently if they were back in their own home country. The findings show that Far East students, ever the pragmatists, behave according to the environment.

Almost all students interviewed claimed to appreciate learning the ability to think critically, defined by Angelo (1995) as 'intentional application of rational, higher order thinking skills, such as analysis, synthesis, problem recognition and problem solving, inference, and evaluation' (p. 6). This skill clearly fascinated Far East students; yet many see it as a distinctively 'Western logic'. Students remarked that when they go back to Asia, they have to be careful with this way of thinking as it may not be acceptable to others. When I asked if learning such a way of thinking is advantageous, they mostly agreed, but one student commented that 'of what use if to put it to practice might land them more into trouble'? The findings also show that Far East students perceive that lessons in critical thinking serve them in two ways: first to learn how to think critically themselves (although they may not wish to practise it in an Asian environment) and second 'at least, we know how the Westerners think, so if we work in a Western company, we know the Western logic'. One student who has worked in a Western company in the Far East added cynically that even so, Westerners working in the Far East tend to follow the Eastern model – they seem to accept critical thinking from Western employees but not from Asians.

Dissonance

There is considerable dissonance detected in these students regarding learning business in the UK, although they cope with the dissonance in many different ways. Since the Western model of business is amoral, many business schools introduce subjects such as ethics and corporate social responsibility so as to bring some degree of social conscience into business, particularly after lessons learnt from major corporate scandals such as Enron and Worldcom. Yet, Far East students often avoid taking such modules. When asked why, three reasons are revealed.

First, many Far East students could not identify with the topics. Students think of themselves not as the company, but merely employees performing their tasks. 'It's not about what I think is ethical', says one student, 'but what I have to do in a company. It's my job, I just have to do it, ethical or not.' When asked about the ethical decisions they might make if they are empowered to do so on behalf of the company, a typical position was that 'the company has to make money: that is more important. If the company is already making money, we can probably afford to be more responsible.'

Second, there is clearly dissonance faced by the students in the study of ethics and social responsibility and what they see as 'the real world of business in Asia'. Interestingly, students manage the dissonance by viewing such studies as 'Western logic'. Asian societies are different, they charge, because we are young and we have different priorities. As one student claimed, 'the competition is keen, the pace is very fast, and we have to be more money-minded. To survive, to compete, we need to set aside ethics and environment and all these things.' Clearly some students accept the amorality of the Western business model, and reject the introduction of 'social conscience' subjects into the curriculum.

Finally, dissonance has led to some students arguing that 'what the Westerners call unethical may not be what we call unethical'. Yet students acknowledge that 'we have to learn what they consider to be ethical, you see, so that if we need to change to suit them, we know how we should change i.e., we know their rules'. Clearly, Far East business students see a dividing line of 'them' and 'us' in the study of business, in part to reduce the level of dissonance.

Students see that a lot of what is taught is 'Western' but they see the value of what is taught – even if they think there is limited applicability – just to know what business is like in the West. They adopt those principles that they think are workable and reject others. When asked if they think instructors are ethnocentric in their instruction and content, students seem to think that it is necessary for instructors to be ethnocentric, so that they can see how instructors think, as they (the instructors) represent the business thought of the West. When asked how they would like it if a Western instructor taught the Eastern style of doing business (if such a style exists) one student said, 'unless you are doing research in Asia, or have worked there a long time, or are an Asian yourself, it's better to teach the Western way and let us decide what could be useful in Asia'.

Epistemology

Learning by rote has made Asians essentially positivistic in their view of the world. There is a right and a wrong way of doing things and an 'objective' way is necessary to ensure harmony, so that there can be a meeting of minds. Hence, everyone is expected to conform to what's 'right'. Knowledge is often seen as received information, and memorization as valuable. This has serious implications when Asian students attempt to deliver a dissertation. Often, dissertations by Far East students are a regurgitation of facts; at the extreme, students blatantly plagiarize. Part of the reason is because they often mistakenly assume that the value of a dissertation is in how much information can be delivered into the thesis. One confused student asked 'if I don't report the facts, what is the value of my work?' Many don't understand why plagiarism is a problem. One student says 'I cite the author and the source in my work; why can't I use his sentences? He says it better!' Another student says, 'if I don't write down all that I've read, how does the examiner know that I've read them? He must know that I have studied, that I have made the effort, right?' Even in examinations, students often misunderstand: in open book exams, students become confused. 'How do I show you what I have learnt, if it's an open book examination?'

Signalling

Students claim that UK education sends the 'right' signal to employers. One student says 'If I am educated in the UK, a Western company will know that I know the Western concepts'. Another added, 'If I have a UK degree, they will know that my English is good'. The latter, ironically, was said by a student whose English was so poor that she had to say it in her native language and her words translated by her classmate. When asked about the learning acquired, the student shrugs. 'Not much. But have to make sure I pass all the exams to get the degree.' Clearly, many students value the certification more than the learning. Employability is always a big issue with students, but strategies (including the type of CV presented) differ if applying to a UK company as opposed to one in Asia: 'UK companies focus on skills; Asian companies focus on your qualifications so you have to modify it accordingly'.

Discussion

My data suggests that cultural habits lead Eastern students to think that there is always a 'right' answer as opposed to a 'good' answer. Compounding the issue is that students are not willing to risk thinking creatively. This is consistent with Gass's (1998) observations of Far East students when he comments that '[students] understand that to think creatively is to risk error, and they'd rather not'.

Cultural habits also lead students into being role-driven. Hence, much behaviour is justified according to where they are and what they are tasked to do. Although some may argue that this is inconsistent and contradictory, it may not be so when one considers the philosophical underpinnings of the Eastern culture – that one's identity is often collective and must be contextual. When an Easterner's identity is linked to the environment, a 'business mode' person is to do what he is required to do in business. This, in their perception, is not relevant to what or who the person 'truly' is (and the notion that there exists such a 'true' person is also debatable in Eastern terms). Past research has shown that it is not a contradiction for a Japanese man to be an aggressive manager in the office, and to be meek and submissive to a wife at home (Fukuyama, 1996). The role-in-context is the dominant driver of behaviour, and pragmatically this role determines what a person should be, within whatever environment s/he is in.

The findings in this study and also from others (e.g., Cheng, 1990; Wang et. al., 2005) show that harmony, above all else, is to be preserved, and the one that disrupts it is not to be given credit, even if what he is saying is right. To say that Easterners care more about harmony than being correct misses the point: the point is *to be right and to communicate it effectively, fitting in with opposing viewpoints and therefore without a need to disrupt harmony.* That is perceived to be the ultimate skill. Students consider that Westerners don't seem to make that effort and that in the West it is only important to be right.

The findings also suggest that much of the education in the Far East is learning by rote. Memorization, and not critical thinking, is therefore the key to academic success. The consequence of such thinking has contributed to Far East students' lack of critical thinking skills which are often necessary in a Western environment. Part of the reason is because Confucian culture necessitates the treatment of teachers' words as the gospel truth. Students have not been conditioned to think critically, not merely because they do not know how, but because students may fear that voicing evaluative thoughts that debate and discuss the issues taught may seem like criticism and may be construed as an insult to their teacher. Set against this background, entering into the UK environment requires considerable 're-conditioning' of the mind.

Clearly, learning critical thinking is a skill highly valued by Far East students, but students felt that they could choose to think in one way or another, depending on the circumstances. There is also dissonance faced in terms of what students value about Western-based business education and what instructors think they should value (e.g., ethics and social responsibility). However, a counter-intuitive finding shows an inherent link between ethnocentricity and the value of business education. Is it wrong to be ethnocentric when business, as a subject that is developed and organized in a Western environment, is valued precisely because of that? While multicultural education aims to be free of inherited biases (Parekh, 1986), would this not conflict with the value of business education which, as a subject, is desired to be specific to Western culture? The findings suggest that students need to be given the right to choose – even if they choose to subscribe to imperialistic notions – as only they themselves can evaluate the losses and rewards that come with their choices. Ironically, it also means that educators who are careful not to indulge in cultural imperialism fall prey to exactly that if they deprive the students of that choice. Far East students, with an intrinsic nature of being drawn to harmony, are often willing to acculturate for perceived rewards (e.g., collective good) that they believe could be obtained from acculturation.

Recommendations

The results also indicate that a lack of understanding of students' cultures may result in instructors misinterpreting students' intellectual abilities. Western instructors often assume that their notion of the value of knowledge and how it can be conveyed and learnt has little to do with culture. However, researchers (e.g., Kimball, 1978) as well as the findings here suggest that culture influences all dimensions of learning. While instructors may think that students show 'poor analytical skills', or are 'slow in learning', it is important to understand that the lack of such skills may be a legacy from a different education culture and the acquisition of such skills may lie in improving students' learning abilities by developing their meta-cognition, i.e., the 'knowledge and awareness of one's own cognitive processes' (Flavell 1976) and 'the ability to monitor, regulate and evaluate one's thinking' (Brown 1978). In other words, students could improve markedly once they are aware of the skills required in a Western context.

Furthermore, when students do poorly in certain subjects, there may be a tendency to blame poor English, particularly when many Far East students do not speak English as a first language. While the mastery of English language remains the most important skill to be acquired to facilitate learning in a Western environment, there is also a need to assist students in understanding the epistemological foundations of Western-based education. Where the design of a course requires students to think in a certain way (e.g., dissertations), students should be made aware of the nature, generation and value of such knowledge, rather than simply be given the rules of behaviour. Of course, there will always be a minority of students who intentionally plagiarize to avoid doing the work, but it is important for institutions to put in place a system to identify these, and to offer assistance to those who require it.

The study also finds the need for a starting point to bridge the gap between Far East students and the applicability of what is taught in business. Dissonance occurs often because students see conflicts and are not given ways to reconcile them – hence they reduce the dissonance in their own way, resulting in the possibility of misinterpreting what is taught. Thus, in line with lessons learnt from multicultural education, instructors could 'start teaching where students are' and 'expand the social, cultural, and intellectual horizons of students' (Gay, 1994: Teaching and Learning ¶9) to reduce dissonance. Education literature indicates that learning is more effective when new ideas are related to previous knowledge and are taught initially in ways familiar to students (Neisser, 1986). Of course, this means that there is a need to increase the cultural competency and literacy of instructors.

Finally, UK universities are obviously valued for quality in education. Yet the results presented here show a worrying trend whereby students value only the certification, and not the learning. Many UK universities are 'old brands', with promises of a pedigree education (though what that means varies with different people). Universities have to understand what that promise involves, and deliver accordingly. The danger is for students to attend UK universities to get a degree simply because the certification promises better job prospects, regardless of the learning experienced. In the extreme, the learning experience becomes a cost, rather than a benefit, to the student particularly when gaps exist that make students perceive the learning to be less relevant towards their employability (Ng & Forbes, 2006). Instructors therefore need to increase the relevance of their courses as well as develop their own cultural competency and literacy, because educational experiences should be perceived as personally meaningful to students. Where a course requires the instructor to make assumptions (and almost all business courses do to some extent), such as applicability towards the Eastern context, it is therefore necessary for instructors to be aware of such assumptions and make them explicit where necessary. Students can then consider whether the assumptions hold in their own cultures, rather than make their own assessments of what can or cannot work. Much of what is taught in business schools is actually relevant across cultures. However, when students do not think so, they lose interest and learning becomes a chore.

Conclusion

In this age of rapid globalization, education has a big role to play, both in terms of being an economic activity and of changing the classroom's multicultural dynamics. This study shows that when Far East students go abroad to study, almost everything is up for negotiation: culture, ethnicity, philosophy, and values. Students evaluate what they like or dislike, and redefine their own identities. They learn how the game is played, and in some cases, willingly acculturate themselves.

The study presented here examines the challenges of learning (and hence teaching) business across cultures, both in terms of difficulties encountered in teaching students of different cultural norms and in terms of what such students value in a Western business education when the application of it is in an Eastern context. These challenges would manifest themselves in all four modes of supply in higher education services according to the General Agreement on Trade in Services (GATS): cross-border supply (e.g., distance learning or e-education), consumption abroad (students studying outside their own country), commercial presence (e.g., branch campus, franchises etc.) and Presence of Natural Persons (mobile instructors) (Knight, 2002). In all four modes, students and instructors would typically come from different cultures. The study raises the question of what instructors should do to develop cultural competency and literacy so that a UK business degree would continue to be valued. Finally, it is not the aim of this chapter to claim that the issues here are generalizable to all Far East students.

Indeed, with globalization, immigration and increasing labour mobility, it would be difficult to discern the way culture, education and lifestyles combine in any one person. This study aims to demonstrate some learning and teaching issues that may arise as students from the Far East go abroad for their studies. Further research could run quantitative tests to examine the prevalence of such challenges, as well as how other teaching techniques such as practice-informed teaching could help increase relevance and reduce the learning/teaching gap.

Reflection questions

1. To what extent are students in your context keen to buy into Western (or other culturally different) disciplinary knowledge/expertise?
2. How do/could we construct the curriculum so that students are aware of subjects being culturally laden even though they are willing to accept its wisdom and teachings?
3. How do/could we assist students in negotiating the applicability of Western-based education in their home country?
4. In what way is your subject area historically and culturally constructed?

Notes

1. We define 'Western' thinking as those originating from the Aristotelian philosophies i.e., European and American cultures.
2. By the term 'Far East', I mean students who come from countries with roots in Confucianism such as Korea, Japan, China, Taiwan, Hong Kong, Singapore and the overseas Chinese in Thailand and Malaysia. Throughout the chapter, the terms 'Far East' and 'Eastern' are used interchangeably.

Resources

Ghoshal, S. (2005). Bad management theories are destroying good management practices. *Academy of Management Learning and Education*, 4(1), 75–91.
This paper is useful to understand the fundamental assumptions of management theories often taught in business schools today. Ghoshal attacks such assumptions as they allow business school academics to engage in a pretence of knowledge where there was none.
Hamilton, G. G., & Biggart, N. W. (1988). Market, culture, and authority: A comparative analysis of management and organization in the Far East. *American Journal of Sociology, 95*, 52–9.
This paper looks at the developed economies of Japan, Taiwan and Korea vis-à-vis three approaches to understanding decision-making in organizations: the market approach (which studies the conditions under which firms operate in a

market economy); the cultural approach (which looks at the role of culture and how economic behaviour is shaped by it); and the political economy approach (which focuses on decision making from the perspective of power and authority).

Watkins, D., & Biggs, J. (eds). (1996). *The Chinese learner: Cultural, psychological and contextual Influences*. Hong Kong: Central Printing.

This book researches the paradoxical question of how Chinese learners can be successful academically when their teaching and learning seems to be learning by rote and memorization. It shows that cross-cultural differences exist in the processes of teaching and learning, and explains the relationship between memorizing and understanding, and the nature of motivation.

Nisbett, R. (2003). *The geography of thought: How Asians and Westerners think differently . . . and Why*. New York: Free Press.

This book proposes that Asians and Westerners 'have maintained very different systems of thought for thousands of years' and that East Asians are more holistic in their perceptions (i.e., perceiving a scene as a whole) whilst Westerners have a more 'tunnel-vision perceptual style' that focuses on selecting objects from scenes and remembering them.

3

Cultural Learning in the Absence of Culture? A Study of How Students Learn Foreign Language and Culture in a Tertiary Classroom

Natalia Yevgenyevna Collings

This chapter represents a qualitative case study of what it means to learn new knowlege and skills in a college classroom. Inspired by this question, I spent three semesters observing a second year Russian language classroom in a large public American university in the Midwest. In this classroom, Russian cultural contexts brought in by the teacher often seemed to be dismissed by students, who limited their work to 'receiving a knowledge base', consisting according to their descriptions of mainly the grammar rules and vocabulary. In the process of observing lessons and interviewing six focal students and their teachers, I came to understand that knowledge of culture (or of any other subject) is a complex concept that students uniquely and individually construct in a constant dialogue with many social sources. Examples and teaching strategies will be shared to help educators understand how students construct knowledge in the context of a tertiary classroom.

Introduction

This chapter starts with a brief account of the context of the study by describing some of the cultural characteristics of the site, its population, and the researcher involved in this study. The literature review explains the theoretical lens used to analyse the results. In particular, the works of Bakhtin and Vygotsky are reviewed. After clarifying the research questions and methodology of a qualitative case study, the results are shared. This part consists of several sections. First, the assertion is made that the focal students conceptualized their learning as receiving a 'knowledge base' of grammar and vocabulary, despite all the teacher's attempts to make classroom learning cultural and contextual. This phenomenon is then explained as constrained by rather rigid genres of classroom communication following the pattern of Initiation, Response, and Evaluation (Mehan, 1979). The reader's attention is drawn to the unique and complex nature of the students' learning practice, which goes far beyond the classroom and rarely has explicit and predictable connections to the teacher's vision of bringing culture into the classroom. The chapter ends with a discussion of how the insights from this study might be applied in a university classroom. It also provides some resources for the readers' future reference.

Context

As a Russian who received a university degree in English language without ever leaving Russia, then as a university teacher of Russian in America, and finally as a Ph.D. student in an American college of education, I always wanted to gain more insight into how it is possible to learn a new language and find out about a new culture while being outside of it. As a result, I designed a study that later became my dissertation and contributed to this chapter. The study was done in a second-year Russian language classroom in a university in the American Midwest. The students in their second year had already gone through the period of initial trial and made a conscious decision to continue studying a foreign language. A year and half of studies allowed them to develop a certain level of language and cultural competency. All students in the focal classroom were Caucasians, with an approximately even number of male and female students. Very few of them had some Russian heritage (e.g., immigrant parents) or had been to Russia before they started studying the Russian language.

I believe that learning a foreign language in a university is a very interesting case for gaining insight into the phenomenon of learning a new culture and language outside of the community associated with them. Russian language in an American university adds yet another angle, taking into the consideration the long and complex historical relationship between Russia and the United States.

Literature review

There are two Russian scholars who are gaining increasing popularity in the modern world of 'soft' sciences: Mikhail Bakhtin and Lev Vygotsky. My study heavily relies on their theories. These theories have been interpreted in many different ways and applied to various fields of inquiry, such as educational research, anthropology, literature and linguistics. In this section, I explain how I understand these theories, and how I connect them to my findings. I hope that my explanations will not only help the reader to better understand my study, but also offer an interesting theoretical lens for thinking about learning and teaching across cultures.

Let me start with Mikhail Bakhtin. First of all, I will ask the reader to think about any familiar definitions of 'monologue' and 'dialogue'. Secondly, I will ask the reader to kindly 'forget' about them for a moment. This is how I offer to interpret Bakhtinian dialogic framework. As you will see in the quote that follows, Bakhtin (1963/1984) states that human thinking (or idea) is dialogic in nature, but monologic in form. By the nature of thinking, Bakhtin means that never-ending process of internal negotiation so familiar to all of us: rethinking certain decisions, contemplating possibilities, hesitating . . . Bakhtin's point is that all these wonderful characteristics of everyday thinking come out as a response to or 'dialogue' with many social sources, such as: people we talk to, classes we take, books we read, media information we encounter, memories that overwhelm us, and so on. Bakhtin further states that people uniquely and individually construct these social sources (he also refers to them as consciousnesses and discourses) in the context of each live event. For example, when you, as a teacher, are explaining a textbook chapter to your students, you are constructing the message of the textbook, the students, yourself, and your thinking according to the situation – different from any other teacher, different from how you will do it next time, and different from what you are going to think in response to this lesson when it is over. Thus, individuality, contextual uniqueness, and dynamic flow come to constitute the concept of a dialogue in Bakhtinian theory.

Now, we all rethink, contemplate, and hesitate – but how often does this receive a true reflection in our routine interactions? Think about teaching and learning again. Would a teacher express hesitation in front of the class while explaining a textbook chapter? Would a student bring out his deepest thoughts and contemplations? If I were true to the thinking that is happening in my head, I, like any author, would have never finished this chapter. Bakhtin explains that in the context of routine interactions such as teaching, learning, or writing a paper we often adopt monologic forms to express our thinking; forms that package our ideas into the neat statements with seemingly closed meanings, such as expressing certainty, beliefs, consensus. Thus, finality, stability and mutuality come to constitute the concept of the monologue in Bakhtinian theory; however, if this consensus is reached, what is there left to talk about? Ability to see beyond the monologic forms of everyday interactions and to contemplate the dialogic nature of human thought is how Bakhtin pieces together the idea and the word:

> The idea . . . is not a subjective individual-psychological formation, with 'permanent resident rights' in a person's head; no, the idea is inter-individual and inter-subjective – the realm of its existence is not individual consciousness but dialogic communion between consciousnesses. The idea is a live event, played out at the point of dialogic meeting between two or several consciousnesses. In this sense the idea is similar to the word, with which it is dialogically united. Like the word, the idea wants to be heard, understood, and 'answered' by other voices from other positions. Like the word, the idea is by nature dialogic, and monologue is merely the conventional compositional form of its expression, a form that emerged out of the monologism of modern times . . . (Bakhtin, 1963/1984, p. 88)

Bakhtin tracks the monologism of modern times all the way back to the Roman Empire (Morris, 1994). In fact, without monologue, there would be no society – no agreement on norms and regulations. Bakhtin describes monologic forms of human interaction as 'speech genres' (Morris). In my study, I was able to identify and illustrate two types of such genres: firstly genres of classroom communication (e.g., teacher's explanation, taking a quiz) that fit into the pattern of 'Initiation-Response-Evaluation' (IRE – e.g., question-answer-feedback); and secondly coherent narratives constructed in conversation.

IRE has been recognized as one of the predominant patterns of communication in classrooms, originally described by Mehan (1979) and recently reviewed by Burbules and Bruce (2001). Burbules and Bruce note that this pattern is predominant in educational practices and institutions and so 'ingrained' in memories of both the teachers and the students, that it is very hard to overcome it. According to their summary, you may also encounter variations on IRE in the literature, including a Teacher/Student (T/S) model and a transmission and recitation model of communication. Burbules and Bruce (2001) identify four assumptions in these conceptualizations of IRE:

1. 'The performative roles of teacher and student are given, distinct, and relatively stable: . . . a teacher teaches and a student learns' (The T/S model, ¶2).
2. The key activities in the classroom are the teacher's acts of 'expressing information, directing behaviour, and evaluating performance' (¶3) – that is, Initiation and Evaluation.
3. 'Teaching is centrally a matter of intentionally communicating content knowledge' (¶4).
4. 'Education is an activity of instrumental practices directed intentionally toward specific ends, and that it can therefore be evaluated along a scale of effectiveness in meeting those ends' (¶5).

Narrative as a genre is a relatively new concept in educational research, often associated with rhetorical and literacy studies (Nystrand & Duffy, 2003). I will elaborate on both IRE and the narrative genres in the 'Results' section. For now, it's important to note that while analysing students' and teacher's words within these genres I received a set of coherent, closed (monologic) meanings of what it means to learn a new language and about a different culture. However, inspired by Bakhtin, I tried to look beyond them and grasp the dialogic nature of my participants' thinking. I was able to do so by employing a theoretical concept of practice developed by Lev Vygotsky.

As I understand it from reading Lev Vygotsky (1962; 1978), *practice* is an organization of cognition with related social activities. Conceived as a practice in this sense, 'studying a foreign language' in a college course is an organization of an individual's thinking which is linked to the social activities of taking a foreign language class and looking for other opportunities to use the language of choice. In traditional socialization studies, 'practice' as a term has a different meaning. These studies attribute practice first of all to a community, a culture, and not to an individual learner. In this sense practices are cultural and defined as 'meaningful actions that occur routinely in everyday life, are widely shared by members of the group, and carry with them normative expectations about how things should be done' (Goodnow, Miller, & Kessel, 1995, p. 1). The problem that I have applying this definition to the context of my study is that participation in the community that

I observe, namely the classroom, does not provide me with answers to what foreign language learning means to the students. Even though the actions that occur there routinely seem meaningful and shared by the members, in each interview that I have conducted the nature of the practice of learning Russian was individually interpreted by the students as embedded in deeper social contexts that varied in every case. These findings led me to shift the focus of my interpretive lens from the practices of a classroom as a culture to the individual practice of the students. I believe that foreign language for my participants 'is not simply a means of expression, rather, it is a *practice* that constructs, and is constructed by the ways language learners understand themselves, their social surroundings, their histories, and their possibilities for future' (Norton & Toohey, 2004, p. 1).

Bakhtinian concepts of *dialogic nature* and *monologic genres* of human communication, together with the Vygotskian concept of *practice*, provide a theoretical lens that can be used to look at the concept of culture that most teachers now routinely operate with. Through this lens, culture looks like a fluid and dynamic dialogic construct, a construct that I urge the reader to recognize beyond its monologic forms enacted within genres of IRE and narratives. Monologic forms definitely constrain human interaction, but it is my belief that instead of seeing them as an obstacle, we should learn to understand them, and thus learn to better understand our students. I hope that the 'Results' will provide an insight into how. For now, let me introduce my research questions and method.

Research question

The main research question of this study was: 'What does it mean for students to learn Russian language and culture outside of Russia, in fact, in a classroom in a large public university in the USA Midwest?' While answering this question, it was important for me to understand and describe the dialogic nature of students' learning practice inside and outside of the classroom, show how this practice was connected to students' understanding of Self, and grasp the connection between this practice and a concept of culture.

Method

This study employs a case study design (Dyson & Genishi, 2005). In order to collect the data for this study, I spent three semesters in a second year Russian language classroom, and also observed and interviewed a few of my focal students from this classroom in Russia during a Study Abroad trip. Ethics approval was obtained beforehand, and all names have been changed. There were two major types of data that I collected: classroom observations and interviews. I typed up field-notes for all classroom observations and transcribed the interviews. Thematic data analysis was an ongoing process happening simultaneously with data collection: I first performed open coding of the field-notes and interview transcripts identifying themes that shaped my then very loose and general research questions. I wrote initial memos to capture these early impressions; when my research questions and agenda became clear to me, I performed focused coding of my data that structured my answers to the research questions, and wrote integrative memos that later transformed into the text presented below as my 'Results'. For a thorough description and examples of such analysis see Emerson, Fretz and Shaw (1995).

Altogether, six focal students and two of their teachers participated in this study for three semesters. However, due to the limitations of this chapter you will encounter only four of the students (Foma, Jacob, Michael, & Sophia) and one teacher in one semester of my observations. I have selected focal students based on criteria of 'internal sampling' (Bogdan & Biklen, 2003, p. 61). All of them sat close enough to my researcher's corner so that I could observe them during class and hear everything they said. My key informants were not a group of friends; rather, they could be described as classmates. As classmates, they provided interesting accounts of each other's behaviour and of events that I observed during class sessions. And finally, all of these students were willing to talk to me and participate in my study.

There are certain limitations to qualitative methodology. First of all, it limits our right to generalize from the results, since the findings are deeply embedded in the social context of the classroom where I studied them, as well as in the various social contexts outside of the classroom that my participants talked about. Secondly, it employs an interpretive mode of inquiry, which means that the data presented here is the result of my own researcher's interpretation of events that I observed. I tried to reflect on this fact by describing words and actions of my participants as my under-standings of their responses to certain social contexts, such as classroom activities and talking to a researcher (me), rather than portraying them as stable characteristics. These limitations do not allow for direct generalization of the findings from one case to others; however, I believe that inter-pretive research is extremely powerful in terms of exercising pedagogical imagination and providing a model for thinking about the importance of small, local, fluid and dynamic details of classroom life.

Results

Culture and 'knowledge base' in classroom learning

While observing the course (Russian 202) it was easy for me – as a previous instructor – to identify routine classroom events and activities. These included grammar, vocabulary, and pronunciation explanations and drills; doing textbook exercises as a class; working in pairs to practise a textbook or teacher-assigned dialogue; watching a Russian movie accompanied by vocabulary tasks; class discussions; and taking tests. The course professor Rimma (to whom I will also refer as 'the teacher'), a native Russian speaker, provided rich contextual explanations for grammar, vocabulary and pronunciation. For example, when students encountered the word 'zaryadka' (*morning exercise*) in a textbook dialogue, she wasn't satisfied with the dictionary translation: she said that morning exercise was 'a very Russian thing', and asked the students if they could relate it to any 'American things'. Rimma also used every opportunity to bring in Russian movies and texts into the classroom, from serious newspaper articles to children's stories.

In sum, I was fascinated by how much cultural context Rimma was trying to bring into the classroom. I was also fascinated with the seemingly less than keen response of the students to these efforts. Rimma's enthusiastic questions and cultural inquiries were often met with silence, uneasiness, and lack of enthusiasm. In the interviews, my participants often talked about receiving a 'language base' in the classroom, and rarely mentioned any contextual or cultural knowledge. Most often, they talked about cultural learning as embedded in communication with Russian speakers, existing or projected into the future. Most students seemed to see immersion as the only way to truly learn the language, but did not seem to believe that it was possible to learn cultural contexts of the language outside of the country where it is spoken. An excerpt from my conversation with Foma demonstrates this attitude:

> *Foma*: I am glad that I waited three years [before coming to Russia]. After three years of studying it's much easier to come here, you know, much, much easier than the first or second year. . . . I know I speak only a little bit better, but I understand a lot, lot better. At first, and before I came here, I would listen to each word and then put it together, but

now . . . I am getting more and more into the language, and it's so much fun, so much fun!

Natalia: Yeah, I talked to many people, I think I talked to you about this too . . . You can't really learn the language being outside the country, right?

Foma: Exactly, exactly!

Natalia: So what was . . . You know, you said that the three year before really helped. What were those three years?

Foma: The three years, you know, learning the basic rules. . . . Knowing the rules helps you understand a little bit more, but now, I know the rules and I know even better the context that they are going to be used in . . . yeah, that's it! I know now, like being here now, like the context makes a lot more sense, a lot more sense! And that's cool.

Natalia: You know, they try to bring the context into the classroom, and they give you all these texts, and literature, and songs . . . Do they help at all?

Foma: Yeah, they do a little, but it's no comparison to being here, absolutely no comparison to being here.

Foma described three years of learning Russian in a classroom as a process of acquiring 'basic rules'. He knew from the beginning that he was learning these rules in order to use them later in Russia. He was 'waiting' to grow context on them. From what he knew about classroom and language learning, one 'couldn't really learn a language outside of the country'. I later concluded that this was why he wasn't looking for this real, contextual learning in the classroom. In another conversation, with Jacob, I received even more support for this finding:

Jacob: You just kind of get a feel for the language. I mean you can't get a feel just studying, but it takes both. For me. I have to study a lot of grammar, but you don't really feel it until . . . the only way you can feel it is being in that culture extensively. At least probably a year or something like that. Inside the culture, at least around people who are speaking it . . . all the time with you . . . because they say it the way that they say it.

Natalia: I remember when we talked before you said that you couldn't learn Russian in Poland when there were Russians around you, because you didn't have the basis . . .

Jacob: I didn't have the basis; now I have the basis and I don't have the people (*smiles*).
Natalia: So you need the basis before you . . .
Jacob: (*joining in*) Before you can do it.

Jacob continued to tell me that he didn't learn a lot about culture in the classroom; rather, he went there in order to be 'forced' to learn grammar, because 'if you don't take a class, you never find time to do it'. When I mentioned a few examples of Rimma's attempts to bring in cultural information to her lessons, he indifferently answered that he 'already knew all that', and even if not, it did not interest him. Foma and Jacob, like most of my other participants, conceptualized their classroom language learning in our conversations as receiving a language base, leaving cultural learning to real and imaginary contexts outside of the classroom. They did not perceive language in the classroom as inseparably connected to cultural learning. I believe that this led to a misunderstanding of what a truly meaningful, authentic context is. This misunderstanding was co-constructed by the textbook material, teacher's vision, and students' conceptualizations of learning. For example, Rimma, following the recommendations of the communicative approach to foreign language teaching, engaged her students in what the textbook recommended as authentic dialogues instead of ordering them to repeat grammatical forms over and over again. However, asking students to compose a dialogue between a movie theatre clerk and a customer cannot be assumed to represent an authentic cultural action of buying movie tickets. The action performed by students as associated with this task in the context of the classroom is quite different from real life ticket-buying.

The students' actions mediated through routine activities in the class-room (most of which are treated as 'authentic' by communicative lan-guage teaching methods) can be described as language practise. When a student is trying to describe in Russian how she spent her winter break, she does not do it to be understood, she does it in order to practice abstract language forms to the point of their recognition by others. This is what's evaluated – the level of recognition, not understanding. Reading Bakhtin, I came to see this situation as a conflict with real-life communication, because 'the task of understanding does not basically amount to recognizing the form used, but rather to understanding it in particular, concrete context, to understanding its meaning in a particu-lar utterance, i.e., it amounts to understanding its novelty and not to recognizing its identity' (Morris, 1994, p. 33).

But students' conceptualizations of classroom learning as receiving a 'knowledge base' did not evolve in a vacuum. 'Knowledge base' represents a coherent concept, a narrative, which the students constructed in the interviews with the educational researcher (me). This narrative was constructed partly within the limitations of the genre of an interview where the interviewee is supposed to provide coherent answers to interviewer's questions. This narrative was also constructed in response to many social sources. I interpreted those sources as constructed under a strong influence of European structuralism, which treated meaning systems within academic subjects as closed, synchronic and universal. These systems evolved from 'comparison of language to the system of mathematical signs' that is concerned not with 'the relationship of the sign to the actual reality it reflects nor to the individual who is its originator, but the relationship of sign to sign within a closed system already accepted and authorized' (Morris, 1994, p. 29). The most powerful social source that influenced the construction of the 'knowledge base' was the Initiation, Response, Evaluation (IRE) pattern, which organizes genres of classroom interaction.

Monologic forms of classroom culture

It is important to keep in mind that both IRE and narrative genres that allowed for the conceptualization of classroom learning as receiving a 'knowledge base' were native cultural forms that the students operated with while trying to make sense of a foreign culture. In this section I describe how I was able to understand classroom culture of Russian 202 as constructed by a powerful IRE pattern of classroom communication. Well in line with Bakhtinian thought, this pattern, or organizing genre, was above all 'conditioned by the social organization of the participants involved and also by immediate conditions of their interactions' (Morris, 1994, p. 55). The social organization of the participants in my classroom placed them into the positions of (a) the teacher with the corresponding actions of teaching the 'material' and checking understanding by asking questions, and (b) the students, who were supposed to learn the 'material' and satisfy the teacher by answering her questions. The immediate conditions for teacher–student interactions were interpreted by students as learning the linguistic, and not cultural material, in other words, the students were receiving a 'language base' instead of learning cultural contexts of the Russian language.

Rimma, as I noted earlier, was a teacher who really cared about her students' cultural understandings of Russia. However, the genres of classroom communication (vocabulary and grammar explanations, class discussion, etc.) into which she tried weaving precious cultural knowledge were quite different from the authentic genres of acquiring cultural knowledge by, for example, observing Russian people and engaging in informal conversations with them. In the process of knowledge co-construction it appeared that the thematic content of Rimma's utterances was not as important as their genre, which students interpreted as vocabulary or grammar explanations in a lesson. As a result, the students limited their work in the classroom to learning vocabulary and grammar, in most cases ignoring the rich cultural contexts that Rimma was trying to provide.

I would like to provide an example of how a genre of authentic communication, in this case, an informal conversation, can become a genre of classroom communication, thus completely changing the social and language themes, goals and rules. During one of my observations Rimma gave students five minutes to practise a dialogue from the textbook. The dialogue was about Brodsky, a famous Russian poet. When the five minutes were over, Rimma addressed the class:

Rimma: Are you ready? Ready? Ready? OK. Who wants to try? (*Silence*).

Rimma: I will start with a Russian and non-Russian. (*Meaning a student with some Russian heritage and one without any. She points at Nadia and Alexandra.*)

(*Nadia and Alexandra each read one line out of the textbook*).

Nadia: What else should we do?

Rimma: Well, I want a conversation between two people about Brodsky. For example, 'I've just read about Brodsky', 'What do you know about Brodsky?' (*She pronounces these questions with enthusiasm and gestures.*) Make it . . . I don't know . . . Normal! And you guys all learn!

(*Nadia and Alexandra exchange two more lines from the textbook and stop. Rimma suggests more directions for the conversations that were not in the textbook but they don't respond, and Rimma calls on the next pair of students. One of these students is Kira, probably the best heritage speaker in the classroom*).

Kira: He wrote about God . . .

Rimma: Not only, not only . . . He didn't work anywhere.

Kira: Ah! And he didn't work anywhere.

Rimma: But you had to work (*in the Soviet Union*)! You couldn't just . . . He was an interesting person, good thinker. You know what he once said? Poetry is acceleration of the mind. . . . He wasn't against anything, he minded his own business, but he wasn't mainstream, he wasn't marching the march, so they thought that there was something dangerous . . .

During this mini-lecture Rimma repeatedly attempted to get students involved and create a conversation, but received only weak responses, or none at all. Sometimes students repeated the words and phrases after her, sometimes provided one-syllable answers. If we apply the IRE model of discourse analysis (Cazden, 2001) to the conversation above, we will see that the students only responded to the teacher's initiations that were addressed personally (as a teacher's call on a student) and required the knowledge of particular information from the textbook. Students also seemed to need some type of evaluation of their utterances from Rimma. Nadia's question 'what else should we do?' proved that Nadia did not know what she, as a student responding to a teacher, was supposed to do except for repeating the lines in the textbook. Kira's first turn was an attempt to use information outside of the textbook dialogue (in response to the teacher's initiation), but it was brief and isolated, and her second response was a translation of the teacher's initiation. Most students' responses during Rimma's closing mini-lecture also focused on translating or repeating Rimma's phrases. All this evidence made me think that the students interpreted the genre and subsequently the theme of the activity as language practice, whereas Rimma was trying to transition it to cultural discussion about life of a nonconformist person in the Soviet Union.

Students' interpretation of vocabulary lessons as linguistic, and not cultural, vividly came out in one of my interviews with Michael. We were talking about 'Adam's Rib' – a Russian movie that students watched in 20-minute increments during the semester. There were handouts for each increment that provided students with the vocabulary lists and exercises. However, Rimma used the movie as a broader opportunity for cultural vocabulary learning. While the students were watching the movie, she was working restlessly at the blackboard, writing down new words and trying to graphically explain their meaning by drawing arrows to the words that the students were supposed to know at their level. By doing this she was trying to model a way of figuring out the meaning of the new words as her students encountered them in authentic communication. However, vocabulary on the blackboard was outside of the unit requirements and not expected to appear on the quiz. As a result, students like Michael often felt confused:

> *Michael*: I understand [Rimma's rationale for contextual learning] . . . But when she explains the new vocabulary, I have no idea. Because I've never used it before, and she uses a ton of context. She says something in English and then she asks a lot of questions in Russian. Or, the same question in Russian, over and over. Then she'll give us one vocabulary word. I don't know if that's very helpful. Because vocabulary is out of context. I mean, it's in context for the movie, but it's just jotting it down, people aren't going to study that. . . . Well, like today, she told us that this thing is very practical to use, but these students will never use it, because they never have to practically use Russian, you know . . .

There were many things that Michael was trying to say here, but I don't think I could pay him enough for giving me this phrase: 'vocabulary is out of context'. The way I interpreted it, vocabulary explanation as a classroom activity, or genre, was out of cultural, conversational context in the context of a foreign language class. Students jotted it down, just like they were supposed to when vocabulary was taught. But because this vocabulary was not going to be on the test, or in exercises, they were not going to study it. Thus, all authenticity of presentation attempting to imitate spontaneous nature of real life language communication did not seem to be helpful.

Sensitivity to cultural contexts that Rimma was trying to encourage by constantly stepping out of the limits of genres of classroom communication proved to be a very hard task to achieve in the context of genres of classroom communication. The following excerpt from my fieldnotes provides another clear example of this phenomenon:

(In the beginning of the class Rimma wrote three Russian sayings on the blackboard and asked the students to guess their meaning. With the help of mostly heritage speakers she discussed the meanings and usage of these sayings. She finished this classroom event by giving students a task to write an essay using one of the proverbs. After this, she announced a vocabulary quiz. Students were expressing anticipation of bad grades while turning in the quiz. When all the papers were collected, Rimma addressed the class.)

Rimma: Did you figure out that two out of five words from your
           quiz were staring at you from the blackboard? (*These two
           words were a part of the sayings that she wrote on the black-
           board in the beginning of the class.*)

(*Several students responded negatively, shaking their heads.*)

Rimma: I can't believe it, it's a phenomenon. (*To me*) Natasha, this
           is something for you to write about.
Students: We didn't get it . . .
Rimma: You didn't make the connection?! I just talked for 15 min-
           utes about it! Raise your hand if you figured it out!

(*No one raised a hand.*)

Alina: But it's on the blackboard, and we were having a quiz!
Rimma: So you were being honest, but you made a connection?
           (*Alina nods.*)
Sasha: We were concentrating on the quiz . . .
Rimma: I just want to say – be cautious!

Even Rimma thought that this case was worth writing about. The
proverbs that she wrote on the blackboard had a purpose of expanding
the usage of the unit vocabulary. However, Rimma did not introduce
them as such, instead streaming the opening event into a homework
assignment of writing an essay. She did not mention that this
knowledge could be utilized in the evaluation part of classroom learning
(the quiz), hoping that the students would figure it out. The test itself
did not matter to her as much as students' flexibility in using Russian.
However, students interpreted the two activities as totally different, and
did not pay any attention to the blackboard, acting within the genre of
writing a test.

Thus, genres of classroom communication (vocabulary and grammar
explanations, taking quizzes, etc.) were expected by students to fit the
pattern of IRE and influenced their interpretation of classroom learning as
'acquiring a knowledge base', instead of as cultural. In Bakhtinian terms,
the genres of classroom communication were the monologic forms of
students' thinking. I believe that monologic genres are very important to
think about when the teacher tries to understand students' work in the
classroom. However, it is also very important to be able to see beyond
these genres, into the dialogic nature of student's thinking. In the next
section I describe this dialogic nature as a unique practice of constructing
cultural meanings that crossed the classroom and went far beyond it.

Dialogic nature of constructing cultural knowledge

Monologic genres of classroom communication can often mislead the teachers into thinking that the students are not interested in learning about culture. The way I understand it, students are interested in culture; however, their interest is of a dialogic nature; i.e., it's constantly evolving, unpredictable and very rarely in a coherent relationship with what goes on in the classroom. Let me illustrate this thought with an example where the students in Rimma's classroom were reading a textbook dialogue referencing the names of several famous Russian poets:

Rimma: Slava, do you know anything about Anna Akhmatova?
Slava: No.
Rimma: Kira, what about you?
Kira: No.
Rimma: You need to fill out this gap in their education. Russians can't live without poetry because 'it's accelerator of the mind'.

'Poetry is the accelerator of the mind' is a famous quote from the Russian poet Brodsky, about whom Rimma talked earlier in the day. Similar to the examples mentioned above, Rimma's commentary about the importance of poetry in the lives of Russians remained without a response. No one asked why poetry was so important for Russian culture and what would be the best way to 'fill in the gap in the education'. None of my focal students, judging from our conversations, picked up a book of the Russian poetry in the library. None of them even continued this conversation with me. Why? This is a complicated question. Judging from my impressions during my conversations with Rimma's students, the answer is not that these students did not care about Russian culture. It seemed to me that the nature of the practice of constructing cultural knowledge related to learning Russian was more complex, taking a unique and individual form for each student. This cultural knowledge involved Russian and Russia, but was not limited to them. In a sophisticated dialogue situated within many societal sources students, as free authors, knitted their own intercultural understandings, picking up the threads and combining them into unique patterns. This view made Rimma's comments on the role of poetry or sports in Russia important. However, who would pick these threads, and what threads they would be combined with, was hardly predictable. The students were not putting on Russian hats and acting Russian.

I have a great example of how unpredictable a connection between a classroom activity and one student's learning practice can be. In the previous section, I provided an excerpt from my fieldnotes describing an attempt of a classroom discussion about Brodsky. Sophia, one of my focal students, was silent in that excerpt. However, a few days after the discussion took place, Rimma told me that Sophia came to her office to talk about Brodsky. Rimma and I streamed this observation into the conclusion that students are, indeed, interested in Russian culture talked about in the classroom and how it is important for the teacher to bring in more of it. However, in my conversation with Sophia this topic came out in a different context:

> *Sophia:* I told Rimma that one of my favourite things to do was to read the transcript of the Brodsky. That was my most favourite thing to do in the whole two years of Russian. There was that transcript of the trial on a poet, and it was abridged, but we had a list of questions and we had to find out everything that was important, and that was so exciting to me, because it was the first time when I felt like that my studying was paying off. I felt like wow, may be I could look at historical documents and study them. Even though it was really . . . they took [the] meat of the document and left the real basic stuff, but . . . it was a most encouraging thing I've done. Because I felt like I have accomplished something as opposed to something like . . . to make a worksheet.

Sophia picked up a thread of the classroom topic covering the Russian poet Brodsky and wove it into her own unique practice of studying Russian, which went far beyond the classroom. Whereas Rimma and I hoped for cultural learning about the importance of Russian poetry, Sophia interpreted reading about Brodsky as working with real historical documents, which was important and meaningful to her because of majoring in history: being a history major constituted the frame of Sophia's practice of learning Russian in the interview. Sophia explained that ideally she wanted to become a specialist in Russian history with the ability to read real Russian documents. She further connected this aspiration with a lack of interest in present-day Russia, including communicating with Russians or following Russian news:

> *Sophia:* Now that I think about that . . . and I think I've been so interested in imperial Russia that I haven't really studied modern Russia, or Soviet history at all . . . I think in a way I was fascinated with old stuff . . . Like, my interest in going to Russia would not be as much for the people and the culture now as for just seeing, experiencing the history . . . I've never thought about it, I don't know . . .

Looking at classroom learning from the perspective of an individual learning practice provides much insight for the teacher. Of course, no teacher will have a chance to become as familiar with her students' histories as myself being a researcher in this study. However, I believe this is not necessary. What is necessary, in my opinion, is to understand that students' learning of academic material is social and cultural: it goes far beyond the classroom and constantly and uniquely evolves in a dialogue with a variety of changing and elusive social sources.

Discussion

I believe that an in-depth ethnographic account such as this study can provide insights for teachers who deal with the idea of culture in their classrooms every day. Understanding culture as a multidimensional phenomenon co-constructed in a dialogue, but a dialogue that often follows the monologic genres of classroom interaction, may help teachers to think of new ways of creatively weaving cultural knowledge into the construction of their unique pedagogies. Understanding student practice of learning classroom material as a dialogic endeavour crossing the borders of the classroom in unpredictable directions may help the teachers to re-evaluate the role of the classroom and their own part in students' learning. Let me illustrate this with an example from my own practice.

As a Ph.D. student of education I taught a course in educational psychology for two years. At the end of my second year I felt a great sense of progress in my pedagogy as I was trying to communicate the complexity of modern interpretations and applications of learning theories, being a strong advocate of those emphasizing social and cultural aspects of teaching and learning. This was when one of my students came to talk about the final project and claimed that she still liked behaviourism. My first reaction was shock: last century's behaviourism after all the discussions about Vygotsky!? But I didn't show this reaction to my student. I thought about several things: the context of our conversation (preparation for a class project that required students to utilize various theories, including behaviourism); the social sources that my student might have been drawing from (perhaps, a reflection of the fact that behaviourism is still very much present in teaching practice and it is pointless to deny it); and the fact that this statement is not a stable characteristic, but a constantly evolving idea. As a reward, I was able to see the complexity of this idea as our conversation continued and as the final project came out. What I hope I was able to achieve as a teacher was to understand the context of a student–teacher conversation as a monologic form that only for a moment packaged a very complex process of my student's understanding of learning theories into a neat, coherent, and (for me) shocking statement: 'I still kind of like behaviourism.' As one of my professors asked to clarify my thought: 'When you talk about monologic, you talk about only the visible part of an iceberg, right?'

Reflection questions

1. What do students in your context see as the essential 'knowledge base' of their course/programme? To what extent does this match the perception of their teacher(s)?
2. To what extent do the genres of communication used in a course/programme in your context lead to the kind of learning aimed for?
3. How could educators in your context become better informed about their students' dialogic learning processes, in the sense described in this chapter?

Resources

Burbules, N., & Bruce, B. (2001). *Theory and research on teaching as dialogue.* Retrieved 16 August 2006, from www.isrl.uiuc.edu/~chip/pubs/dialogue.html. Also in V. Richardson (ed.), *Handbook of research on teaching* (4th edn). Washington, DC: American Educational Research Association.
This article provides a great overview of the concept of dialogue in theoretical literature and practical applications.
Cazden, C. B. (2001). *Classroom discourse: The language of teaching and learning* (2nd edn). Portsmouth, NH: Heinemann.
This book will help you understand the genres of a classroom culture by using the IRE model of analysis.
Morris, P. (ed.). (1994). *The Bakhtin reader. Selected writings of Bakhtin, Medvedev, Voloshinov.* London: Arnold.
This book will help you to familiarize yourself with Bakhtinian theory in a concise and informative manner.

4

Perception of 'Self' and 'Other': Social Boundaries that Influence Teaching and Learning in Increasingly Diverse US Classrooms

Silvina Ituarte and Garth Davies

This chapter examines the role that social boundaries play in the university learning environment. As the composition of classrooms in the United States becomes increasingly diverse, the culture, background, and knowledge students bring into the class notably influence how they learn and interact. In a survey of 1694 students at two American universities, respondents were asked to examine their perceptions of social groupings and boundaries among students. Student responses indicate that grouping behaviors are occurring within learning contexts such as classrooms, study areas, and class projects, and that the most prominent social boundary factors are language, ethnicity, race, and appearance. The implications on teaching and learning are discussed and recommendations suggested.

Introduction

This chapter examines the perceptions of social divisions among students attending two United States university campuses and proposes a framework for exploring best practices in creating positive educational environments. First, this chapter examines the concept of social boundaries as developed by the Southern Poverty Law Center and its relation to the shifting demographics of the student populations attending US colleges and universities. A discussion of identity formation theories follows in order to contextualize how individuals' perceptions of themselves and others shape their campus experiences in ways which may influence their educational achievement. Next, the responses of 1,694 students regarding their perceptions of social boundaries and grouping behaviours are analysed followed by a discussion of how these social divisions may influence the learning environment. Through the examination of two primary questions, the researchers examine students' perspectives on the campus social climate and analyse the results to suggest strategies to build expertise for fostering pro-social learning environments within classes.

Context

Over several semesters teaching an upper division undergraduate course entitled *Prejudice, Violence, and Criminal Justice*, a recurring theme emerged year after year: students in the class continually questioned why individuals segregate themselves according to an assortment of social cliques. They perceived certain settings (e.g. cafeteria, classroom and library) as segregated according to race, ethnicity, international student status, athletic ability, student government affiliation, or other social stratification categories. While the researchers wondered whether this perception was unique to the campus, an examination of the Southern Poverty Law Center's (SPLC's) *Mix It Up* home page (Southern Poverty Law Center, 2006a) revealed that this dialogue was taking place not only in this course, but also within classrooms throughout the United States. According to the SPLC, school students across the nation were witnessing social divisions taking place on their campus, particularly in the cafeterias.

The SPLC, a US organization which creates tools for teaching tolerance and monitors bias-motivated violence, initiated a campaign in 2001 called 'Mix It Up' with the hopes of encouraging students to break down the social boundaries that keep individuals isolated from one another (Southern Poverty Law Center, 2006a). The aim of the campaign was to have students from various ethnic, religious, and social backgrounds interact at lunch and commence a dialogue that promotes understanding and acceptance among diverse persons. While the 'Mix It Up' campaign was principally geared toward primary and secondary school learners, the researchers of this project sought to probe the perceptions of university students regarding social boundaries. The researchers wondered: 1) Do students at the university level experience social boundaries which keep them from interacting with students of different backgrounds, cultures, or experiences? and 2) Do these social boundaries impact the students' overall educational experience (and so potentially their learning)?

Literature review

Identity: 'self' and 'other'

As the demographics of the United States population change, diversity among the student body of college campuses alters as well. It is estimated that in the next decade, Latino/as will comprise the largest US minority group, followed by African Americans, with Asian Americans continuing as the quickest growing immigrant population (Kirkwood, 2002). While it is uncertain exactly what percentage of each demographic group will attend US colleges, today's classrooms comprise students who are more ethnically, linguistically and experientially diverse than ever before. Many classrooms in the new millennium consist of non-traditional age learners returning to school, countless non-native English speakers, increasing numbers of women, pupils with different preferred styles of learning, and many first generation college students. These students bring an array of experiences, traditions, responsibilities and lifestyles. Yet, while colleges and universities 'may have a diverse student body in terms of the presence of a large number of students of varying ethnicities, races, and cultures . . . the question remains whether the diversity in numbers is reflected in a diversity in interactions' (Cowan, 2005, p. 49; cf. Eisenchlas and Trevaskes, this volume).

For many of these students, the college experience represents the first opportunity not only to interact with individuals who are different from themselves, but also to explore their own identity. Tajfel and Turner's (1979) *Social Identity Theory* proposes that people formulate their self-concept by evaluating themselves according to identification and comparison with others. Individuals use categories to simplify the world and use a set of norms by which to respond to particular groupings. When an individual encounters a new person, that individual is instantly assumed to share some characteristics associated with those belonging to his or her gender, occupation, economic status and so forth (Tajfel and Turner, 1979). Through this categorization process, people identify with certain groups (in-groups) and compare themselves to others (out-groups). The outcome of this process is best captured by Nelson (2002):

> Dividing people into groups to which we either belong or do not belong has a number of implications for how we think about a given individual. Individuals who are part of an out-group are perceived to share similar characteristics, motives, and other features. However,

when it comes to our own in-groups, we like to think that our groups are composed of unique individuals who happen to share one (or two) common features (e.g., one's occupation). Thus, we think that the out-group members are 'all alike,' whereas our in-group members are as different as snowflakes. (p. 29–30)

According to Tajfel and Turner (1979), by identifying one's in-group with positive features and the out-group with negative characteristics, membership with the in-group naturally signifies one's positive self-worth. In essence, individuals establish their self-worth and determine their place in society by constructing a 'self' in contrast to 'others'. Students who have had little contact with diverse groups of people may experience 'little motivation to be accurate in their assumptions, expectations, and generalizations' (Nelson, 2002, p. 229) regarding others and may therefore fall prey to stereotypes that inhibit authentic exchanges among students. In these cases, stifled comments, censored statements, and inhibited interactions impact and alter learning environments such as classrooms.

In order to examine how *social boundaries* inhibit interactions among students, it is necessary to examine 'the dynamic *live* interactions between majority and minority group members, and how their thoughts, feelings, and behavior both *change the interaction* and *are changed* by their perception of the interaction on a moment-by-moment basis' (p. 143). The presence of members of oppressed groups, as well as those belonging to the dominant culture, changes the types of interactions that take place within the classroom. The presence of one, or a small number of students belonging to a different group, will impact the awareness of the remaining students. If the classroom setting is such that the few students representing a marginalized group express their thoughts, they increase the awareness of those who might not otherwise recognize the invisibility of the experiences of those outside the dominant culture.

Links between social boundaries, self-identity and learning

While social boundaries between individuals in a school, work or neighbourhood setting may appear normal, expected, and insignificant, one must recognize that in the case of students, the perception of an uninviting environment may result in students distancing themselves emotionally from school, thereby disengaging from the campus, student social networks, and from learning in general. In a review of the experiences of Muslim college students (Nasir & Al-Amin, 2006), students described feeling burdened with the need to constantly contend with others' perceptions of them. According to Nasir and Al-Amin (2006), 'this identity management process required energy and time that could have been devoted to their studies' (p. 24). How students experience their self-identity within the social context of the university environment can either lessen or heighten feelings of alienation on campus and ultimately influence their ability to learn.

A common belief espoused by *Intergroup Contact Theory* (Williams, 1947) suggests that divisions and prejudice between groups can be reduced through constructive exchanges among members of differing groups. Allport (1954) and Pettigrew (1998) also acknowledged the significance of different variables related to the type of contact exhibited in the interaction, and recognized the significance of the experiences, biases and personality characteristics which shape the perceptions and experiences of each individual involved in the interaction. They recognized that students segregate themselves according to various social cliques and groups: 'A classic example is the tendency of members of ethnic minority groups, which are often a small percentage of the student body, to eat together in the dining facilities' (Asante & Al-Deen as cited in Cowan, 2005, p. 50). While there may be some comfort in being among a group of similar people (i.e. racial or ethnic background), it is an error to expect

> that people who share a common culture or language also share the same attitudes, beliefs, values and behaviors. It must be emphasized that culture is not the only, and in many instances not even the most, important or salient variable when differences or potentially conflicting situations arise in diverse settings. Socio-economic status, educational background, religion, gender, age and worldview are some of the determinants that influence *who* and *what* we are, but also *why* we react in a particular way in certain situations. (Roux, 2002, p. 42)

While limited research exists regarding the exact connections between segregation and learning outcomes, both professors and students can attest to the inhibitions that take place in classroom settings when students do not feel safe to share their thoughts or vocalize their concerns. Each quarter students enrolled in a *Prejudice, Violence, and Criminal Justice* course repeatedly claimed to walk into the university cafeteria and witness students grouping themselves into different cliques and social groups. As a result of this discussion, the researchers embarked on a venture to examine a list of possible social divisions using an adaptation of the survey created by the Southern Poverty Law Center's 'Mix It Up' campaign. By identifying social boundaries, this project represents a first step toward recognizing the impact of social divisions on the daily lives of university students and their academic learning.

Research questions

1. Do students at the university level experience social boundaries which keep them from interacting with students of different backgrounds, cultures or experiences?
2. Do these social boundaries impact the students' overall educational experience (and so potentially on their learning)?

Methodology

In the Spring of 2003 and 2004, the researchers surveyed students attending two mid-sized (12,000–14,000 students) universities located within approximately 25 miles of two metropolitan cities in the United States: one on the east coast (New York City in New York) and one on the west coast (San Francisco in California). In total, 1,694 responses were collected from students ranging from first-year students to graduate students across a wide range of majors and varying age groups. Students were asked to evaluate which, if any, social categories inhibited social interactions among students. The questionnaire explored student perceptions of the daily impact of social boundaries such as race, ethnicity, age, national origin, sex, sexual orientation, physical ability and social economic status.

An email and letter explaining the project were sent to faculty in each of the academic majors at the east coast university requesting the professor's cooperation in allowing students enrolled in the class fifteen minutes to complete a brief questionnaire consisting of 15 questions. The questionnaire was modelled after the one created by the SPLC during the first national 'Mix it Up' event (Southern Poverty Law Center, 2006b). While the questionnaire used in this analysis utilized many of the same social categories defined in the survey created by the SPLC, the questions were slightly modified to address the experiences of college students (e.g., the inclusion of dormitories). Additionally, in the original SPLC's survey participants were asked to mark which of the listed categories created social boundaries on their campus, whereas the participants of this study were provided the list of categories and asked to state whether each individual category created a social boundary on their campus by marking the box labeled 'yes' or 'no'. The following represents one of the questions in the survey: 'Have you noticed people grouping themselves and others in the following areas: cafeteria, classroom, sports teams, class projects, dormitory, recreational activity, spectator event, study area, or other.' Tables 4.1 and 4.2 provide an overview of the main questions examined in this analysis. Once an affirmative response was received from individual faculty members agreeing to include their students in the research, a date and time to distribute the questionnaires was established. The same process was followed at the west coast university in spring of 2004.

Results

The demographic characteristics of the sample are presented in Table 4.1. The sample is made up of more females than males, and is skewed toward the youngest age category (17–24). In light of the age skew, subsequent analyses are dichotomized, with 17–24 constituting

Table 4.1: Demographic characteristics

	Total		East coast campus		West coast campus	
	N (1,694)	%	N (877)	%	N (817)	%
Sex						
Female	972	57.4	482	55.0	490	60.0
Male	681	40.2	370	42.2	311	38.1
Missing	41	2.4	25	2.9	16	2.0
Age						
17–24	1146	67.7	622	70.9	524	64.1
25–30	270	15.9	123	14.0	147	18.0
31–40	154	9.1	68	7.8	86	10.5
41+	89	5.3	43	4.9	46	5.6
Missing	35	2.1	21	2.4	14	1.7
Ethnicity						
Caucasian	599	35.4	388	44.2	211	25.8
Latino/a	266	15.7	168	19.2	98	12.0
African American	240	14.2	150	17.1	90	11.0
Asian/Pacific Islander	331	19.5	51	5.8	280	34.3
Other/UK	258	15.2	120	13.7	138	16.9

one category and all higher ages comprising the other. The distribution of sex and age are very consistent across research sites. Overall, just over one-third (35.4 per cent) of the sample is Caucasian, while respondents of Latin, African American, and Asian or Pacific Island descent are roughly equally represented. In contrast to sex and age, however, the ethnicity of respondents is much more varied across sites. The east coast campus respondents are more heavily Caucasian, and there are considerably fewer Asians. Conversely, Asians comprise the largest group for the west coast campus. The potential relevance and impact of these differences is explored below.

Two groups of questions were used to explore students' perceptions of social boundaries. The first proposed a variety of school settings and asked students whether they had noticed people grouping themselves and others by categories within these settings. The percentages of respondents answering in the affirmative are presented in Table 4.2.

Although the range of responses (from a low of 35.9 per cent for *Dorms* to a high of 84.3 per cent for *Cafeterias*) is substantial, processes of division and exclusion are evident across all settings. Consistent with research done in other educational settings, *Cafeterias* are characterized as highly segregated areas. From the perspective of learning environments, the results for *Classrooms*, *Study Areas* and *Class Projects* are particularly troubling. These areas are most directly relevant to the students' learning experiences, and, outside of cafeterias, these are the places that respondents most consistently identify with grouping processes. If learning is positively associated with perceptions of inclusivity, this is a concern. More generally, all of these facets of the university experience are identified as being divisive. In fact, the results suggest that there are few aspects of campus life that are untouched by considerations of social boundaries; even sports and recreational activities do not appear to be immune.

In terms of addressing diversity, it is important to note that these findings are dynamic and differ by context. Chi-square analyses reveal significant differences between the two universities examined in this research: in every instance, perceptions of grouping are significantly higher for the western campus.

There are no noticeable gender differences with regard to extra-curricular events, and males and females are equally as likely to recognize such behaviours in cafeterias. There are, however, important differences between males and females related to classrooms, study areas and class projects. Specifically, in each of these settings, women are more likely than men to identify grouping behaviours.

Table 4.2: School settings where you have noticed people grouping themselves and others by categories

	Total %	Site		Gender		Age category		Ethnicity			
		East coast campus %	West coast campus %	Female %	Male %	17–24 %	25+ %	Caucasian %	Latino/a %	African American %	Asian %
Cafeteria	75.4	67.2	84.3**	76.5	74.4	77.4	71.0*	73.0	72.9	72.1	84.6
Classroom	46.6	24.1	70.9**	49.1	43.6*	44.5	51.7*	42.1	40.2	43.3	62.2
Study areas	42.8	15.8	71.7**	45.2	39.9*	40.8	47.8*	35.9	36.1	34.6	67.1
Class projects	39.3	14.1	66.2**	43.0	34.2**	38.3	41.5	29.4	30.5	39.2	63.4
Sports teams	34.8	21.7	48.8**	34.7	35.2	38.6	26.5**	31.4	32.3	32.5	45.9
Recreational activities	34.2	14.9	54.8**	35.1	33.3	35.6	32.0	29.4	27.4	28.8	52.9
Spectator events	31.4	13.7	50.4**	30.8	32.9	33.6	27.5*	25.7	26.3	31.7	43.8
Dorms	28.2	21.1	35.9**	27.8	28.9	32.3	19.9**	23.9	22.6	31.3	36.9

Note: * $p < .05$; ** $p < .001$

The pattern of difference among age categories is less straightforward. Whereas more 'traditionally-aged' students (17–24) notice grouping relative to sports teams, spectator events and dorm life, nontraditional or returning students are more apt to perceive these behaviours in contexts that more directly impact their education, including classrooms and study areas. In comparison, the breakdown of perceptions by ethnicity follows a singular pattern. Specifically, Asian respondents were significantly more likely than respondents of other ethnicities to notice people grouping themselves.

The second set of questions asked respondents to identify what categories create group boundaries at school (See Table 4.3). Four of these items – language, ethnicity, race, and appearance – were noted by more than a quarter of the students. It is likely not coincidental that the top four categories all correspond to immediately obvious traits. As with the previous analysis, these results vary markedly by location. In contrast to Table 4.2, however, the pattern of variation is less consistent. The proportions of variance tend to be higher at the west coast campus, but for some categories, most notably ethnicity and race, the reverse is true. This makes generalization with regard to location difficult.

The complexity of these issues is further underscored by the gender and age breakdowns. Surprisingly, there were no differences between males and females relative to the top categories. However, younger students were consistently more likely than older students to perceive category differences based on language, ethnicity and race.

In sum, these respondents are indicating clearly that processes of group creation are occurring in virtually all areas of university experience. Moreover, these differences are fostered by a continuum of categories, the most prevalent of which are language, ethnicity, race and personal appearance. Finally, the dynamics of these perceptions of social boundaries are fluid and complex, varying by location, gender, age and ethnicity. In order to address the effects of these dynamics on educational attainment and learning outcomes, one must be sensitive to, and take into account, the diversity of these effects.

The focus of this study emphasized student perceptions of social boundaries and did not directly evaluate, measure, or assess student learning. The researchers recognized that *learning* as a construct is difficult to measure within varying academic courses across disciplines and that learning is dependent on multiple factors that are difficult to isolate for this type of analysis. Instead, the researchers focused on student perceptions of social divisions and social groupings framed within the context of past research and psychological theories that speak

Table 4.3: Categories that create group boundaries at your school

	Total (%)	Site		Gender	
		East coast campus (%)	West coast campus (%)	Female (%)	Male (%)
Language	41.9	44.4	39.3*	40.1	44.3
Ethnicity	38.5	47.7	28.6**	36.5	41.7
Race	31.9	39.0	24.4**	30.2	34.7
Personal appearance	26.3	20.1	33.0**	24.5	29.5
Beliefs	24.8	18.0	32.1**	23.1	27.5*
Academic achievement	24.1	17.2	31.5**	24.2	24.5
Style	22.3	20.3	24.4*	21.0	23.9
Hobbies	20.0	17.1	23.1*	17.3	23.8**
Athletic achievement	19.9	23.5	16.0**	18.0	22.9*
Gender	18.7	14.7	22.9**	18.1	19.4
Religion	16.4	13.1	19.8**	15.7	17.5
Sexual orientation	15.0	15.4	14.6	12.1	18.8**
Home neighbourhood	13.6	9.0	18.6**	11.6	16.4*
Musical interests	12.6	9.1	16.4**	10.7	15.1*
Family income	8.7	7.0	10.6*	6.9	11.0*

Note: * $p < .05$; ** $p < .001$

to how social contexts (e.g., social alienation, peer acceptance, validation and inclusion) influence one's comfort, sense of safety and ability to learn. Learning, as a discussion construct, was also expanded to comprise more than academic content to include skills such as collaboration, multicultural awareness, social sensitivity, team work, etc. which are generally not included in typical learning outcome assessments.

Discussion

Perceptions of grouping behaviour

The authors specifically conducted this analysis at two similar universities on opposite coasts with the expectation of discovering some differences.

Age category		Ethnicity			
17–24 (%)	25+ (%)	Caucasian (%)	Latino/a (%)	African American (%)	Asian (%)
43.5	38.0*	46.4	43.2	32.9	39.3
41.2	33.1*	38.6	38.0	42.1	37.5
34.2	27.3*	34.2	28.2	35.8	31.7
28.4	22.6*	28.7	17.7	27.5	29.3
24.5	25.3	25.5	19.5	25.0	26.0
23.9	25.0	20.7	18.8	22.9	33.8
24.3	17.5*	23.7	16.9	25.0	25.1
22.8	13.3**	18.4	13.2	16.7	29.6
22.8	13.6**	23.0	18.8	19.2	17.5
18.2	19.5	17.4	13.2	20.0	24.5
16.1	17.0	17.4	12.4	14.6	18.7
14.8	14.6	15.7	11.7	17.5	12.7
14.1	12.3	13.4	6.0	15.4	19.0
13.3	10.9	11.0	7.9	17.9	15.4
8.1	9.9	9.2	6.8	8.8	9.7

Although it is difficult to almost impossible to speculate regarding the exact underlying causes of the dissimilarity between the two campuses, the differences might be due to regional peculiarities. While the name 'United States' implies uniformity in one set of beliefs and way of life, the regional differences between the east and west, as well as north and south, are quite distinct. During times of political discourse or political elections, it is evident that the nation is divided often into shades of red and blue (the colours used to represent the Republican and Democratic parties). While both the northeastern states and the west coast are typically representative of the Democratic Party's position, general socio-cultural differences still exist. For example, many east coast residents characterize native Californians as fake and too laid back, while some California residents describe New Yorkers as irritable and brash. Similarly, individuals living in southern states view visitors from other regions of the United States as unfriendly when compared to what has been traditionally known as a culture of 'southern hospitality'. In these instances, it becomes clear that the United States is diverse in its beliefs, values, ideals and lifestyles. Countless generalizations regarding the differences between east and west coast perspectives could be made, yet what matters when discussing teaching and learning is the impact of these regional differences on professors and students. While the east coast may be viewed as having a lengthy history complete with the cultural roots of many early immigrant populations, the west coast is typically perceived as having a more progressive ideology. The important fact to recognize is the complexity this poses for professors teaching diverse student bodies within different regions. Diverse populations in different parts of the country may respond differently to certain classroom activities, assignments, teaching styles or classroom formats. For professors, teaching techniques that are effective in one location may have a completely opposite effect on students in another region. More importantly, how students perceive the professor's acknowledgement or denial of diversity may be radically different and thereby alter the interactions in the class.

With regard to participants' gender, women are more likely than men to identify grouping behaviours in each of the settings examined in this study. The findings of this study would suggest that professors should mitigate the perceived groupings by assigning groups that are equally divided among the sexes.

Differences among non-traditional, or returning students, in contrast to more traditional 17 to 24 year old students, pose various challenges. Of concern for professors and those involved in the learning process is the disparity in the perceptions of separation in the cafeteria, classroom and study areas. When the cafeteria, the area ranked to be the most divided by social boundaries is removed from the analysis, the classroom and study areas are the next two regions in which non-traditional learners perceive a division among students. Possibly, the perceived divisions are the result of a disconnect in attitudes toward learning between younger and more mature students. Quite often the level of commitment to learning, the amount of participation in class discussion, and the eagerness to engage in scholarly dialogues differs among students. In some cases, returning students with a renewed commitment to their education feel taunted or mocked by the students who are more interested in the social aspects of college life and express frustration over conversations initiated by more mature students. On the other hand, younger students may be inhibited in their responses for fear of revealing their limited life experiences. For professors, this creates a challenge in inspiring the motivated and engaged students while not abandoning the less experienced students who may feel inhibited in speaking or may view college as largely a social gathering. Professors need to make sure that the classroom is a safe environment for all students to speak freely without feeling taunted, mocked, discouraged, or put off by others.

In relation to perceptions of boundary creation, it is possible that Asian respondents have a heightened consciousness of social boundaries due to the greater cultural differences between eastern and western cultures. Overall, most diverse students of western cultures share similar alphabets, clothing articles, and religious philosophies. For Asian students from the various parts of the Asian continent including India, China, Cambodia, Vietnam, Thailand, etc., the transition from an eastern culture focusing on 'communal values' to a western culture that emphasizes 'the individual' may be more difficult. Students need to overcome not only language barriers, but also cultural ways of thinking about how individuals interact with one another.

Social boundary categories

Language, ethnicity, race and appearance rank as the four strongest social boundaries to overcome at both university campuses. It is logical that language presents the largest social barrier for individuals to interact. Communication is the basis of any interaction, and if one or both parties are afraid of miscommunicating or unable to express themselves accurately due to language barriers, it makes sense that the interactions will not take place. Whether it is the fear of not expressing oneself appropriately, a fear of being misunderstood, or a self-conscious discomfort regarding a strong accent, language is an overwhelming social barrier for students.

Social boundaries extend beyond typical demographic categories to seemingly innocuous categories such as athletic skill, academic excellence, or even physical appearance. While personal appearance as the fourth strongest social boundary is a bit surprising, it is possible that this category is laden with social meaning. It is possible that personal appearance is the more 'politically correct' manner of addressing economic differences as well as social role expectations of attractiveness, or of being 'in' with the latest trend. The mere fact that appearance was perceived as significant by over a quarter of all the students surveyed reveals that pressures with regards to beauty, size, hipness, and economic ability to maintain a certain level of expectations pose a significant amount of pressure on students that could result in the alienation of some students and consume others. In either case, student learning is not the focus of either the student who experiences alienation, or of the student who is consumed with 'fitting in'. Whether it is one's hairstyle or clothing, these simple characteristics convey meanings and messages regarding one's attitude, affiliation, identity or sexual availability. For younger students especially, 'peer acceptance or rejection has the potential to be the significant factor in the development of adolescents' attitudes towards their formal education in the process of schooling. Perceived or real rejection can contribute to the development of a significant sense of alienation on the part of individual students and groups of students' (Brady, 2004, p. 352). For example, 'hairstyles represent a physical characteristic, which can create positive or negative impressions and has considerable cultural implications' (Roux, 2002, p. 42). Furthermore, peer pressure has the potential to influence one's desire for uniqueness, conformity or assimilation. For example, students may feel significant pressure to either wear, or not wear, African Kinte cloths, traditional Indian saris, or Muslim hijab.

The most significant differences in the perception of social boundaries by female and male students were in the categories of hobbies and sexual orientation. In both cases males perceived these two categories to be powerful barriers. While the category of hobbies may represent an innocuous category with which male students communicate and share their interests with their male peers, sexual orientation as a barrier could create a hostile atmosphere for some students. In these situations, a greater onus is placed on the professor to foster a safe environment of inclusivity in which all students feel comfortable and safe to express his or her thoughts and experiences. For example, the presence and disclosure of a gay man in a political science class could inform the other students' awareness of the impact of current legal debates regarding legalizing same-sex marriage. Similarly, the presence of a Latina student could add a new dimension to discussions of immigration in a social work course.

Conclusion: socially responsive professors

Can professors foster constructive learning environments that limit the impact of social boundaries without losing sight of the course content? While providing the most favourable learning atmosphere for students of varying social, cultural, experiential and linguistic backgrounds may appear daunting, one must recognize that the shifting demographics of student populations reflect a microcosm of an emergent society. By integrating efforts that challenge social boundaries within the course content, students become better prepared for the changing social, political and economic world. Irregardless of the academic discipline, simple techniques that challenge social boundaries can be implemented.

This chapter discusses three main areas in which professors can confront social boundaries in their classes. While most professors may selectively choose to incorporate only one of these suggestions, one must recognize the collective impact of individual efforts by numerous professors on the educational experience of students. Professors, the facilitators of the class, have the ability to challenge social boundaries and foster prosocial learning environments through the use of the following techniques: 1) modelling inclusivity through language and behaviour while also generating authentic interactions and exchanges that focus on collaborative learning rather than competition, 2) introducing service learning activities, and 3) seeking out resources and information on best teaching practices with diverse student populations from their Centre for Faculty Development.

First, through *modelling inclusive language* and validating the experience of all students, properly equipped professors possess the ability to generate authentic exchanges among students within the safety of the classroom. Providing an education to students represents more than teaching content material. 'It is also about values, assumptions, feelings, perceptions and relationships. No education can take place without interpersonal communication. Effective teaching can thus be qualified in terms of relating effectively in the classroom' (Roux, 2002, p. 37). Professors not only serve as educators and conveyors of knowledge, but also as role models who model and facilitate human interactions.

> Students from different cultural backgrounds may view, interpret, evaluate and react differently to what the teacher says and does in the classroom. Teachers therefore have to constantly bear in mind that the more substantial the differences in cultural background between the sender and receiver involved in the communicative process, the more substantial the differences in the meaning attached to the message and the social behaviour will be. (Roux, 2002, p. 37)

Teaching and learning occurs in an exchange of communication between the professor and the students. As educators and specialists in an academic discipline, professors rarely receive much instruction or training on how to teach university students, in particular a student population consisting of diverse backgrounds, skills, abilities and learning preferences. Professors who are socially responsive recognize student diversity extends beyond culture, ethnicity, and religion into areas of physical abilities, sexual orientation, gender identity and other categories. While professors may typically focus on the course content and the material to be taught, effective teaching and learning can only take place once the professor is better informed and aware of the impact of diverse backgrounds and experiences on the student's learning. The professor should be the one

> . . . who is aware of, and sensitive to, the reality of diverse backgrounds, viewpoints and needs in the classroom. Central to effective teaching and learning in any classroom is the communicative relationship between teacher and the students individually, but also his or her relationship with the class as a group. . . . Effective formal education or schooling is not simply a matter of teaching and learning curriculum content. It is also about values, assumptions, feelings, perceptions and about relationships. Often students achieve and behave according to how they perceive themselves to be through the eyes of others. The teacher is such a significant person in the lives of students. (Roux, 2002, p. 47)

The climate and respect espoused by a professor influences the social climate students experience while at a school. Feelings of alienation can have an impact on the educational experiences of students. Through challenging social boundaries and providing a validating campus climate, students have the ability to focus on their education. Furthermore, the manner in which a professor includes materials and selects his or her words (e.g. *he, she, partner*) creates an atmosphere in the class that validates the existence and experiences of marginalized groups while fostering awareness among other students. Inclusive language that acknowledges non-mainstream holidays (e.g., Eid or Yom Kippur), gender-neutral occupations (e.g., firefighter, police officer, or flight attendant), and a variety of family configurations (e.g., same-sex couples, blended families, etc.) validates the existence of many students and informs their peers of the significance of acknowledging all individuals.

Once a professor has made efforts to communicate effectively and responsibly with his or her students, it becomes evident that students have different preferred learning styles. Through the use of *service learning projects*, students are able to have a hands-on view of how the academic content relates to real-world issues. For example, students in a finance course may participate in a project that trains local residents in personal budgeting. While experiential learning has many practical, social and educational benefits for students, one must not underestimate the significance of such educational activities for students with learning disabilities, non-native English speakers, and students who have not interacted with others different from themselves. Service Experiential learning activities provide an alternate means of understanding the connections between scholastic endeavours and real life contexts while also extending the role of the educator from the professor to incorporate other students as well as community members. Through these collaborations and interaction between, and among, students and community members, additional social boundaries are confronted and shattered.

Finally, as the demographics of students enrolled in institutions of higher education have changed, the population of professors continues to change at a slower pace. Many of the professors have not been exposed to the same experiences as their students. In order to keep up with the changing needs of the student populations, as well as to maintain freshness in teaching, professors are encouraged to *consult their Centre for Faculty Development*. Often, by attending workshops at the Centre for Faculty Development, professors can learn about the cultural differences that may result in misunderstandings in the class. For example, the degree to which students ask questions or remain quiet may differ across varying cultures.

> . . . many professors might view constant questioning as aggressive or dependent behavior or interpret a reflective, observing child as withdrawn or slow. It is typical for white, middle class, school minded parents to constantly ask their children questions that they already know the answers to: . . . children with other backgrounds may not be used to an adult asking questions, unless the adult does not know the answer. (Oakes and Lipton, 1999, 78)

As evidenced by the findings of the two student populations, social boundaries do exist on university campuses. Student responses indicate that grouping behaviours are occurring throughout the university experience including campus contexts specifically focused on educational attainment such as classrooms, study areas and class projects. Although the exact relationship between social boundaries and educational achievement remains unclear, it is evident that professors have the opportunity to challenge social divisions and promote pro-social learning within the context of authentic exchanges among students.

Reflection questions

1. Are any social boundaries prominent among students in your context? Which social boundaries can you identify? What (if any) evidence do you have that these boundaries influence student learning?
2. What steps could professors in your context take to establish a pro-social learning environment in class?
3. In what ways do professors in your context show that they value being socially responsive educators?

Resources

Nelson, T. D. (2002). *The psychology of prejudice*. Boston, MA: Allyn & Bacon.
   This book not only offers an overview of varied forms of prejudice, but also provides a theoretical framework by which to understand some of the connections between prejudice, identity formation and group interaction.
Oakes, J., & Lipton, M. (1999). *Teaching to change the world*. Boston, MA: McGraw-Hill.
   The authors of *Teaching to Change the World* emphasize academic rigour and a social justice perspective. In the process, they discuss how to effectively teach for all students and examine how teachers can better prepare to become culturally competent educators.
Roux, J. E. (2002). Effective educators are culturally competent communicators. *Intercultural Education*, *13*(1), 37–48.
   Roux emphasizes the significance of communicating effectively in the classroom, explores the challenges of effective expression within complex and diverse contexts, and stresses the value of educators becoming 'effective communicators and thus culturally competent in cross-cultural encounters' (p. 37).

5
Intercultural Postgraduate Supervision: Ethnographic Journeys of Identity and Power

Catherine Manathunga

As growing numbers of international students enrol in research degrees outside their own countries, intercultural postgraduate supervision is becoming increasingly common in Western universities. This chapter applies post-colonial theories to interview data collected from ethnically diverse faculty supervisors and Ph.D. students at an Australian university. It argues that in the contested and unstable pedagogical contact zone of intercultural supervision, supervisors' and students' identities become altered. Recommendations for students and supervisors are provided based on the rich data the study unearthed. In particular, this chapter challenges assumptions about Asian students as dependent learners and about Western supervisors as providing insufficient guidance and support. It also suggests that holistic supervision strategies that seek to recognize the role of identity (re)formation are both part of an Eastern approach to supervision and an enactment of more recent Western notions of supervision as mentoring.

Introduction

This chapter explores the educational context of intercultural postgraduate supervision and the reasons why this is an intriguing form of pedagogy. The burgeoning literature on intercultural supervision is investigated, the postcolonial concepts of contact zones, transculturation, unhomeliness and identity are delineated and a series of research questions generated. The major section of the chapter will address elements of intercultural supervision evident in interviews with supervisors and students. Finally, these results are discussed in order to determine some of the implications of culture, identity and power for effective intercultural supervision.

Context

Postgraduate research supervisors have different titles and roles within research education programmes across the globe. Supervision in this case refers to the guidance of research students in Australia, New Zealand and the United Kingdom (and other former British colonies) by academic mentors referred to as dissertation supervisors in Canadian and US contexts. This research was conducted in an Australian university and involved five supervisors and two Ph.D. students from different social science and humanities disciplines. Three female and two male supervisors and one male and one female student were interviewed.

Three Anglo-Celtic Australian supervisors, two Asian supervisors from Japan and China and two international students from Vietnam and Malaysia participated in this research. The selection of students from Asian cultures reflects the fact that they are a large percentage of Australia's international student body. These international students were based in Australia for the duration of their Ph.D. programmes, although they planned to return to their home countries to conduct their field work. They were located in the disciplines of social work and applied linguistics. I have deliberately not outlined my participants' gender and ethnicity together or presented my participants in their supervisory duos or trios, in order to preserve their anonymity and harmonious supervisory relationships. While I am wary of using homogenizing terms such as 'Australian' or 'Asian', I have had to use them to maintain this anonymity. Sometimes this means that I have had to gloss over intriguing intersections of gender and ethnicity or the particularities of culture, which is problematic for this kind of research.

Exploring intercultural teaching and learning experiences within postgraduate supervision is an interesting endeavour for a number of reasons. Doing a Ph.D. represents a 'threshold moment' in the (re)formation of their academic and personal identities (Green, 2005, p. 154); hence its powerful transformative effect. Students are in the liminal, in-between space of becoming a researcher. Their evolving identities can be nurtured, crushed or developed during the often intense interpersonal interactions involved in supervision. Although there is no denying the asymmetrical power dynamics between supervisor and student, the operations of gender, age, ethnicity and culture invest power in all protagonists in diverse ways. Part of the intensity of the supervision also comes from its location, at least in the inherited British model, as a pedagogical space private between the student and the supervisor (Manathunga, 2005a). Until recently, the supervisor's role in this pedagogical space was characterized by either 'benign neglect' (Lee & Williams, 1999, p. 17) or close scrutiny. Although many supervisors are now seeking to provide a balance between guidance and freedom for students, the process of helping students to (re)shape their academic and personal identities as independent researchers is simultaneously fun and fraught for supervisors and students. There is also the potential for clashing cultural assumptions about the roles of supervisors/teachers and candidates/learners in Western and Eastern pedagogical traditions. Traditionally, it is believed that Western educational systems focus on the individual learner and value independence in students. It is also assumed that some 'Asian' educational systems endorse the authority of the supervisor/teacher and value obedience and respect in students, who may regard their supervisor as a parental figure. While neither of these stereotypes is accurate, there is a need for more critical research to explore how these dynamics may interact within intercultural supervision.

Literature review

Western supervision discourses are moving away from the traditional British elite 'magisterial distain' approach characterized by 'neglect, abandonment and indifference' (Riemer cited in Johnson, Lee & Green, 2000, p. 136) towards a mentoring discourse, where students are provided with active pedagogical guidance and support (Pearson & Brew, 2002). These changes in supervision have spawned a growing body of literature seeking to advise supervisors about how to empower their culturally diverse students. Much of this research, however, is firmly located within what B. Smith (2001) calls the 'administrative framing of supervision' (p. 26): a fundamentally liberal discourse about responsibilities of supervisors and students. Consequently, one can find many articles that provide practical tips about intercultural communication. However, there is often a tendency towards liberal *disavowal of difference*, where authors argue that the needs of all students are the same regardless of culture (Chalmers & Volet, 1997; Geake & Maingard, 1999). Further, there is a failure to tackle the more challenging issues of power, identity and culture in supervisory relationships (e.g., Ballard & Clanchy, 1991; Ryan & Zuber-Skerritt, 1999; Wisker et al., 2003), although some articles have challenged stereotypes that position all Asian students as dependent learners (Lau et al., 1998; McClure, 2005; Pang, 1999; Wu, 2002).

Some scholars are beginning to investigate the issues of identity and power in intercultural supervision in more nuanced and reflexive ways that will form a basis for this chapter. In particular, Kenway and Bullen (2003) have used postcolonial theory and Pratt's (1992) concept of the university as a 'contact zone' to explore how female international students in Australia and Canada negotiate their identities as research students. They found that the women adopted a range of identity positions from pragmatic adoption and assimilation to resistance in response to representations of themselves as Others. While many of them experienced affirmation, some also felt ambivalent in both their host and home countries.

The impact of intercultural interaction and migration on students' and supervisors' identities is particularly explored in the work of Aspland (1999a & 1999b), Cadman and Ha (2001) and Venables et al. (2001). It is worth reviewing some of their findings about identity because they form a rich basis to this chapter. Aspland (1999b) found that all of the Asian women that she interviewed were forced to interact in uncomfortable ways with their supervisors. She also describes the experiences of Mei, a Chinese student, who in her initial supervisory relationship was expected to assimilate to Western practices. Fortunately, Mei changed supervisors and in the second supervision relationship she experienced 'both-ways supervision' where the cultural differences between the supervisor and the student were drawn upon as 'sites of possibility' (p. 37 & 38). Cadman and Ha (2001) explore intercultural supervision, with Cadman, an Australian supervisor, exploring how she had to modify her supervision style to become more directive in working with Ha, a Vietnamese student. Ha describes how difficult their initial supervision meetings were and how he appreciated Cadman's attempts to change. He also reflected on how he changed during Cadman's supervision to become more independent.

Venables et al. (2001) use postcolonial theory to explore the impact of migration and engaging in supervision and doctoral education on their diverse subjectivities as South African women (a supervisor and two research students). The supervisor, Jenny, writes about how her identity shifts and changes with each new supervision. Her students, Sharifa and Eleanor, describe how their Ph.D. and migration journeys require them to 'grow new mind states, new emotional and conceptual landscapes' (pp. 243–4).

Postcolonial theory

To offer a fresh perspective on identity and power in intercultural supervision, I will summarize postcolonial theories about contact zones, transculturation, unhomeliness and identity. These theories allow an exploration of the colonial overtones or stereotypes about people from diverse cultures that may subconsciously impact upon the ways international students are perceived by Western supervisors. Each of these terms will be explained and linked to supervisory practice. To begin, Pratt's (1992) notion of the contact zone will be discussed.

Contact zone

Pratt (1992) describes the *contact zone* as 'social spaces where disparate cultures meet, clash and grapple with each other, often in highly asymmetrical relations of domination and subordination' (p. 4). This is applicable to intercultural supervision, where asymmetrical power dynamics between supervisor and student are overlaid by different cultural assumptions about pedagogy. For example, culturally diverse students may feel they have very little power in the supervision relationship not only because the supervisor has greater authority as the teacher, but also because the supervisor and student may have very different cultural expectations about how supervision should work.

Kenway and Bullen (2003) extend the idea of the contact zone to higher education, arguing that 'the goal of those teaching in . . . the contact zone is . . . to focus on . . . how students, texts or cultures might come together in productive dialogue – without glossing over difference' (p. 10). This is similar to Aspland's (1999b) description of productive 'both-ways' intercultural supervision. Thus, the contact zone becomes a place where transculturation is possible.

Transculturation

Transculturation describes how

> subordinated or marginal groups select and invent from materials transmitted to them by a dominant . . . culture . . . Subjugated peoples . . . determine to varying extents what they absorb into their own and what they use it for. (Pratt, 1992, p. 6)

In other words, culturally diverse students can have power and agency in their interactions with their supervisors. But transculturation is not a one-way process. It also describes how marginal groups' cultures and practices impact upon those of dominant groups. Therefore, supervisors' identities can also be changed in the process of working with their students. Transculturation is more than a strategy of temporary accommodation or resistance: it is also a form of adaptation and the creation of new cultural possibilities. For example, culturally diverse students may select those parts of Western knowledge that they find useful and blend them with their own knowledge. If supervisors are open to the cultures and ideas of their students, there is the potential to learn and grow. As a result of this mutual experience of transculturation, creative new knowledge can be formed. For example, Mei, the Chinese student in Aspland's (1999b) chapter, describes how she and her second supervisor were able to build a bridge together between her ways of learning and Western approaches to build her critical analysis skills. While there are exciting moments of change and growth for both students and supervisors, it can also be an uncomfortable or 'unhomely' experience.

Unhomeliness

Unhomeliness is a concept used by Bhabha (1994) to describe 'the estranging sense of the relocation of home and the world – the unhomeliness – that is the condition of extra-territorial and cross-cultural initiations' (p. 9) that migrant workers, refugees, Indigenous peoples and cultural minorities experience. This concept tries to capture the cultural alienation, sense of uncertainty and discomfort that people experience as they adjust to new cultural practices. It seeks to identify the ambivalence people may feel about themselves in this process. Culturally diverse students experience this not only in adjusting to the Australian context, but also in adapting to the Western educational system and the implicit cultural expectations supervisors may have of them. Supervisors who are seeking to adapt their supervision style to their students' learning needs in a culturally sensitive way may also become uncomfortable as they adopt unfamiliar strategies and roles.

Research questions

This chapter investigates the intercultural experiences of a small number of supervisors and students in several humanities and social science disciplines at an Australian university. In particular, it seeks to explore instances of:

1. transculturation experienced by supervisors
2. transculturation experienced by research students
3. students' agency
4. students' assimilation to Western practices
5. unhomeliness or ambivalence described by both students and supervisors.

It is important to explain these research questions in more detail. Firstly, in terms of transculturation, I am particularly looking for instances where Australian supervisors seek to enhance their own understanding of their students' cultural practices and pedagogical expectations rather than expecting students to conform to typical Western patterns. I am also looking for examples of transculturation where students' identities have been changed by the experience of studies in Australia. These questions particularly investigate whether intercultural supervision is a liminal contact zone for both supervisors and students, where both become transcultural hybrids and can learn from each other. I am also keen to explore examples where students have been expected to assimilate to Western norms. Regarding agency, I am looking for examples of empowerment for students, when the supervisor accepts their identity or authority on a topic. Regarding ambivalence, I am seeking to investigate 'unhomely' moments of uncertainty, turmoil or discomfort when the student's or the supervisor's sense of self is questioned.

Methodology

A semi-structured interview was taped and transcribed for this ethically cleared study, with five supervisors and two students participating. Two of the supervisors and two of the students were from Asian countries while three of the supervisors were Anglo-Celtic Australians. Their broad disciplinary areas included social work, applied linguistics, languages, sociology, psychology and cultural studies. They were selected because of their disciplinary diversity and because of their different levels of supervision experience. The students were studying full time in Australia, although they were planning to return to their home countries for field work. The majority of their supervision was face-to-face, supported by additional emails. I also gathered additional comments about supervision from one of the students, in whose country I was about to deliver an educational development programme. In some cases, the supervisor had taught the student in other degree programmes before supervising them, while in other cases the supervisors had been recommended to students by the school's postgraduate coordinator. Their supervision meetings were a mixture of formally scheduled appointments and informal interaction.

The interview questions explored aspects of supervisors' and students' supervision experiences (e.g., 'Do you think your student feels part of your School's research culture?', 'What has been particularly helpful about your supervisor's style of supervision?'). Additional questions about Asian supervisors' experiences as students were asked (e.g., 'How has your own experience of being supervised impacted upon your current supervision practice?') in order to broaden the number of international student perspectives included in the study. Australian supervisors were not asked about their experiences as students because it was assumed that they had been supervised by people of similar cultural backgrounds to their own.

In order to alter the dynamics of the interviews, my research assistant, Maryam (Shirin) Jamarani, who is an Iranian Ph.D. student in an Australian university, interviewed all of the Anglo-Celtic Australian supervisors, while I, as an Irish Australian supervisor, interviewed two international students and the Asian supervisors. We chose to do this because we wanted to continue the intercultural dynamic by interviewing people with different cultural backgrounds from our own. A triangulation of perspectives was also planned through investigating not only Australian supervisors working with international students but also Asian supervisors working with local Australian students. However, while invitations to the two Australian students to participate in the study were issued, they were unable to be interviewed because of time constraints.

The interview data was initially subjected to a content analysis that investigated student and supervisor perceptions. In three cases, both the supervisors and the students were interviewed, and in the two other cases, the supervisors only were involved in the study. If the student mentioned an issue in their interview, this was tracked within the supervisor's interview as well. So too, if the supervisor made claims about their supervision practices, then verification was looked for in the student's interview. From this, a number of significant themes were identified. These themes were then framed by the postcolonial theoretical constructs of transculturation, assimilation, agency and unhomeliness.

Results

The interview data provide an intriguing, rich insight into the tensions and pleasures involved in intercultural supervision. Evidence of power, culture and identity found within the interview data will be presented.

Transculturation for supervisors

Several supervisors in this study discussed experiences of transculturation. This term refers to the changes both supervisors and students experience as a result of engaging in intercultural supervision, where, in seeking to understand each other's cultural perspectives, they begin to co-create new cultural knowledge and perspectives. Two of the Australian supervisors made conscious attempts to discover more about their international students' cultural practices. In particular, one supervisor indicated that 'I spend a lot of time asking about their own countries and I have read a lot about their own cultural practices'. Where possible, he sought to visit their countries, and talked with pride and pleasure about visiting a number of former students 'they were . . . proud to show me their place and I was entranced by the framework in which these very intelligent sensitive people had been formed before they come to us' (Australian supervisor 3). Another Australian supervisor indicated that 'you really need to have some kind of understanding of the [student's] context' especially when they are conducting fieldwork in their own country (Australian supervisor 1). Interestingly, she had also asked her international students about their countries but found them curiously evasive, although because of the social nature of their research she learnt more about their cultures indirectly. She speculated that their reticence could be related to their gender as males, and had sought to include male supervisors in the supervision team. Another Australian supervisor had also deliberately sought female associate supervisors when his students were female (Australian supervisor 3). This is a recognition that students may experience moments of gender unhomeliness as well as cultural unhomeliness.

Without being prompted, one Australian supervisor indicated that his international students 'offer me some new things'. He amplified on this point:

[I am] constantly reminded the way I look at things is not the only way . . . I've come to understand . . . how intellectual activity looks when you start from different cultural positions . . . and in some cases different gendered positions . . . I've learnt heaps from them about . . . about intercultural sensitivity . . . the validity of different ways of doing intellectual things. (Australian supervisor 3)

He spoke passionately about the need to understand 'from my . . . international students the steps it takes . . . to accommodate to working in an Australian cultural and intellectual framework but also the steps which I can take towards them which will help to narrow the gap'. He agreed that he had become 'a different person because of [intercultural] supervision' (Australian supervisor 3). Another Australian supervisor also agreed that she had changed – 'I have become much more relaxed . . . I have lived my life [before that] according to time frames and deadlines and dates and structure' (Australian supervisor 1).

Interviews with these two supervisors' international students confirm their appreciation of these attempts to accommodate their supervision style to their needs. One student described how 'I can always talk about [anything] with [my supervisor] and give insights into [my country's] culture and before he ask me to do anything he always ask for [my] perspectives and he tries to understand why I am thinking the way I am thinking' (Student 2). The other student also described how he felt 'more at ease' with one of his supervisors – 'I try to express my feelings. And . . . my ideas with her. And I know that she would not be judgmental and she would be accommodating to me' (Student 1).

The other Australian supervisor did not refer to a desire to know more about her students' cultures. It was only when prompted by questions about what her international students have taught her that she indicated she had learnt more about professional practice in her students' countries. She agreed that knowing more about her students' cultural backgrounds would have helped, although she was 'not actually sure if that would have helped with the supervision process once you are into it'. She was also more inclined to deny the relevance of culture, instead focusing on 'personality' (Australian supervisor 2).

In summary, these findings about transculturation within intercultural supervision suggest that effective intercultural supervision occurs when the supervisor recognizes the student's cultural perspectives. While it is often assumed that international students will change and develop better understandings of western culture during their international studies, this research also highlights the cultural growth and change experienced by the supervisor in effective intercultural supervision.

Transculturation for international students and Asian supervisors

The international students and Asian supervisors interviewed in this study reveal instances of transculturation, where they actively incorporated aspects of Western ways of thinking into their own intellectual repertoire. Their words demonstrate the agency and power with which they select which Western ways to adopt. They engage in creative collage, where parts of Western culture that they find useful become connected with their own worldview.

One student spoke about the typical role of the supervisor in her home country, saying 'the supervisor is the only means of information'. She now believed 'it's not right [to] rely a lot on teachers and the supervisor'. She revelled in the freedom her supervisor gave her. Her supervisor 'always appreciate what we are doing and even when he doesn't particularly like the idea he has [laughs] very good way to ask us to improve it . . . he never really impose his ideas' (Student 2). This same supervisor had inspired her during her Masters studies to change her own supervisory practice. When she returned to her home country, she began to give her own Masters students more autonomy, while understanding their need for guidance and direction. She encouraged them to explore their own ideas but also made sure she gave them enough structure within which to practice their new-found independence (Student 2, additional comments).

All of the international students felt that they had changed as a result of their studies in Australia. They both spoke of gaining more confidence. One student's views about social issues such as gender had been challenged by his interactions with one of his Western supervisors. While he did not choose to speak about this, one of his supervisors spoke about how he had had 'to move out of [his] comfort zone' to study 'a different religious perspective'. She also spoke about how she had been 'very upfront with him about my . . . particular belief system [. . . which] would be absolutely opposed to his'. He was able to accept this difference and they were able to develop 'a good relationship [because] we . . . respect each other' (Australian supervisor 1).

The Asian supervisors interviewed also described their experiences of transculturation both as former international students and as supervisors in Australia. One Asian supervisor described her own difficulties as a Ph.D. student in reconciling her values about collectivity, reciprocity and holistic connections between her mind, body and spirit with Western individualistic and rational approaches to research. She described her experiences of transculturation where she was able to adapt largely Western postmodernist theories about identity and subjectivity and blend them with her values to produce her original contribution to knowledge. Her experience is similar to those of the current international students', whose comments are explored above. In writing her thesis, she had 'huge difficulty of seeing these people as my subjects . . . I just felt like it was a real intrusion and exploitation' (Asian supervisor 2). After meeting an anthropologist who 'introduced me to some new areas about . . . how to see subjectivity', she was able to recast her thesis as 'my own journey . . . questioning of my own identity'. This ensured that it was a 'kind of collaborative project . . . so long as it's a collaboration and reciprocal relationship, then it's ok' (Asian supervisor 2).

This experience also shaped her philosophy as a supervisor. She always asks students 'why you wanna do this? And who you are? And your identity as a researcher and what kind of role you going to play.' She spoke about the Western tendency to 'over-theorize everything' and believed it was very important to 'talk about how you feel about things'. She has found with her students that this approach 'seems to work quite well' because it brings 'you and students closer'. Without being prompted, she also spoke about supervision as 'a collaborative process', where 'I learn as much as they learn' (Asian supervisor 2).

This supervisor also spoke of her initial difficulties as a student with responding to questions like ' "what do you think?" . . . that was the question I was so so scared of because we never . . . had that sort of experience'. She described how gradually she began to realize that everyone has 'that piece of opinion that you only can contribute' and she laughed as she realized that 'now I'm asking students "what you think" or "what you feel is the important thing"'. She now finds that students respond really well to her encouragement to find 'something that *you* can only say' (Asian supervisor 2).

In summary, the international students in this study experienced moments of transculturation when they were able to blend their own cultural knowledge with selected aspects of western knowledge to create new knowledge. This gave them a great deal of confidence. For some of the international students, who had later become supervisors, their cultural world view was shaped by notions of reciprocity and collaboration that encouraged them to interact with their research participants and their research students in holistic ways.

Students' agency

There were a number of instances in the interview data where supervisors were keen to empower students to identify their own unique contribution to knowledge. All of the students in the study were eager to seize the opportunity to demonstrate their independence, even if at first such an opportunity felt a little uncomfortable. This contradicts the stereotype that Asian students are always less independent than Western students. These were not, however, instances of neglect where students were left on their own to navigate through confusing research waters. Instead they provide powerful examples of scaffolding: the guided exploration of ideas where the supervisor gradually allows the student greater freedom. While this is a supervision strategy commonly used in socializing all research students into postgraduate research culture, what is particularly interesting here is that stereotypes of both Asian students as being dependent and Western supervisors as not providing sufficient direction are challenged.

One Australian supervisor described this process as 'I will spend a lot of time with them just trying to . . . find out . . . about their intellectual backgrounds and goals'. He also spoke about trying to 'see where [students] are coming from . . . so I don't impose my view on it I just help her to build hers' (Australian supervisor 3). His student amplified how he gave students' agency. She described how he

> leads other people in the way that is most beneficial . . . he draws out their strengths . . . he asks questions like 'why don't you do this and see what will happen?' . . . and if I say 'I think it is not a good idea', then he will say something like 'can you say why you don't think it is a good idea?' (Student 2)

These supervisors provided guidance for students to experiment with their independence and freedom in a supported learning environment. This involved treating each student differently according to their own learning styles and culture. This was achieved through:

- scheduling regular formal and informal contact
- dealing with personal issues if they arose
- including students in a supportive research culture.

One supervisor described how he recommended that his students record supervision sessions so they could concentrate on chatting about their ideas in the session rather than having to take notes. He also begins an email message to each student at the beginning of the meeting and gradually records 'things we talk about' and then he sends that to the student at the end of the session. He also believed ongoing informal contact was important, describing how he often 'pop[s] in on them', although he was aware that some of his international students found this a bit 'disconcerting' at first (Australian supervisor 3).

Several of the supervisors in this study believed it was important to be available to discuss personal issues with their students if necessary – 'I invite them to tell me personal circumstances which affects their ability to study . . . [and] I give them my [home] phone number and say 'if there's anything bugging you or whatever . . . ring me first' (Australian supervisor 3). The students in this study expressed their appreciation about being treated as whole people with external lives and pressures. Interestingly, one of the Asian supervisors in the study indicated that this more personal approach was closer to Eastern approaches to supervision, where the supervisor was expected to be like 'almost a parent . . . counseling . . . giving them advice'. Particularly because of his own difficult experiences as an international student, he 'felt very close to international students' and discovered that many local Australian students also began to rely on his personal approach to supervision (Asian supervisor 1).

Several of the supervisors in this study also worked very hard to build a supportive research culture for students. One supervisor had set up a research group for his students, which was both face-to-face and online so that, even before students arrived in Australia, they were able to make contact with other students. This provided both intellectual and social integration into a research community. All of these scaffolding strategies were designed to be gradually removed so that the students were able to eventually develop into independent researchers. As one supervisor explained, 'it's like a scaffolding [where] with their agreement I remove bits of the scaffolding and see how they go' because his ultimate goal was to 'basically . . . make myself irrelevant . . . [to] see them set sail under their own steam without needing further sustenance from me' (Australian supervisor 3). His students really appreciated this because he is 'some one I can rely on academically and other aspects . . . I feel um more confident that way' (Asian student 2).

This interview data also provided some interesting insights into the issue of independence among international students. Firstly, one supervisor indicated that he had found Asian students more independent than local students – 'I think they will try to nut it out on their own longer than Anglo [Australian] students who will be more likely after hitting their first brick wall [to] bring me the brick wall for comment'. He also found that gender played a role in levels of independence. His international female students especially tried 'for too long to work it out for themselves' (Australian supervisor 3). So too, another student in the study had specifically asked for critique – 'I did mention out . . . if I'm out of the track . . . it's ok for you to comment me on things . . . Don't just say that I'm good . . . because that way I won't learn much' (Asian student 1).

In summary, this section highlighted examples of international students demonstrating their agency in their research studies. In particular, it challenges both assumptions that Asian students tend to be dependent learners and that Western supervisors do not usually provide sufficient guidance.

Assimilating students to Western norms

There was also some evidence among the interviews that some supervisors sought to assimilate international students to Western norms. One supervisor spoke a great deal about the problems associated with supervising international students, particularly their difficulties with written English. She described international students' writing as 'difficult and strange . . . [it] needs an awful lot of editing' (Australian supervisor 2). By making continual references to 'not treating them like idiots', she seemed to reinforce rather than deny her deficit view of international students. She also believed that all students should be treated in the same way regardless of their ethnicity:

> I don't believe that they should get any less . . . compared to local students. It just means that you have to work harder . . . I will expect the same intelligence and ability . . . as I would from other Ph.D. students. But I give the time and effort to talk it through with them . . . And that may make it a bit stressful. But in the end they realize that you are treating them like others. (Australian supervisor 2)

She defended this point of view using a recurring discourse about the importance of maintaining academic standards of English.

There is also evidence that some Western supervisors may blame the difficulties they have with their international students on what they perceive as different cultural expectations about male and female roles, rather than accepting that the supervision strategies they use with domestic students may not be as helpful in supervising international students. Being treated 'the same' as domestic students may only serve as a painful reminder to international students of how different they actually are and sap their confidence in themselves. This can make it harder for international students to communicate their thinking. It also can deny the value of their pre-existing cultural knowledge so that their only option is to learn as quickly as possible to conform to Western ways of thinking.

The interviews with both Asian supervisors also indicated that, as international students, they had experienced efforts to assimilate them to Western norms. For example, one Asian supervisor described how in her past experience as a student she 'didn't know what to expect from the supervisor . . . and there was no way of discussing what the role could be'. This was because her supervisor basically let her 'explore and wander around' and she was supposed to 'just come and ask . . . if you have question'. She described her feelings of being 'very lost . . . I was so desperate I actually nearly gave up' (Asian supervisor 2).

This experience of being assimilated into Western approaches not only continued while the Asian supervisors were students. One supervisor described how, initially, her local Australian student did not take her advice very seriously because she was 'an [Asian] person, female'. She felt that 'he had that kind of I can get away with it' attitude to her until his confirmation of candidature was postponed because his progress had not been up to standard. Since then 'he has become more serious' (Asian supervisor 2).

In summary, this section highlighted the difficulties some of the international students and Asian supervisors in this study experienced when they were forced to conform to Western ways of thinking or when their students took them less seriously because of Western stereotypes about Asian women. For international students in particular, this kind of assimilation can destroy their confidence in their own ability to such an extent that they may withdraw from or abandon their studies all together.

Ambivalence for both supervisors and students

The experience of intercultural supervision also left both supervisors and students feeling ambivalent about their identities and roles. Several participants reflected on the reverse culture shock they or their students experienced when returning to their home countries. Studying internationally was a transformative experience, leaving them feeling unhomely when they returned to their own countries. As one supervisor indicated, some of his students' parents had said to him that they had sent him their child 'as a nice obedient Japanese daughter and . . . [she's] come back argumentative'. He elaborated on this point, suggesting that 'cultural practices have a way of leaking in . . . and it takes a while to leak them out again' (Australian supervisor 3). Another supervisor made a point of pre-warning her students that 'you are not exactly the same person that you [were when] you came here' and that international studies were an opportunity 'to find out who they really are . . . to explore' (Australian supervisor 2). While these experiences could be positive, they certainly provoked a great deal of questioning of identity, leaving some students feeling doubly displaced.

One Asian supervisor also expressed his ambivalence about the extra burden he believed non-Western supervisors faced because of their difference. He described how not only international students but many local Australian students approached him for assistance. He believed that he had developed a reputation as 'Mr Fix-It' because he adopted a more caring approach to supervision than many of his colleagues. His approach was more in line with Eastern expectations about supervisors as parental figures and was appreciated by all students. This ensured that his supervision workload doubled but in a hidden inequitable way (Asian supervisor 1).

In summary, this section highlighted the feelings of ambivalence that international students may experience as a result of their adoption of some Western ways of being and thinking. It also uncovered the extra supervision burden Asian supervisors may experience because of their focus on caring for their students as whole people.

Discussion

This research has investigated how identity and power may play out within the complex, liminal contact zone of intercultural supervision. In particular, this study emphasizes the importance of:

- transculturation for supervisors so that they are able to engage in 'both-ways' supervision
- creating opportunities for transculturation for culturally diverse students
- encouraging international students to develop agency
- providing scaffolding and support within which students can practice their independence
- valuing cultural difference as a dynamic for growth for supervisors and students.

Many of these findings have extended the work of previous authors. The instances of transculturation and accommodation by supervisors described in the interview data elaborate on how supervisors are able to engage in the 'both-ways' supervision that Aspland (1999b) identified. Other authors have also contributed to this notion (Cadman & Ha, 2001; Venables et al., 2001). By recognizing that there may be a cultural gap between Anglo-Celtic approaches to supervision pedagogy and international students' expectations and seeking to move towards a transcultural supervision style, supervisors become more effective. They are also able to adopt some of the positive aspects of Eastern supervision highlighted by one of the Asian supervisors in this study, particularly the close role as a supportive parental figure desired by many students. This helps to promote a holistic approach to supervision that nurtures the mind, body and spirit of research students rather than limiting the interaction to Western rational approaches. It is also closer to more recent Western notions of supervision as mentoring (Pearson & Brew, 2002). It values the collaboration and reciprocity that are significant in collectivistic cultures as well as the individualism associated with the West. In this way then, cultural diversity is valued in the intercultural supervision contact zone as a possibility for new learning for both supervisors and students rather than as a barrier between them or as a feature of supervision that should be ignored or denied.

Creating opportunities for culturally diverse students to adapt elements of Western ways of thinking into their own intellectual repertoire is also an important outcome of this study. Kenway and Bullen (2003) also delineated useful elements of transculturation. It is through this creative process of cultural and pedagogical collage that culturally diverse students demonstrate their agency in drawing on many intellectual traditions in their work. They become able to learn both 'square and round', as Aspland's (1999b, p. 25) participant evocatively described. As an Irish Australian supervisor brought up in the Western intellectual tradition, I can learn a great deal from culturally diverse researchers who have access to many worldviews and perspectives. This type of transculturation becomes possible when supervisors encourage students' agency and provide them with support to test their growing independence as researchers.

Some of the supervisors in this study worked to empower students by accepting and facilitating their perspectives, identities and authority about their own research area. Rather than assuming international research students were somehow devoid of experience or deficient in Western knowledge and language skills, these supervisors constantly sought to understand more about the student's own approach to their research, their motivations for exploring their topics and their unique insights. This facilitative supervisory style enabled students to enhance their confidence as a researcher. This type of supervision was also achieved through regular formal and informal contact with students, dealing with personal issues if they arose and including students in a supportive research culture (Manathunga, 2005b). They valued and tried to build on students' agency rather than merely expecting their students to conform to stereotypes of dependent international students, which have also been challenged by other authors (Lau, 1998; McClure, 2005;

Pang, 1999). So too, they did not expose their students to the excesses of traditional Western supervision where students were required to be 'always/already independent' (Johnson et al., 2000, p. 138) at the beginning of their candidature. Instead they provided the supportive structure within which students could gradually test their independence that Wu (2002) wrote about.

This research also highlights the problems created by Anglo-Celtic Australian supervisors when they seek to impose Western norms on their culturally diverse students (Aspland, 1999a & b) and Anglo-Celtic Australian students when they impose Western stereotypes on their culturally diverse supervisors. In particular, this process of assimilation debilitates the student's sense of identity and saps their confidence. It also ensures that supervision becomes stressful for both the student and the supervisor.

The onerous cultural burden experienced by Asian supervisors does not seem to have surfaced in the literature, although it is sometimes acknowledged in work on Indigenous supervision (Budby, 2001). There are colonial overtones embedded in this dynamic that will require additional research and more equitable approaches to workload planning and other forms of recognition. Finally, this research illustrates some of the unhomeliness associated with intercultural supervision, especially for students who may feel doubly displaced by their international education experiences. Understanding the role that ambivalence and inner turmoil plays in intercultural supervision is vital in enhancing our knowledge about the complexities of supervision relationships (Grant, 2003).

This research seems to suggest that effective intercultural supervision could include:

1. Experiencing cultural change as supervisors as well as students
   a. supervisors need to monitor their supervision strategies and think seriously about whether they need to modify their supervision styles to work effectively with culturally diverse students
   b. supervisors need to enhance their knowledge and understanding of their student's cultural practices, educational systems and approaches to learning.
2. Creating opportunities for students to blend their existing cultural knowledge with particular aspects of Western ways of thinking
3. Providing scaffolding and support within which students can practice their independence as emerging researchers

4. Viewing cultural difference as a dynamic for the mutual growth of both students and supervisors.

This research has confirmed the usefulness of using postcolonial theories about the contact zone, transculturation, unhomeliness and identity in seeking to extend our understandings of intercultural supervision in the humanities and the social sciences. By applying these constructs to interview data, I have not only identified some of the cultural possibilities inherent in intercultural supervision but also have begun to explore culturally diverse approaches to supervision, which have been largely neglected to date. This study could serve as the basis for a much larger study of Asian, Indigenous and other non-Western supervision pedagogies. Further research also needs to be conducted into the experiences of Anglo-Celtic Australian students who have culturally diverse supervisors. It would also be interesting to test the applicability of these theoretical constructs in the sciences. As an academic developer specializing in supervisors' professional development, this study has a number of significant implications for my future supervision development work. This research has particularly demonstrated that intercultural supervision has the potential to be a fascinating, challenging pedagogical contact zone that may enable mutual learning for supervisors and students.

Reflection questions

1. How does your cultural identity and that of your students impact on your supervision relationship?
2. In being supervised as a student, or in supervising students, have you experienced moments of transculturation (creating new knowledge by blending your own cultural ways of thinking with those of other cultures)? Or unhomeliness (uncertainty or uneasiness in working in a different environment or culture)? What did they feel like?
3. What support is provided in your context for students to test their own independence as researchers?

Resources

Aspland, T. (1999b). 'You learn round and I learn square': Mei's story. In Y. Ryan & O. Zuber-Skerrit (eds), *Supervising postgraduates from non-English speaking backgrounds* (pp. 25–39). Buckingham: The Society for Research into Higher Education & Open University Press.

This chapter provides an excellent insight into 'both-ways' supervision approaches that see cultural diversity as a dynamic for learning for both supervisors and students.

Kenway, J., & Bullen, E. (2003). Self-representations of international women postgraduate students in the global university 'contact zone'. *Gender and Education, 15*(1), 5–20.

This article provides a powerful exploration of the experiences of several international female research students and a helpful insight into the postcolonial concept of the contact zone.

Wu, S. (2002). Filling the pot or lighting the fire? Cultural variations in conceptions of pedagogy. *Teaching in Higher Education, 7*(4), 387–95.

This article recommends an excellent way of providing research students with both structure and freedom so they can gradually develop their independence as researchers.

6
Mobile Students, Flexible Identities and Liquid Modernity: Disrupting Western Teachers' Assumptions of 'The Asian Learner'

Catherine Doherty and Parlo Singh

This chapter examines international students' accounts of their educational journeys and their personal motivations using interview data collected from Asian international students enrolled in preparatory TESOL programmes in an Australian university. A selection of these interview accounts are analysed to demonstrate how these students carefully negotiate the contradictions and possibilities of globalizing times, their investments in diverse cultural capitals, and the restrictive cultured identities made available to them in the internationalized university. We argue that Asian international students may at times strategically take up essentialist versions (Spivak, 1990) of Asian learner identities that are discursively constructed and influential in Western TESOL practices. At the same time, these students also disrupt such narratives of Asian learner identities that circulate in TESOL classrooms, and offer alternative imaginings through discursive re-articulations (Hall, 1996a). Both of these tactics may be used strategically by students to further their project of appropriating new resources as they travel across transnational educational routes. The paper concludes by reflecting on the implications of new theorizations about the flexible identities of mobile students under conditions of liquid modernity for educators in internationalized education.

Introduction

In this chapter we analyse interview accounts of educational journeys provided by international students from Asia enrolled in preparatory TESOL programmes in an Australian university in order to understand the identities being constructed by these mobile students. We begin with a brief explanation of the internationalized yet Australian context of the study. Our review of relevant literature about international student identities challenges past theorizations that nevertheless continue to strongly influence the field of practice. We then identify key concepts to inform the analysis. These three concepts are: (a) investments in identity projects, (b) strategies of essentialism and re-articulation to navigate scripts and models of the 'Asian learner', and (c) the cultural politics of representation. Next, we analyse the interview data and present the results that, in the discussion, prompt a rethinking of the identities of globally mobile students, the identities made available in TESOL classrooms, and, more importantly, the identities that are constructed in their process of becoming. We end the paper by considering the implications of new theorizations about the flexible identities of mobile students for educators in internationalized programmes.

Context

In the Australian higher education sector, approximately 24 per cent of the total student population are now full-fee paying international students (Department of Education, Science & Training, 2005). The flow into Australian institutions has predominantly been students of Chinese heritage from Southeast Asia nations (Nesdale, Simkin, Sang, Burke & Frager, 1995). Thus, the international student in this context is widely imagined, constructed and known within a discourse of 'the Asian learner'. The term discourse is used here to refer to the set of ideas and premises generating possibilities for classroom practices (see Bernstein, 2000). In other words, curricular texts, pedagogic designs, and classroom practices are constituted by and within discursive rules which govern what can legitimately be spoken/written, when, where, how, and by whom (see Foucault, 1990). Moreover, pedagogic discourses are not only ways of talking and thinking about learners. They are also 'practices that systematically form the objects of which they speak' (Foucault cited in Ball, 1990, p. 17). Thus discourses serve a double function – both prescriptive and performative (Bourdieu, 2003). In their prescriptive mode, discourses constitute ways of thinking about 'the Asian learner', and in their performative mode they produce the reality of classroom practices, shaping what pedagogic designs are do-able or construct-able with Asian international students.

The research reported in this paper took place inside the institutional programmes offered to international students to prepare them for the Australian mainstream university's mode of pedagogy. The designs of curricula and pedagogy in these transitional spaces reveal how the institution understands or constructs the needs of its international student body, and how their problematic 'cultural difference' is managed. As an example of such performative productions of the dominant 'Asian learner' discourse in the Australian context, the generic one or two semester 'Foundation' programme has become well established across the Australian higher education sector as a reception pathway for international students into mainstream undergraduate programmes (Coleman, 1998; Doherty & Singh, 2005; Singh & Doherty, 2004). It includes disciplinary studies and academic skills programmes with an emphasis on cultural briefing, but entry and exit standards are typically expressed in levels of English language competence.

Thus when it comes to 'knowing' the international student, it may not necessarily be any intrinsic truth about their identities that will impact on pedagogic design; rather it will more likely be a matter of who they are habitually constructed as and believed to be by those managing the internationalized Australian university. Such institutional understanding will determine what learner identities are made available to these students with which to articulate their personal identity projects in pursuit of their imagined futures. We use the term 'articulate' here following Stuart Hall (1996a) to examine how identities are not just produced and projected by the individual, but are negotiated in the fit between personal dispositions and the possibilities for that individual offered by the social setting. A theory of articulation thus makes us question what work the discursive category of 'Asian learner' does in this context, and moreover, what subject positions it offers the international student in Australian universities.

Literature review

Over the history of Australia's increasing involvement in Asian educational markets, the discursive category, 'Asian learner', has been produced and reinforced in an influential stream of 'how to' literature (for example, Ballard & Clanchy, 1984; 1988; 1997). Such literature invokes a set of problematic, essentialized attributes arising from notional cultural difference, such as an over-reliance on rote or surface learning and passive classroom behaviours. These attributes are understood to require pedagogic intervention and amelioration from Western teachers. The cultural traditions producing the 'Asian learner' are usually described in a stark binary contrast to Western traditions, with the East and the West understood to be mutually exclusive:

> In Western education it is axiomatic that knowledge is gained and extended through critical analysis, by individuals working with increasing independence . . . yet such a view, we often forget, is culture-bound . . . In Asia, for example . . . knowledge is not open to challenge and extension in this way, and academic education may have little to do with the beginning of wisdom. . . . Similarly, the written or printed work carries great authority. (Ballard, 1987, p. 114)

Critiques of this long standing 'Asian learner' discourse are emerging (for example, Biggs, 1997; Chan, 1999; Kubota, 2001). Kubota critiques cultural difference theory which essentializes the practices of ESL/EFL learners and classrooms and constructs an unproblematic self for BANA (British, Australian, North American) teachers and classrooms. Such schema of broad, predictable cultural differences overstate commonalities within any group and overstate differences between groups. They also tend to oversimplify and 'fix' social practices as timeless givens, rather than understanding them as produced in particular historical times, places and relations that are subject to change. Such a focus on difference is understood to be a process of Othering, meaning:

> the ways in which the discourse of a particular group defines other groups in opposition to itself: an Us and Them view that constructs an identity for the Other and, implicitly, for the Self. Othering of another group typically involves maintaining social distance and making value judgements (often negative) based on stereotyped opinions about the group as a whole. (Palfreyman, 2005, pp. 216–17)

Despite their growing number, these critiques have yet to impact on institutional TESOL and higher education practices in Australia which continue to regard Other international students (Bullen & Kenway, 2003; Singh, 2004) as passive, reproductive learners who need generic, preparatory programmes to induct them into the classroom practices of the Western academy.

From our point of view, any critique of the discourse of 'Asian learner' has to deal with both its prescriptive and its performative aspects. While the literature cited above addresses the prescriptive processes of Asian learner identities, we are interested in understanding how the students deal with the performative aspects of this dominant discourse, that is, how they manage to negotiate the practices and positions that the orthodox discourse of 'Asian learner as a problem' has produced for them. In addition we are interested in challenging the premise of mutually exclusive cultures that underpins any such Othering discourse, in recognition of the accelerating interpenetration of cultures and overlapping lifeworlds in today's globalizing interactions. A number of theorists argue that the new affordances of instantaneous communication, global travel, electronic finance, and mobile capital have produced a new, more flexible or fluid social condition (Castells, 1997; Urry, 2000). Bauman (2000) terms this condition 'liquid modernity', extending the 'liquid' metaphor to characterize the 'melting' of previously 'solid' bonds of collective identity into the less determined, more vicarious forms of 'individually conducted life policies' (p. 6).

To engage with this larger context of significant social change, we outline three theoretical concepts which offer possibilities for rethinking the learner identities of mobile Asian international students under conditions of liquid modernity. These three concepts, discussed in the following order, are: (a) investments; (b) strategic use of essentialism and re-articulation in navigating the scripts, narratives and operative models of the mobile 'Asian learner'; and (c) the cultural politics of representation.

Investments

Norton (2000) highlights the role of 'investments' made by the cross-cultural language learner, to further identity-shaping processes across time and space towards future goals. Norton extends Bourdieu's (1986) notion of different types of capital, to derive this metaphor of 'investment':

> If learners invest in a second language, they do so with the understanding that they will acquire a wider range of symbolic and material resources, which will in turn increase the value of their cultural capital. Learners expect or hope to have a good return on that investment – a return that will give them access to hitherto unattainable resources . . . Thus an investment in the target language is also an investment in a learner's own identity, an identity which is constantly changing across time and space. (p. 10)

Through her ethnography of a group of language learners negotiating their class, gender and linguistic positioning as newly arrived immigrants in Canada, Norton demonstrates how identities are not given, essential and fixed, but rather, are constituted in a context's particular configuration of power relations and the various parties' investments in those particular relationships. Similarly McKay and Wong's (1996) study discredits the 'generic, ahistorical "stick figure" of the learner' (p. 603) to paint a much more complex picture of the interplay between operative discourses and the individual's strategic agency to pursue their investments while conducting 'delicate social negotiations to fashion viable identities' (p. 603).

For our purposes, these studies highlight firstly, the importance of educational careers in 'the process of becoming' (Hall, 1996b, p. 3). Educational choices can thus be understood as 'biographical solutions' (Beck, 1992, p. 137), that is, active choices to invest time, money and effort in the hope of realizing imagined futures and new identities. Secondly, these studies demonstrate the complexity of articulating identity projects with the institutional subject positions made available, and the multiple fronts on which students must construct their identities (see also Hall, 1996b). In educational settings, this will not be a unilateral process. Both teachers and students can make, or fail to make, investments in any pedagogical relationship, and choose to engage either more or less with the way the other party positions them.

Asian middle-class strategy

With regard to more fluid identities in Asian settings in particular, upwardly mobile capitalists are no longer reviled as mere 'merchants' but are now applauded for their entrepreneurship, their economic leadership, and their international networks (Pinches, 1999). Pinches highlights the strategy of accruing international educational credentials as important status markers for these groups, and their pursuit of such as a strategy to achieve the less tangible cultural capital associated with social refinement. For Pinches, these strategies (that sustain much of the flow of international students into Australia) are not fixed cultural traits, but newly acquired tactics (that is, biographical solutions) arising from the significant cultural and economic changes of 'liquid modernity'.

Against this backdrop of social change, Pinches (1999) explores the rhetorical tension between competing accounts for the Asian middle class's economic success. On one hand their success is often attributed to their intrinsic cultural difference and 'traditional Oriental values', while on the other hand, it is also equally attributed to the rampant spread of Western consumerism and capitalist markets. Pinches argues that this seeming dualism overlooks the relational nexus between these two representations, and how the individual can strategically elect to invoke either global or local identities and rationales:

> Each of these representations of the new rich in Asia needs to be understood in reference to both the global and the local, and, most significantly, the interplay between them. . . . mediated through the unprecedented movement across state borders of people, capital, consumer goods, fashion and lifestyle images, and contending politico-religious ideologies . . . (p. 10)

In this vein, Ong (1997) uses the term 'self-orientalization' to highlight the opportunistic take-up of triumphal Orientalism by Chinese diaspora capitalists and Asian leaders to strategically produce transnational solidarities when so desired. Ong argues that such self-orientalizing is a strategic discursive response to certain settings, deployed by the transnational capitalist to further their ends opportunistically, distinct from any claim or expression of some intrinsic cultural truth. For our purposes, the idea of such middle-class strategy highlights how individuals can choose at times to articulate with traditional scripts and narratives of essentialized cultural identities, and at other times, in other settings and for other purposes, to invoke more global identities and global cultural resources.

Politics of representation

Spivak (1990) uses the term 'strategic use of essentialism' to signal two ways of representation – representation as delegation in the political sense, and representation as portrait or depiction. Crucially, Spivak suggests that it is 'not possible to be non-essentialist' (p. 109). She suggests that we should think about the ways in which individuals represent themselves, and in the process represent members of particular social groups. In other words, it is important for teachers to engage in the cultural politics of representation – who is being represented, where, how, when, and for what tactical or strategic ends? Consequently, TESOL teachers may engage students in conversations about home and host countries, self and group identity, and at the same time question and critique the accounts given by students rather than accept them as authentic accounts. Re-articulation is another such strategy for disrupting Othering and Orientializing discourses in the global terrain of cultural politics (Hall, 1991; 1996a). Here the ideological elements that have been articulated or sutured together to cohere into a discursive unity are prised apart and re-articulated or re-assembled. Thus students may in one situation give an account of themselves as culturally determined and their need to be 'acculturated' to the Western university, an account that would be publicly acceptable to Australian teachers and interviewers, in line with the script that has been provided to these students in the 'cultural briefing' of their preparatory curriculum. At the same time, the students' account may work to disrupt and challenge this type of account and question whether Australian classroom practices actually do provide them with critical thinking skills and English language proficiency.

Research questions

These studies of 'investments', 'middle-class strategy' and representation strategies provoke a more problematic and multi-faceted concept of identity that fractures any overriding ascription of cultural identity with considerations of such dimensions as class positioning, gender, educational background – notable silences in the institutional construction and literature regarding the 'Asian student' in Australian higher education. Thus from a variety of fronts, we arrive at the realization that identities can no longer be adequately understood as fixed, or ascribed by membership in collectivities, but rather need to be understood as more fluid works-in-progress, meshing the positions and resources on offer with the biographical solutions of the individual (see Hall, 1996b). With this conceptualization of increasingly fluid life-politics, we can now more clearly articulate the research task through a series of preliminary questions working towards the final broader question:

- What investments, identity projects and strategies are mobile students pursuing through a common strategy of international education?
- How do institutional understandings of who these students are shape who they can be in these settings?
- How do students work with or against such institutional understandings?
- Who are these internationally mobile students, and how can we know them?

Method

We conducted 24 semi-structured interviews with groups of two or three students studying in EAP or academic preparation courses at an Australian university. These interviews constituted one part of a larger study into the curriculum and pedagogy designed for international students which also involved video-taping sequences of classes, and teacher interviews with stimulated recall accounts of episodes in their teaching. For this paper, interviews with 32 students attending a generic 'Foundation' academic preparation course were selected. Informed consent was sought before the conduct of classroom observations and student interviews. The interview questions probed students' reasons for studying in Australia, their experiences learning English, the variety of pedagogy they had experienced, how they understood 'Asian' and 'Western' values, and their expectations of the preparatory programmes. These students came from Taiwan (eight), Hong Kong (six), Singapore (four), Indonesia (four), Japan (two), with individuals from East Timor, India, Korea, Malaysia, Philippines, Papua New Guinea, Thailand, plus one whose nationality was not recorded. In our content analysis[1] of these interview accounts, we were interested in firstly, what investments the students were making, with what purpose in mind; and secondly, how any essentializing or 'Orientalizing' discourse was either invoked or challenged by the international students. We cannot erase the possibility that the interview setting and the framing of the questions contributed to the 'cultured' positioning of the student. Our purpose here, however, is to show how the students negotiated the cultural politics of such discursive positioning to represent their motivations and experience. Quotes are reported verbatim here to retain the students' voices as much as possible.

Results – analysing self-reports

Investing in Western cultural capital and English language competence

In the students' accounts, it was difficult to analytically separate their quest for a 'Western' education from their quest for English language competence. The latter is necessary for the former if undertaking studies in Australia, but is acknowledged by the students to be a valuable commodity in itself, and could be considered as adding value to their investment strategies: 'Yes, I can get the degree, can get a knowledge, also I can get English language with me.' Thus in terms of investments, the quest for English language competence temporally precedes, then can be conflated with, the 'Western' higher education qualification.

By their accounts, the students had already made long-term investments in pursuing English language competence as a biographical strategy prior to their arrival in Australia. Many students report 'six or seven years' of effort to develop their English language proficiency, some much longer: 'since at kindergarten'. This personal investment is matched by the significant investment made by their home schooling systems, with English language courses offered in junior and senior secondary, sometimes earlier, and English competence exams required for university entrance in some settings. This formal systemic investment was reportedly often supplemented by the individual with private tuition, or their own informal effort; 'English is very important so even though when I studying degree we have no English subject but I still studied by my own like listen to the programme'.

This sustained investment should be understood as an expensive and arduous commitment. One student reported having already spent two years in preparatory English classes at the Australian university. Others could be considered early investors, with five of the 32 students taking three to five years of their high schooling in Australia: 'so that's why students start early. It's a good advantage for them'. That such students were still required to undertake a preparatory programme casts a shadow over that particular investment strategy.

The students often reported poor returns from much of their home country schooling investment in English, with frequent complaints about the limited competence gained in such programmes: 'but we start on the basic English, like A, B, C the alphabet and we never speak English in school and that is quite difficult for us to learn how to speak'. On the other hand, some students also voiced frustration with their preparatory studies in Australia, given the limited opportunity to mix with native English speakers and their separation from the 'real' university practices:

I feel like because we are learning English and we need to be able to use it to speak and to listen to someone speaking in English. I don't feel like if we have more time to participate in real situation like, say, being given some chances just to go into a lecture hall you know like there were 300 students and sit there and just listen and see how people are participating.

These interviews did not sample students who had decided to cut their losses and return home without realizing their investment. Others however, such as the dissatisfied customer quoted, seemed prepared to undergo the required programme, in order to serve their longer term plans: 'I just want to get it over with.'

In terms of their capital investment, many students suggested that Australian university places were relatively cheap and close by, offering good value for money: 'Yeah, if I studied in America it's going to be double the price.' In addition, Australian university places were sought for specialized offerings not available in the home country, and with regard to a general perception of better quality. Such quality claims were represented in some accounts as reflecting inherent qualities, such as the currency of the course content, the technology facilities and its 'open mind of thinking' for postgraduate studies. For others, it was more a matter of quality measured by 'brand power' or symbolic capital, in terms of future employer perceptions: 'and I also chose to study here because I think people back home and even the companies back home would like to receive employees with an English background'. Ironically, such accounts were produced alongside others that reported easier entry into higher education in Australia, due to the extreme competition for limited local places: 'and it's near and it's easy to get in. I mean if I try to study in Indonesia it's really difficult because we have a test to enter the uni and it's very difficult.' Thus, international study emerges as a second option, a fall-back solution: 'I think that it's actually an alternative to my local uni. Maybe that's when I didn't get in so I sought opportunities'.

What did the cultural capital of English language competence and 'Western' credentials mean to these students and their life chances? Students often referred to the value English language competence would accrue for their employment prospects: 'English is important there for all the job in Hong Kong'. The 'inner circle' (Kachru, 1996) status of Australian English also meant that students from 'outer circle' settings aimed to acquire the privileged dialect of the Centre: 'So one of the reasons I came here because I wanted to speak proper English as well.' A higher education qualification also carried its own meaning/value, which made its pursuit overseas necessary if local opportunities were limited: 'so the only way I can get out [leave the home country] is to study in other country'. In addition, students mentioned broader biographical agendas informing their mobility, such as participating in an internationalized community, learning languages in general, gaining independence, and pursuing their academic interests in specialized disciplines.

Another pattern that emerged in the students' interview accounts of their investment strategies was the frequent mention of established family routes that made their study in this Australian university a routine biographical solution, as they follow in the footsteps of siblings, relatives or friends: 'It goes like we have relative and apparently like she study in (university) and she make it and she study in (town) and also my younger sister and then my turn.' The presence of relatives or family friends studying at the university, or more generally in Australia, was cited by 14 of the 32 students in this sample as factors precipitating their choice of location or institution. Fathers in particular featured as influential in the decisions leading to students' enrolment: 'My Dad chose it for me . . . I don't have any interest in English . . . He thinks it's better to study abroad instead of studying in my home country.' This patterning supports Ong's (1999) thesis of the disciplinary structure of the Chinese diasporic family regime, and the patriarch's transnational strategies played out through the relocation of children to further familial and business opportunities.

Significantly, one student expressed an interest in gaining permanent residency in Australia. One other aimed for an international career, but the vast majority constructed their routes as circuits, leading back to their nation of origin. This pattern can be read in two ways with regard to the moral panic historically associated with the risk of illegal or 'backdoor' migration into Australia by international students (Nesdale et al., 1995). Firstly, the students may have strategically chosen not to make such plans public and chose to represent their motivations in the legitimated discourse compatible with temporary study visas; or secondly, the imagined 'risk' is overstated, and Australia overestimates its attractiveness to this mobile population.

This section has explored our first question regarding the nature of the investments made by these students and the strategies they are pursuing, and gone some way to explore our broader question of how we can 'know' these students. To summarize, this first analysis has purposefully employed a metaphor of 'investment' following Norton (2000) to describe the biographical solutions made by the students from Asian nations to plot personal trajectories in a global field of educational opportunities. Their long-term investments to gain English, as both an end in itself and as the gatekeeper to the cultural capital of a Western qualification, demonstrate how embedded such a global frame of reference is in these echelons of Asian societies. Their imagined life-worlds are not adequately contained within local or traditional cultural scripts. English is in their world (Pennycook, 1995), for better and for worse, and its acquisition is now becoming a routine aspect of preparation for local employment markets, an institutionalized 'biographical pattern' (Beck, 1992). Their goal to acquire English competence demonstrates a transnational imaginary driving cross-border investments to appropriate the resources of one national setting and deploy them advantageously in others. Though their strategies involve long-term risky investments, these students have pursued an enterprising solution to circumvent restricted local opportunities, and capitalize on global markets in order to engage with global flows of knowledge and economic opportunity. Their sojourn in Australia emerges not so much as their ultimate goal, but more as a stopover en route. National boundaries are immaterial to those with the necessary economic resources, which allow them to circumvent local strictures on higher education opportunities and access other nation's systems, albeit by playing by those rules temporarily. A fixed, static interpretation of cultural identity no longer adequately represents these variegated 'life-policies'.

Fulfilling the orthodox script: the self-orientalizing account

This second research step sought to identify how students took up and located themselves within the orthodox institutional discourse of 'culturally different Asian learner' and constructed an 'East' vs. 'West' binary in their accounts. We have suggested that such binaries of essentialized cultural difference inform much of the institutional response to their presence. Such accounts were understood to indicate how students can take up the cultured positions offered by this discourse, and Orientalize themselves as the 'Asian' student, while valorizing the Western parallel construct.

In general, the majority of students from Asian nations slipped easily into this orthodox framing. The majority of such self-Orientalizing accounts referred to different educational practices, precipitated by the question, 'Is the teaching here the same as the teaching in your home country?', or similar wording. The recurrent difference constructed was in regard to the regulative order of classroom interaction – being high in oral participation with more parity between students and teachers in the West, while teacher-dominated with a markedly higher status for the teacher in the East:

> Maybe in Australia the teachers always will ask you to talking and then make sure enforcing (that in) the class but in Hong Kong it's just all the time the teacher's talking and you're supposed not to talking and just listening.

Related to these aspects, is the difference reported in the desired relationship to curricular knowledge: 'Um – I think my country and I think most Asians the education style is input . . . You know like

Western country like Australia is output.' It is significant that in some accounts of contrasted pedagogies, the students often expressed self-criticism and an inherited sense of the 'East' needing fixing: 'in Singapore I think they are not open enough, we are not open up enough to actually like raise question across during lectures . . . but I think of here you're actually encouraging that.' Other accounts couch the differences in more relative terms of temporary contextual adjustments to be made, 'and adapt to the system'. Students also drew contrasts between the East and the West in regard to the wider social sphere, including family relations, censorship, fashion, recreation, religion and work ethic. However, most students limited their claims to 'in my country', and avoided making broader claims regarding pan-Asian attributes.

Intervening in the orthodoxy: autoethnographic re-articulations

Our focus in this third analysis was on how aspects of students' accounts worked against the orthodox 'culturally different Asian learner' discourse through strategies of re-articulation in their cultural represen-tations – that is, by using the terms and logic of such discourse to re-present themselves in challenging and problematized ways that reassembled parts of the discourse in order to disrupt the orthodoxy. In their interviews, the students were asked whether or not they had encountered cultural differences between the 'East' and the 'West' in the classroom and beyond. Some of their responses troubled this binary in a number of ways.

Firstly, the interview question regarding difference often provoked responses that constructed similarities rather than difference, in curricular knowledge and educational practices: 'But it's not so differ-ent . . . because when in my generation we, you can see we accept the Western style education, yeah. It's not the traditional Asian value.' Some students referred to their home countries' colonial legacies to fore-ground similarities rather than differences 'because in Hong Kong basi-cally is used to be controlled by the British so the education system is based on the British. So I come to Australia. It's about the same to me.' Students also told of changing, intersecting, impure and intermingling lifeworlds ('the Phillipines has had many influences like so many years of people staying there') in which the categories of 'West' and 'East' could no longer be held apart due to global flows of media and consumer products: 'Like nowadays in India the Western culture is a big influence . . . All that stuff is in India nowadays.' Thus the scope and scale of difference was pointedly reduced in these accounts. The pan-categories of 'East' and 'West' were themselves repeatedly troubled. Some students fractured the 'West' into its UK and US origins, with Australia understood as a hybrid: 'I think Australia sits more, they may have British culture but they also have American technology . . . and those things.' Similarly, the 'East' was fractured into national categories with different resourcing levels in their educational sectors. Other students suggested that students from both Australia and Asian nations shared similar problems when faced with the transition to higher education: 'This my first time in there (tertiary education) . . . So I think that would be the only difference but I think if I were like in high school or something it would be relatively the same.'

Secondly, interviewees gave different rationales for the 'cultural traits' attributed to the 'Asian learner' in the orthodox discourse. In this vein, classroom interaction patterns in their home settings were explained with reference to class size, rather than cultural dispositions: 'Um they're kind of similar . . . but the main difference, I think, is the class size because in Hong Kong the class size usually bigger around 40 students in the class. It's really big . . . And here it's around 20.' In their Australian educational settings, the passivity understood to be a cultural trait of the 'Asian student', was repeatedly constructed as an artifact of language learning processes rather than cultural learning traditions. Students were hesitant to ask questions because they were unsure of their English-language competency:

> he (the lecturer) says the Asian country, the student from Asian country they don't like to join the discussion in class because they feel shy and they're scared to do that . . . Because I think the big problem (is) because the English that they learn is not that good.

By reconstructing their needs as learning about language, not about cultural scripts, they essentially reconstructed the premises for curricular design. In this vein, one student demanded more explicit and pertinent linguistic feedback in these courses. Another complained that they didn't need to learn about Asian culture, 'someone need to tell us what is Western culture but I don't think they need to tell us what Asian culture'. Another student resented the curricular focus on cultural briefing, as irrelevant to future studies: 'It's just a waste of time and money, you know?'

A third tactic was to disrupt the ascription of relative value. In this way, some students engaged with the logic of difference, and reported such difference but did so without ascribing any superior value to the 'West': 'So like there are differences. Like you don't say to discriminate but because there is a difference.' Other accounts offered harsh critiques of their perceptions of the West, reversing the 'West is best' bias in the orthodox account: 'most Asian like they want to try harder and get better education that's why they come to Australia . . . And the Western they like they just want to get a job and be able to get to earn money.' Finally, for some students the mobile self was constructed as adaptable, quite the opposite to the orthodoxy's culturally circumscribed student: 'I'm able to adapting to different environment quite easily because I've also been to international service so . . . so you will go into a different environment and you have to remember talking like that.'

This analysis demonstrates how some students could work both within and beyond their orthodox discursive positioning to represent themselves and their needs in a variety of ways. It should be noted that not all students disrupted the orthodox framing. Our point, however, is that the sample of re-articulated interventions reported above are enough to unsettle the resilient determinist logic of difference between the binary categories of East and West and warrants fresher theorizations that can engage with social change, entangled routes and historical interpenetration. Such revisiting is timely and necessary in order to tackle the stale orthodoxy and its constraints on how institutions can know their mobile students, and thus promote more effective learning.

Discussion

Our analyses demonstrate how the identity projects of these internationally mobile students have outgrown homogeneous cultural labels. In order to know them and address their needs, educators need to engage with their accounts of class dynamics, family strategy for social mobility, changing global/local labour markets, educational quotas and complex, stratified language ecologies. These students embark on these routes through internationalized universities not to realize or live out notional cultural identities, but to forge new strategic and speculative identities by investing in a global language, symbolically branded credentials and educational knowledge. They are seeking 'biographical solutions' to protect and promote personal interests in liquid modernity. Their accounts show how they are in some ways willing to temporarily submit to the limited imagination of institutional offerings that define who they might be in that setting. However, their accounts also show how these students can talk back and dispute such polarized constructions, by undermining and re-articulating these versions of themselves. If we renovate how we as educators understand the routes of these mobile students, we can renovate and better tailor our institutional responses to their educational needs.

Who then is this mobile student en route through the Australian university system? And how can we as TESOL researchers and practitioners 'know' this student group in order to inform any pedagogic model of the learner? We have offered an alternative framing of their educational routes and motivations as biographical solutions to newly emergent and contradictory pressures in their lifeworlds, pursued through diasporic spaces and transnational investment strategies. This account can acknowledge how students variously negotiate the global flows and the relations of family regimes, class strategies, local job markets, national educational systems, and language ecologies. This is a more complex identity palette than 'cultural difference' theory would recognize.

What are the implications of this way of knowing for the day-to-day practices within the fields of TESOL and internationalized education? Who educators understand their students to be is a crucial matter in any pedagogical design, producing knowledge and models that will underpin any curricular design. We have argued that such underpinning models need to be constantly monitored and re-examined in regard to their currency in a context of rapid social change. In this way, we have scrutinized the presumption of 'cultural difference' and how it has been built into pedagogical designs that the students have to pass through. This analysis has revealed that the students make huge investments in the resources of English language proficiency and Western academic capital. Such investments however do not always accrue the intended linguistic and educational returns. A one-stop preparatory programme constructs international students too simply as Other, and implicitly as deficit by reference to what they are not (that is, non-Western). Such pedagogic designs provide students with the 'catch-up' linguistic and educational socialization needed to perform appropriately in 'Western' university classes. Our analysis has shown how students can submit to such one-dimensional typecasting to serve their longer term strategy, but should they have to? Such constrained understandings of international students do not take into account the motivations, transnational identities and resources these students bring to the Western university, and how these resources may be exploited to construct less parochial, more global or internationalized educational spaces. In another sense, such nostalgic understandings of mobile students also overlook the shift in the institution's own student body, a shift which makes claims of 'pure' pedagogical traditions increasingly spurious.

More nuanced and flexible alternatives to the model of the front-end, one-size-fits-all preparatory programme are needed, so students can engage with the Western university in diverse ways and from a number of positions. Indeed, relevant English language skills might better be taught by integrating international students with other students in their shared chosen fields of study and supporting them in these more targeted contexts. This would be more productive than the existing strategy of relegating them to the parallel universe of separate, generic preparatory programmes that address over-generalized constructions of 'cultural difference' through polarized scripts of pure pedagogic traditions. Under the conditions of liquid modernity, such mutually exclusive worlds no longer exist, and educational routes through the Western university have become a common part of the Asian middle class's solution for living in globalizing times.

A more nuanced understanding of who internationally mobile students are, and more importantly, who they are in the process of becoming, could disrupt educators' preconceptions about what this group need. We suggest that TESOL practitioners be deployed more strategically as 'embedded' consultants to work in partnership with academic staff to enrich curricula and pedagogy within faculties. More flexible, embedded engagements could open up the overly fixed, unified and nostalgic discourse of 'Asian learner' that has been performatively produced and sustained in the designs of separate preparatory programmes. Rather than generic course offerings, preparatory courses could be attached to faculties and deal more specifically with the target discipline's language and entry point texts. Rather than one-size-fits-all curricula designed around the premise of fixed cultural differences, programmes could offer modular topics and allow students to assemble and personalize their own programmes around their particular needs and interests.

Reflection questions

1. What does the design of your programmes say about your institution's construction of international students?
2. What do international students have *in common* with local students in your context?
3. What diversity is there within the category of 'international student'?

Note

1. The analytic questions asked of the interview accounts were: (1) What investments has this student made? (2) What does the education capital (language, credentials) mean to them and their life chances? (3) How do their accounts take up the cultured identities offered? (4) How do their accounts disrupt orthodox versions of the 'Asian' student identity?

Resources

Bullen, E., & Kenway, J. (2003). Real or imagined women? Staff representations of international women postgraduate students. *Discourse: Studies in the Cultural Politics of Education, 24*(1), 36–50.

Kenway, J., & Bullen, E. (2003). Self-representations of international women postgraduate students in the global university 'contact zone'. *Gender and Education, 15*(1), 5–20.

(The above two articles should be read together, because their contrast is telling. The first shows how staff at an Australian university construct the female international student. The second shows how the students themselves represent themselves and their journeys. The two articles tell very different stories).

Giddens, A. (1999). *Runaway world: How globalization is reshaping our lives*. New York: Routledge.

This book is a series of lectures Giddens gave on the radio. In an engaging style, Giddens reviews the radical changes underway in the global social fabric as we entered the twenty-first century.

Acknowledgments

The study was funded by the Australian Research Council. An earlier version of this work was presented at the AARE Education Research Conference, University of Western Sydney, Parramatta Campus, Australia, *Creative Dissent: Constructive Solutions*; 27 November–1 December 2005.

7
Cross-cultural Engagement in Higher Education Classrooms: a Critical View of Dialogue

Alison Jones and Kuni Jenkins

This chapter takes a critical view of the ideal of face-to-face dialogue between cultural groups in higher education classrooms. It takes as its point of discussion some New Zealand Pākehā (White) students' expressions of anger at feeling 'left out' during a course where the instructors divided the class into two groups based on their ethnicity: Pākehā students and Polynesian (in particular indigenous Māori) students. The instructors (the authors of this paper) felt this division was in the interest of progressive teaching as well as providing learning opportunities for the students. In examining the different responses of the two groups, the authors ask higher education instructors to reconsider the ideal of cross-cultural dialogue and the fantasies on which it rests; they also offer an alternative to dialogue in postcolonial classrooms.

Introduction

Our work might be said to be both *within* and *against* the literatures in 'cross-cultural education' and critical pedagogy. On the one hand, our writing and teaching is always motivated by the ideals of cross-cultural educational engagement and of progressive social change. On the other, we are critical of the fantasies of engagement on which cross-cultural and critical pedagogy often rest. These fantasies are the focus of our chapter.

The ideal of cross-cultural engagement underpins most progressive educational work. It is recognized by liberal teachers and educators that modern democratic education systems must enable and promote dialogue and understanding across cultural differences. The ideals of 'multiculturalism', 'empathetic understanding across diversity', and 'cultural sensitivity', which are commonly the focus of educational discourses, are often easily spoken, and easily desired. But it is possible that the sharp differences between social-cultural groups, including indigenous and colonizer peoples, and our painful – and sometimes shameful – shared histories, become sidelined as too uncomfortable as we focus on 'understanding each other'. In this chapter, we ask: What does it mean in higher education classrooms to foreground *difference* as we contemplate mutual understanding based on face-to-face engagement?

While this chapter takes a critical approach to 'empathy' and 'multiculturalism', we are optimistic about engagement across cultural differences in postcolonial higher education settings (where colonizer and indigenous groups share educational spaces). But we are not persuaded that good cross-cultural work is necessarily made possible by face-to-face dialogue or empathetic sharing in classrooms. As a result, we do not call for better communication; we do not suggest ways of listening better. Rather, we argue for three elements that offer more convincing possibilities for developing cross-cultural engagement: (a) a *reflexive* element: a critical consideration of why 'we' might desire dialogue between indigenous peoples and others in postcolonial education settings, (b) an *ignorance* element: including a recognition of the limits of knowing and an acceptance of the possibility of not knowing, and (c) a *knowledge* element: including the necessity for knowledge of our shared and differing colonial and social histories. Each of these elements (see sections below) raises difficult and discomforting questions, but each provides opportunities to think through what is at stake in the calls for dialogue and cross-cultural engagement between differently-located groups in higher education classrooms.

Context

Because we write from New Zealand, we may need to explain the cultural context of this chapter. The authors, Alison Jones and Kuni Jenkins, are respectively Pākehā (with White settler ancestors) and Māori (with indigenous and White settler ancestors). For a number of years, we have taught together in New Zealand university classrooms. Although New Zealand is increasingly multiethnic, our chapter focuses on the relationship between indigenous and colonizer (Māori & Pākehā) groups in our higher education classrooms.

We are conscious of the problems of using certain concepts in writing about our students. Pākehā students are unlikely to understand themselves as 'colonizers' (because colonization, they often believe, is now in the past). They may not even see themselves as 'Pākehā', but rather as 'European' or 'Kiwi' (the term 'White' is rarely used in New Zealand). We use the term 'Pākehā' (a commonly-used term, first coined by Māori to name the early British people in New Zealand) because in our view it better reflects those aspects of 'European' New Zealanders' identity with which we are concerned here. It also indicates a cultural difference from our White North American readers. Another problem with using simple ethnic categories is that the boundaries between 'Māori' and 'Pākehā' are blurred through inter-marriage; indeed, most Māori have Pākehā ancestors. But we persist with the troublesome terms and binaries to avoid getting bogged down in other complexities. Our use of the term 'postcolonial' in our chapter title contextualizes our work in a modern country (New Zealand) which is a product of colonization authorized 167 years ago by a Treaty between the indigenous (Māori) chiefs and the British crown. Māori now comprise almost 15 per cent of the population, compared with about 80 per cent for 'European' people (Statistics New Zealand, 2005).

Literature review

Most researchers and commentators in the field of 'education and diversity' write positively about how diverse higher education settings develop attitudes and provide experiences which contribute to a more tolerant and equitable society and workforce. For instance, Bowen and Bok's (1998) large-scale, long-term study argues for ethnically diverse intakes to North American colleges and universities, indicating improved attitudes to other race groups for both Black and White students, as well as other social benefits. Chang (2003) and Millem (2003) argue similarly, that 'students who are exposed to diverse experiences, perspectives, and ways of thinking that truly reflect the multiracial and multiethnic society . . . will be better prepared to participate meaningfully in it' (Chang, p. 13; see McConaghy, 2000, for a good discussion of perspectives on indigenous education).

Amongst the many voices raised in praise of culturally diverse colleges, universities and classrooms, we find muted commentary from minority teachers and students about their experiences. Some of the minority voices that do speak about culture in the classroom make ambivalent or negative comments. For instance, Cheryl Johnson (1995), a North American 'black womanist intellectual professor', in an oblique and grimly humorous account, considers that the best way to avoid tensions inevitably produced by her 'black body' is to keep her teaching 'sanitized'. She speaks of her dialogue with her white students and colleagues as 'marked by the desire for cleanliness – for no odors, no germs; it is a sanitized, deodorized, bleached (no pun intended) interaction' (p. 129). In deciding not to make her students face difference as difficult, complex and dirty, she keeps the pedagogical environment 'safe' for them – and for herself – by avoiding what she sees as the confronting aspects of cultural difference (see also Narayan, 1988). In response to the problems of some groups feeling silenced in the classroom, another university teacher, Aruna Srivastava (1997) says that 'there need to be working groups consisting of students of color, working class students' but she is 'scared' to set up such segregated groups in her university because it would 'transgress all sorts of boundaries' (p. 122). By forming separate groups based on ethnicity or cultural difference she fears antagonizing those who demand 'togetherness' and who oppose 'segregation'.

These writers suggest that the benefits of cross-cultural engagement cannot be simply assessed. The experiences and meanings of cross-cultural work may differ across the groups in higher education classrooms. We consider some of these meanings, and how interaction between diverse groups in classrooms may be problematic, especially for minority or non-White groups.

We focus on problems of classroom dialogue partly because 'dialogue across difference' has become such an uncritically accepted sentiment in critical pedagogy (see Darder, Baltodano, & Torres, 2003). Paulo Freire's (1972) model of dialogue, which is at the heart of much critical pedagogy, is one where teachers and students, and students and students, enter into reciprocal critical conversations, as opposed to monologue-based 'banking' education where the student receives the words of the teacher. Freire's original notion of dialogic education was intensely idealistic. Dialogue, he stipulated, is not a simple exchange of ideas 'consumed' by participants, nor a hostile polemical argument, nor a manipulation of one by another; it cannot be a crafty instrument for domination, nor exist in the absence of profound love and humility (p. 62). It cannot happen if one is closed to or offended by the contribution of others; it requires intense faith in others, and develops trust: 'Founding itself upon love, humility and faith, dialogue becomes a horizontal relationship of which mutual trust between participants is the logical consequence' (p. 64). Good cross-cultural pedagogy, on this model, aspires to have diverse groups and individuals equitably share the educational space; boundaries between indigenous–colonizer, Black–White, are reduced. Or at least, the boundaries are challenged by 'border crossing' students and teachers as they expose and examine power relations between the participating groups (Aronowitz & Giroux, 1991; McLaren, 1995). Outcomes of such dialogue are supposed to range from 'awareness' of, or sensitivity to, the cultural values of others, to a politicized orientation to social justice (Burbules, 1993).

Our experience of attempts at cross-cultural engagement in higher education classrooms has led to our being sceptical about such claims for dialogue. Teachers' and students' desires for 'crossing borders' or 'hearing the voices' and 'sharing realities' may be heart-felt. But those desires can never stand untouched by the political, economic and cultural differences which continue to characterize most societies. These differences mean that students' experiences of dialogue, and their desire for dialogue, may not be the same at all – and may in fact be negative.

Questions

In response to our third-year undergraduate course 'Feminist Perspectives in Education', which attracted a significant number of Māori students, some Māori women argued for separate classes where they could discuss course questions in their own group. We decided the next year to run the course in two streams, with Māori and Pacific[1] students in one group, and Pākehā in another. We, the regular class teachers, each taught sections of the course, in turns, to these two parallel groups – each of which were made up of about fifty students, all women of varying ages. About one quarter of the classes were taught with the groups coming together. All the students wrote in their 'learning journals' about the pedagogy of the divided course.

We were startled by the very different reactions of the two groups of students. While most of the Māori students actively enjoyed the structure, relishing the opportunity to develop ideas alone, many of the Pākehā students were very angry and disappointed that they were separated from their Māori peers. These reactions led us, as teachers in this classroom, to some interesting questions about the ideal of cross-cultural dialogue in classrooms: Who is the 'we' that desires dialogue in higher education? What if the indigenous students do not particularly want to engage in dialogue, preferring to speak amongst themselves? To what extent can we know each other, anyway? How might our teacherly desires for cross-cultural engagement between our students (and between students and teacher) be met, or are they an impossible fantasy?

Methodology

Our separated class was an experiment, in a sense. We only did it for one year, and we did it to get a sense of how it might 'work'. We decided later that, because of the Pākehā students' strongly negative responses, divided classes were not viable in the longer term. We analysed the students' journals, with their permission, and we wrote articles about the students' responses to our separating them (Jones, 1999, 2001, 2004; Pihama & Jenkins, 2001). We build on these analyses in this chapter; our 'methodology' here is to use what we learned from our students' responses in order to address the question of 'learning and teaching across cultures'. To illustrate our argument, we take a few of the comments made by our university students about our pedagogy. We then explain our theoretical approach to the students' reactions to the divided classes – an approach we hope will assist other higher education teachers in thinking about the ideals of cross-cultural engagement. Finally, we introduce our practical responses to some of the problems of face-to-face dialogue.

The next sections of this chapter consider three elements (mentioned earlier) that we think can contribute to critical thinking about our desires for cross-cultural engagement in higher education classrooms. These are: (1) a *reflexive* element, (2) an *ignorance* element, and (3) a *knowledge* element. Each will be reviewed.

Dialogue element: a reflexive element

First, we reconsider the *desire* for cross-cultural engagement in higher education classrooms: Why do progressive teachers want cross-cultural conversations amongst students from different ethnic and cultural groups? The typical answer focuses on reducing barriers and inviting those who do not usually speak in classrooms to have their views heard. It is usually assumed that a better flow of talk may allow the interests of all to be served, and lead ultimately to a more just and democratic, and less divided, classroom and society. It is believed that if people do not connect across difference, divisions and misunderstandings are increased. Some higher education teachers may be enthusiastic for a face-to-face engagement because classrooms bring together groups who may not normally converse about the social and political questions which affect them differently.

Before we ask whether such conversations are even *possible*, let's first return to the *desire* for talking across difference – focusing now on indigenous and colonizer groups. It is rare to find calls for cross-cultural dialogue ('we want to hear about you') coming from indigenous peoples, or other minority ethnic groups. Indigenous groups may want colonizer groups to understand indigenous peoples' histories, experiences, and feelings in order to garner political support and recognition, but do they need to engage in *dialogue* about these things? That is, do they need to *exchange* information with colonizer individuals in order to tell their own experiences? Do they need to hear the colonizers' views as part of dialogue? Surely these dominant views are the ones with which indigenous peoples are already over-familiar.

It was this ambivalence about mutual engagement that we saw in our university classroom. While the Māori students might be happy to talk with their Pākehā friends about their shared social experiences at the café or last night's party, as indigenous subjects they were generally unenthusiastic about intercultural classroom dialogue. They found it a daunting task to have to explain or justify repeatedly their culture and perspectives to those who were confused by Māori practices. How do they answer questions which already assume a particular dominant perspective? How do they reply to questions (which are more like accusations) such as 'why do you [Māori] always focus on the past?' 'Can't we just get on with the present and look to the future?'

It may be that the Māori students could explain to their Pākehā classmates that cultural difference in relation to time often creates confusion among Pākehā. Māori understand the past (*mua* = ahead) as in front of us, and the future (*muri* = behind) as coming after us. (The future cannot be seen; the past is all that is in view. Therefore it is on the basis of the accessible past that we can move into an unknown future.) This apparently logical response assumes that Pākehā students will, as a result, revise their view that Māori are 'stuck in the past', and 'backward looking'. But the Māori cultural explanation may not stop Pākehā saying: 'We know that you think the past is "in front", but that does not get us anywhere with trying to move towards to a better future!' For Māori students, such a response from Pākehā is disappointing, perplexing and hurtful.

The Māori students can be hurt in other ways. Explanation of Māori perspectives by Māori students requires that those students have such explanations available to them. The vast majority of young Māori in our classes are in the process of discovering their Māori identity, including acquiring knowledge about Māori language and meaning. These Māori students may want to articulate their own history but they are only familiar with dominant ways of thinking – including ways of thinking about time and history. In other words, one reason indigenous students may not desire dialogue with non-indigenous peers is rooted in the effects of colonization. For many indigenous students, the mixed classroom cannot be a 'safe' place to speak as an indigenous person because they do not yet have what they see as a 'proper' indigenous voice. They may be learning their own language, history and culture; to display this lack of knowledge – to be the 'inauthentic' indigenous person – in front of one's own group is bad enough; in the company of curious outsiders it would be unbearable. Better to be silent – or seek an educational place within one's own ethnic group. Amongst indigenous peers who share the difficult process of gaining a voice in one's language and culture, there is at least more potential for growth in confidence as an indigenous self.

If indigenous groups, and individuals as indigenous subjects, generally do not prize dialogue with colonizer groups, what might be said about the enthusiasm for cross-cultural, face-to-face engagement? Jones (1999; 2001) (as well as others such as Roman, 1993; 1997) has argued that the call for classroom dialogue comes from dominant groups who seek to hear the voices of the Other[2] – voices not usually available to them. In a country like New Zealand where Māori and Pākehā regularly interact in their work and social lives this may sound odd, but we are not referring to casual daily interactions. Rather, we are referring to speaking *as* Māori or *as* colonizer subjects – that is, when we speak of our experience and knowledge as indigenous persons, or as Pākehā settlers. When Pākehā desire to hear indigenous voices 'first-hand' in classrooms, Māori peers are under significant pressure: first, that they exist as indigenous subjects (when many Māori students are still struggling with this) and second that as indigenous subjects they *teach* their peers who often have little real ability to comprehend difference. This demand for teacherly attention was expressed by some of our Pākehā students in their journals (Jones, 1999, p. 301):

. . . it would [have been] interesting for all the students to be able to share their unique cultural perspectives with each other. . . . I am sometimes quite ignorant and intolerant of other view points, so a wider input would have been educational.

Could we not learn from each other? Wouldn't it be valuable to share our differences in experience? . . . It is different reading about it in books, or having it taught by teachers. It is better to hear it straight from the women who are having the experience.

On the face of it, these students merely desire to 'learn' from their peers about Māori beliefs and experiences. Such confessions of need and ignorance seem to signal an 'openness to know' on the part of the colonizer individual. A confession of needing to learn is often a plea for assistance, which positions the guileless speaker as helpless, hapless, in need of sympathy, compassion and understanding, even love. 'I am not powerful,' the confession seems to say, 'not threatening, only sadly ignorant. Care for me! Teach me!' Thus an apparently benign educational request becomes a significant demand for interaction and attention, requiring the needy dominant group be taught by indigenous knowers.

When Pākehā students ask to be given the opportunity to 'learn' about others, they position themselves as open to new knowledges. It was interesting to us, therefore, to hear Pākehā students' responses to the classes where a Māori teacher (Kuni) taught the class. Many of the Pākehā students found this teaching difficult. They complained of marginalization, of being left out, of feeling unwelcome, of being disconcerted and uncomfortable (Jones, 2001, p. 282):

> I felt marginalised in this class . . . As a Pākehā, I get tired of reading and hearing about how we assimilated the Māori. It is as if they want to keep making us feel guilty out of payment back. What can I as one person do now?

> Of course people have different views, but I felt quite uncomfortable when I heard the *korero* [talk] about all the gods and 'spirituality' of the *marae* [meeting house],[3] because as a Christian I worship only one God . . . I felt like I did not belong.

> The activity[4] in which we were asked to pick out and comment on an aspect of the meeting house made me feel extremely uncomfortable and stupid. I thought it served to emphasise rather than diminish my status as an 'outsider'. The activity assumed a prior knowledge which I did not have . . .

These Pākehā students seem to express a disappointment: their hopes for cross-cultural understanding and inclusion were not met in this class session. They had wanted empathetic engagement with their indigenous peers from whom they want to learn. But when they were taught by an indigenous teacher who spoke as such, these Pākehā students felt marginalized, offended, uncomfortable and resistant. The hope that we could all be brought together inside a shared conversation was unfulfilled when Māori spoke *as Māori* rather than as caring friends, or empathetic teachers.

These Pākehā students' responses provide further understanding of indigenous students' resistance to dialogue with their White peers. If White students feel uncomfortable and 'left out' when indigenous people speak as such, then cross-cultural engagement is likely to be difficult. The onus comes on the indigenous speaker to maintain the 'comfort levels' and the inclusion of their classmates or students. Alternatively, 'sharing' might become for indigenous students an opportunity to defiantly 'speak back'. In either case, the focus is on the needs, feelings and concerns of the dominant group, who are enabled to define the agenda, again.

Is the desire for dialogue, then, actually only the desire of dominant groups? Do those who want dialogue recognize that the ultimate pedagogical benefits of cross-cultural engagement may lie with the dominant group, and that the key role for minority groups in cross-cultural classrooms is to educate their mainstream peers? Take, for instance, a Supreme Court argument for ethnically diverse universities. Chang (2003) reports on Supreme Court Justice Powell's view of admissions policies for the medical school at the University of California (at Davis), which reserve spaces for 'diverse' students. The judge ruled in 1978 that this policy was fair. Chang says that 'explaining this decision, Powell stated that qualified students with a background that is diverse in some way, whether it be ethnic, geographic, or economic, may bring to a professional school experiences, outlooks, and ideas that enhance the training of the student body and better equip the institution's graduates' (p. 4). Chang adds 'people of different racial and ethnic backgrounds are likely to bring different experiences, perspectives, interests, and analyses to a college campus' (p. 13). Powell and Chang appear to imply that a key argument for diversity is its benefit to White students. After all, as we have already argued, Black or other minority students do not need to be exposed to the views of White students (they are already surrounded by those views). It is largely the White students who need access to the views of diverse others for their own 'enhanced' and rounded education. As Black or indigenous students are normally already very familiar with dominant White views and interests, it becomes difficult to see the direct pedagogical value for minority students in hearing White viewpoints yet again in classroom exchanges.

While we are not questioning the importance of diverse classrooms for exposing all students to the views of others, we point out that the *value* of cross-cultural engagement may differ considerably for differently-located groups. It may be very valuable for dominant groups, but have limited value for indigenous or minority groups. We argue for an element of reflexivity for teachers seeking cross-cultural dialogue. We suggest that as higher education teachers we consider our own desires and interests in demanding cross-cultural engagement, and think carefully about whose interests may be served. It may be useful to check out our assumptions about the value of dialogue by asking groups of students to write about their views of 'talking across difference' or ethnicity, or history or any topic which is relevant to the course. Even getting 'reading responses' to a chapter such as this one may open avenues for discussion. Colleagues from several countries report that their students' responses to the possibility of ethnically-divided classes tend to reflect the patterns we identified amongst our students: the minority students are keen to meet and learn separately, at least some of the time; the White students are angry, and upset, at the idea that Black or minority students might meet in separate groups. What does this difference mean for teachers wanting to forward the interests of all our students?

Desire for dialogue element: ignorance and the other

Given these complexities, as teachers in higher education we have become curious about the *possibilities* for learning about the Other in cross-cultural classroom encounters. To consider this question in more depth, we return to comments from our Pākehā students' journals, already reproduced above from Jones (1999; 2001).

> I am sometimes quite ignorant and intolerant of other view points, so a wider input would have been educational.

> The activity [in a Māori context] . . . made me feel extremely uncomfortable and stupid. . . . [It] assumed a prior knowledge which I did not have . . .

Both these Pākehā students appear angry. Both seem to confess to ignorance. The first seeks to be taught by her indigenous peers (something she believes she is deprived of in the separated classes). The second finds the indigenous teaching – which she may have desired originally – unbearable. The confessions of ignorance by both of these students do not appear to be confessions of shame, humility or even curiosity; they seem to be demands for knowledge and inclusion. Their comments can be read as a desire to be saved from their ignorance by the indigenous others – who in this case are either absent peers, or disappointing teachers.

As we have already argued, in confessing their ignorance and therefore their desire to know, Pākehā students often position themselves as 'good' and 'open' students, ready to hear the voices of others. There is another possible interpretation of such confessions. While Pākehā students may profess to want to understand their peers' experiences of indigeneity, many express feelings of 'marginalization' because they want to know only on their own limited terms. The desire to 'know' others through being taught by them may be at the same time a *refusal to know* or, paradoxically, a desire for ignorance. It may be a refusal to recognize one's own implication in the racialized and colonized social order, where indigenous knowledges are submerged. And it may also be resistance to the possibility that indigenous peers may not *want* to be empathetically 'known' by their Pākehā classmates, or to teach them. These desires for ignorance sit uneasily alongside the desire to know others through dialogue in higher education.

A common teacherly impulse in multicultural higher education classrooms might be to attack this refusal to know. But Felman's (1982) now-classic work on ignorance and learning suggests teachers' refusal of students' refusal to be pointless. Through a psychoanalytic frame, Felman sees learning as proceeding (as did Kuhn in his critique of scientific progress) 'not through linear progression, but through breakthroughs, leaps, discontinuities, regressions, deferred action' (p. 27). Teaching and learning, says Felman, are inevitably uncomfortable, unruly and non-rational processes. Teaching is certainly not in the happy business of ensuring an ordered and progressive 'growth of knowledge', and the increase in certainty and stability. All teaching, she suggests, whether in a progressive classroom or not, is inevitably unsatisfactory – or impossible – because it is based in the persistent pedagogical fantasy about the linear and cumulative increase in knowing. Nevertheless, as another psychoanalytic theorist Deborah Britzman (1998) puts it, education continues to offer tidy stories of 'happiness, resolution and certainty' (p. 79).

Of course, narratives of resolution and happiness are central to cross-cultural teaching and learning, based as it is on desires for improved social relations. Cross-cultural classroom engagement wants to banish ignorance about the Other. But Felman (1982) insists that ignorance is something always present in knowing. Ignorance she days, 'is less cognitive than performative . . . it is not a simple lack of information, but the incapacity – or refusal – to acknowledge one's own implication in the information' (p. 30). Teaching, then, has to deal not so much with a lack of knowledge as with resistances to knowledge. Ignorance, Felman argues, is simply an interminable desire to ignore – or a passion for ignorance. This is where Felman's work raises interesting questions for talk about cross-cultural teaching and learning. Can we understand the Pākehā students' response to their indigenous peers and teachers in terms of a passion for ignorance? Is it that many White people in cross-cultural educational settings (unconsciously and consciously) refuse to know their implication in cultural difference and its oppressions? As a dominant group, do they have a cultural incapacity to recognise that they assume they can know (everything)?

If we follow Felman's (1982) logic, teaching by peers or teachers in multicultural higher education cannot ultimately mean giving students information they lack, or trying to get students to understand through dialogue. Filling-in-the-gaps of students' knowing so they finally understand is nothing other than an impossible fantasy of mastery (Ellsworth, 1989, 1997). This is particularly the case in classroom scenes like the one we have been discussing, where anger, defensiveness and hope all limit as well as produce the possibilities for teaching and learning. When pedagogy is so slippery and interminably difficult, and all learning is 'more or less traumatic, surprising, uncomfortable, disruptive, troubling, intolerable' (Ellsworth, 1997, p. 59), it is unsurprising perhaps that our Pākehā students resist the loss of the fantasy of knowing and its promise of unity, certainty and 'peace'.

While Felman (1982) assists in thinking through the impossibility of teaching, other philosophers have addressed directly the problem of learning about the Other. Following Levinas, Sharon Todd (2003) considers the limits of empathetic understanding of the Other (in our case, indigenous experiences, perspectives, knowledges). Her book *Learning from the Other* provides a powerful critique of teaching that tries to generate empathetic learning about the Other through listening to others' accounts (say, of the Holocaust) or through 24-hour famines (to learn about starvation in Africa). Todd recognizes that within social justice education, the notion of the Other has often come to refer to an attribute of social injustice: the Other is that which is disadvantaged, and unknown. This position implies that education may contribute to a reduction in Otherness through a togetherness/sharing/equality born of sharing ('I know how you feel'). Todd argues that we cannot learn *about* the Other, because we inevitably 'shroud' the Other with our own interpretation. We can only learn *from* the Other about our difference from others.

If we take the idea that the dominant group know others only obliquely, and that they can only learn from others about their own experience of difference, it follows that dominant group members must develop an openness to, or acceptance of, our inevitable ignorance about others. They might need to understand that they cannot remove this ignorance by asking others to fill the gaps they find in themselves.

Desire for dialogue element: knowledge of our shared social histories

If we had been able to, we would have continued with our segregated classrooms, and used the students' written responses as a basis for teaching on the subject 'teaching and learning across cultures'. But for a range of reasons, including the negative reaction by our Pākehā students, we returned to regular classes the following year. In our subsequent classes we took a new approach to learning and teaching across diversity. Rather than 'facing each other' and sharing stories, we encouraged our students to metaphorically 'stand side by side' to consider stories of a shared past. Something that indigenous and settler peoples 'share' in a colonized society is our historical relationship. That relationship might be very differently interpreted by those on either side of it, but histories are such that the stories of the colonizers are the ones that most people (including many indigenous people) are familiar with. For Pākehā/colonizer students, a relationship in the present with indigenous peers requires recognizing and claiming one's place in the historical relationship. But for Māori teachers, such as Kuni, a goal necessarily prior to any 'cross-cultural communication' is to enable indigenous students to recognize and claim *their* histories. This is difficult to do in a setting where Pākehā and Māori students learn together – for all the reasons mentioned above about identity, knowledge and 'safety'.

Claiming one's own indigenous history presupposes claiming one's indigenous identity. This sometimes painful process occurs only in an indigenous context; hence the limitations of the shared classroom. Indeed, Kuni has more recently extended her engagement in Māori education by taking a leading position in a Whare Wānanga, a Māori higher education institution. Educational institutions such as these enact the desires of Māori for a 'learning community' outside the constant challenges of Pākehā groups and individuals,[5] where indigenous identities and knowledges can be (re)formed and (re)claimed.

It is worth mentioning here the question we raised at the beginning about the problems of the indigenous–colonizer dualism, when the dividing lines between the categories Maori and Pakeha are often blurred by relationships, as well as by the sheer homogenizing force of colonizing education. Many Māori individuals may not wish to claim their Māori or indigenous identity and history. We do not suggest they *must* make this claim. We are simply interested in a pedagogy, such as that below, which gives oxygen to indigenous identities and histories, at the same time recognizing that indigenous identities, knowledges and experiences are never genuinely outside colonization. In addition, we argue that to engage in learning and teaching across cultures in a postcolonial context requires the Pākehā/White/colonizer groups to recognize their own knowledge, identity and experience as shaped by colonization.

What does it mean to 'stand side by side' rather than face-to-face? Many possibilities for such pedagogy suggest themselves. We have taken an approach, in mixed classrooms, which requires three readings of a key event. The first reading comes from our students' historical imagination: we ask them to imagine, in writing, certain events in the past where Māori and Pākehā interacted (such as the first sermon in New Zealand by a British missionary, or setting up the first school). The second reading comes from research where students find out what has been published in historical and fictional accounts of these events. Then, third, Kuni and Alison as teachers attempt other interpretations of these shared events. We consider these reading exercises as a form of pedagogy which does not demand face-to-face encounters between Māori and Pākehā peers, but which asks questions about the implications of different interpretations of our relationship. These interpretations potentially map on to the ways we think about current cross-cultural or postcolonial relationships.

Here is an example (from composite reconstructions of student responses), which the students share with each other:

First reading: imagined scene of the first sermon

[*A Māori student imagined*]: 'A Pākehā man gave the sermon, in English, referring to the Bible. Mostly Pākehā settlers were present, and Māori were resistant to listening. Once key relationships were built, this may have changed.'

[*A white student imagined*]: 'This sermon was by an English missionary in the early 1800s. It was a blessing on the land and saying that God loved everyone. Māori would have wondered what was said. They would have been confused and maybe resentful.'

Second reading: a historical story of the first sermon

The standard account of the first sermon in New Zealand tells that the English missionary Reverend Samuel Marsden preached from

St Luke: 'Fear not: for, behold, I bring you good tidings of great joy, which shall be to all people' on the slopes above a beach in the north of New Zealand, on Christmas Day 1814, a few days after his arrival. This first formal mass event took place before several hundred attentive Māori people who had been assembled by the chief who had invited Marsden to his land. When Marsden had completed his sermon, the people rose in a massive *haka* [*vigorous 'dance'*]. (Sources for historical accounts might include Belich, 1996; King, 2004; Nicholas, 1817; or Salmond, 1997)

Third reading: a Māori account of the first sermon

[*Kuni tells this story*]: Few people present would have been able to understand Marsden's sermon, so it was Ruatara, the interpreter, the young chief who had invited Marsden to New Zealand, who was the real speaker that day. Neither we nor Marsden can know what he said to his countrymen. It was unlikely that Ruatara relayed the Christian message about 'good tidings'. His interpretation of Marsden's words would have been the words he, Ruatara, wanted his people to hear. Ruatara's interpretation of the sermon would have been passionate, of necessity building on Māori knowledge of the spiritual realm. Ruatara would probably also have talked of the implications of Marsden's settler 'family' for the material possibilities for the people. Thus, on the occasion of Marsden's sermon, the people did not hear the Gospel, as such. Although Marsden would have been highly respected by Māori as a man of authority, he was, in a sense, merely Ruatara's helper during the sermon – assisting Ruatara to bring new knowledge and ideas to his people. The people heard Ruatara's words, not Marsden's, and it was to Ruatara's words they responded. The *haka* would have been an affirmation of Ruatara's authority and an emotional response to their leader who, in directing them to accept the new arrivals, was setting a new path for them.

The stories about the sermon provide a shared moment in history where Māori and Pākehā students learn about their relationship, and how it might be variously understood (see Jones & Jenkins, 2004). Kuni's story which suggests there were two, not one, speeches allows us to see the ways Māori and Pākehā are positioned in the other readings. The story of Marsden's sermon positions Māori as bemused recipients of Pākehā authority and ideas; the story of Ruatara's sermon positions Māori as actively working through and with Pākehā ideas to further their own interests. Such 'opposing' stories allow students in higher education classrooms to consider a range of cross-cultural questions: what do we know about our historical (and contemporary) relationship – what have we learned from reading? What are the effects of different accounts of the relationship between us? Who are the actors in our mutual relationship, and how do we know?

In the side-by-side pedagogy, we still allowed Māori and Pākehā students to work in small separate groups on their interpretations. But in this less dramatic segregation, Pākehā tended not to get so anxious, and Māori students found satisfying ways to engage with their history. The Pākehā and Māori students were not required to focus on, or face each directly. They did get to hear others' interpretations, and these were taken up by the teachers as material for further interpretation. The more oblique engagement satisfied all the participants through disembodied discussion, as the text became the main focus, rather than the experience and knowledge of the members of the class.

Discussion

Drawing attention to those things we would rather overlook, our chapter considers the difficulties inherent in the ideal of cross-cultural dialogue in higher educational settings. It is in the tense and difficult places of dialogue, we believe, that the most unexpected and penetrating insights are possible. We raise questions for those seeking engagement between members of different ethnic groups, about ethnic difference (our focus is on indigenous and colonizer students). A commonsense approach to learning about others in higher education is to speak directly 'across cultures' to one another in 'safe' classroom settings. Such engagement, it has been argued, offers the possibility of improving democracy, reducing silence, and increasing knowledge and tolerance of ethnic others. We take a contrary position, and advocate for a critical consideration of allowing a separation of ethnic groups in classrooms, at least for a proportion of the course, in order to enhance the possibilities of confident, informed cross-cultural interaction. We suggest that a posture of *parallel* rather than *joint* critical inquiry into relationships between groups – particularly indigenous and colonizer groups – offers a powerful opportunity for learning 'across cultures'.

Our separation of White and indigenous students in our university course led to anger as well as celebration. Pākehā students tended to be dismayed that they were separated from their indigenous peers from whom they wanted to 'learn about other people'. Most of the indigenous students on the other hand were delighted to have the sanctioned opportunity to debate and develop knowledge with other indigenous individuals, outside the interrogating gaze of their Pākehā classmates.

As teachers, we recognize that the Pākehā students' desire for face-to-face dialogue is also a desire to be taught by their indigenous friends, to receive 'understanding' and attention from them, and in this way be relieved – at least to some extent – of the colonizer's burden. While such attention may be positive for Pākehā students, we saw it as another case of dominant groups determining the pedagogical agenda. When dominant groups lose control of the pedagogical agenda, there is often trouble. Indigenous teachers in our classroom were not always successful with Pākehā students; these teachers' attempts to teach as indigenous subjects were criticized and resented by some Pākehā students who felt excluded when the Māori teacher referred to ideas outside their experience and knowledge.

We have considered three reflexive elements in our thinking-through of these difficulties. First we interrogated the desire for cross-cultural dialogue, which raised the question of who most benefits from face-to-face engagement in higher education classrooms. Then we ambivalently accepted our inevitable ignorance. Learning *from* the difference of the Other, instead of attempting to learn everything *about* the Other, suggests that ignorance is a feature of knowing – that openness to the Other's otherness enables an engagement, particularly by colonizer students with their indigenous peers, which is less demanding and more open. Finally, we foregrounded the pedagogical value of addressing the shared relationship between the diverse groups – in the case of indigenous and colonizer peoples, this is the relationship of colonization – and how its multiple narratives must provide quite different memories and different knowledges across cultures.

In summary, we suggest that higher education professors interested in interaction between diverse groups:

- may have to reduce their expectations of face-to-face engagement. In our experience, minority and non-dominant ethnic groups may not benefit from this form of sharing. Dialogue, we argue, is often in the interests of the dominant group only.
- may find that other forms of pedagogy, in which the ethnic groups in their classrooms are not forced into direct engagement but into a more oblique form of knowledge-production and sharing, may work better to address the relationship/s between the groups represented in the classroom.

- might consider asking (in careful ways) their minority group students whether they want to caucus or meet separately to debate and develop their own knowledge and interpretations (and then be prepared to protect those students from the possible attacks or demands of the others).
- might also ask their dominant group students to consider how their ethnicity and /or colonizing history is significant to the development of their own knowledge and stories about the past and the present.
- may, in the face of inevitable opposition to possible separation of their students into ethnic groups, need to consider in depth the logic of their own pedagogies and whose desires and interests those pedagogies express.

Reflection questions

1. When and how did face-to-face dialogue across cultures 'work' in your experience? How do you know it worked? What drawbacks might such an approach have?
2. How might students of different ethnicities or backgrounds respond to the idea of separating classes or discussion groups on the basis of their differences?
3. What written histories or stories might be useful to encourage a critical consideration of the historical or social relationship between diverse groups in your class?
4. How might you respond to the charge that separating students for study groups on the basis of ethnicity is 'racist'?

Notes

1. Although elsewhere we refer to the Pacific students as well as Maori in this classroom, for simplicity's sake in this chapter on postcolonial classrooms we refer to Maori students and White students only. We recognize that this simplification is problematic, and skates over the important complexities of the 'multicultural' nature of contemporary higher education classrooms. However, our focus in this chapter is on the possibility of a dialogic relationship between indigenous and colonizer peoples.
2. We have used the capitalized Other in the sense used by Todd (2003, p. 1): 'Social justice education has been and continues to be marked by a moral concern with those who have been "Othered" and marginalized through discriminatory relations that are seen as violent, both in symbolic and material terms. Often defined through social categories of identity, difference, and community, this figure of the "Other" occupies a special, and central, place in both theoretical and practical approaches to such pedagogical initiatives.

3. Marae refers to the Maori carved 'meeting house' complex. The students visited the University's marae as part of their studies in this course.
4. This activity, supervised by the Maori lecturer, required the Pākehā and Maori students (in mixed groups) to talk collectively to the class in any way they wanted about their shared reactions to and knowledge about any carving in a Maori meeting house.
5. Whare Wānanga are open to enrolments from any ethnic group, but their pedagogies and knowledges are based in Maori approaches.

Resources

Boler, M. (2004) (ed.). *Democratic dialogue in education: Troubling speech, disturbing silence*. New York: Peter Lang.
This edited collection raises some challenging questions about dialogue and why it might be problematic, for a range of groups, including ethnic groups.
Fine, M., Weis, L., Powell, L. C., & Wong, L. M. (eds). (1997). *Off white: Readings on race, power and society*. New York: Routledge.
This useful and courageous edited collection raises some challenging questions about dialogue and why it might be problematic, with a focus on ethnicity and difference and White people's responses to ethnicity.
Smith, L. T. (2001) *Decolonising methodologies: Research and indigenous peoples*. London and New York, Zed Books.
This book, written in accessible language by a leading indigenous (Māori) scholar, outlines some key issues for those engaging in research for or about indigenous people. Many of the points Smith raises are relevant to thinking-though the politics and practice of indigenous education.

Part 2
Practice

Preface to Part 2: Practice in the Multicultural Tertiary Classroom

Dawn Lorraine McBride

The second section of *Learning and Teaching Across Cultures in Higher Education* focuses on the interplay between theory and practice, as it relates to the university and college classroom. Two resonating themes in the second half of this book are for instructors to exercise flexibility in their teaching practices and to be open to self-discovery when working in cross-cultural settings. The following chapters demonstrate how innovative, creative and flexible approaches to learning can promote intercultural competence.

The authors in this book have considerable experience in the classroom and are active in providing innovative opportunities for students to work across cultures. Although each chapter focuses on a particular domain of study, the reader is invited to reflect on how the teaching strategies and tools can be adapted to other areas of study. Reflection questions at the end of each chapter may be helpful in this examination process.

The first chapter, 'One Size Fits All?' addresses a very relevant and timely question: How can university teaching centres respond to the challenges of helping faculty become competent in eliciting and facilitating rich intercultural dialogue in the classroom? The author's review of Hofstede's (2001) five dimensions of culture and Hall's work (1976) on cultural influences provides a strong foundation for adapting faculty development training sessions in multicultural settings. In Smith's case, she relates her work to providing these workshops at a university in the United Arab Emirates (UAE). Unique to the context of Smith's work is the cultural makeup of the faculty and students. Faculty come from around the world to teach in the UAE, often only remaining for two to three years on temporary leave from their home country university. The students also have diverse backgrounds, and in many cases are more aptly described as being 'third culture' students. As described by Pollock and Van Reken (1999), these students reside overseas (e.g., UAE) as expatriates, where they are not eligible to obtain citizenship, yet they have spent most of their lives in this host country. In reading Smith's work, it becomes readily apparent that educational developers need to give careful consideration to the cultural complexities involved in offering training to faculty from diverse backgrounds, who are working in a multicultural setting, so that classroom interactions are elicited, understood, and appreciated.

In an Australian context, Eisenchlas and Trevaskes advocate, in their chapter 'Intercultural Competence', the need to develop university programmes to actively encourage international and local students to work together. This type of intercultural engagement promotes cultural understanding and connectiveness. To enhance intergroup communication in the classroom, these two instructors describe a number of very useful and innovative assignments they have piloted in their courses. The assignments are well explained allowing the reader to adapt the assignments to their course material to foster their own cultural exchanges in the classrooms. The theory presented in this chapter provides a strong rationale for the need for instructors to be open to changing their teaching practice to better accommodate learners who are benefiting from globalization.

The issue of instructors being flexible in their teaching practice when working in a foreign country is very evident in the chapter by Cronjé, 'Afrikaners and Arabs'. This South African professor, with some of his colleagues, implemented a tutored masters IT programme in Sudan. His chapter outlines, in narrative form, the efforts which the teaching team had to make to be culturally sensitive and attuned to the learning needs of the Sudanese students. Although at times Cronjé's narrative invites a chuckle (e.g., electricity being turned off /on in waves to conserve energy and how Cronjé adapted to teaching IT skills in these circumstances), it does highlight the critical importance of working with, not against, the cultural elements.

The remaining three chapters offer more specific examples from instructors who created courses with the clear objective of promoting intercultural awareness and competence. Professor Schuetze, from Canada, wrote the chapter 'Assessing Intercultural Dialogue' based on his work of creating an online course where Canadian and German university students learning a second language worked together to develop their language and cultural skills. In his chapter he discusses the rationale and development of a comprehensive and practical assessment matrix to evaluate the progress of students' cultural awareness and the intercultural quality of their submitted work (e.g., online discussion forums, assignments). In addition to the valuable assessment tool described in this chapter, Schuetze documents how cultural awareness was invited and fostered in this innovative course.

The chapter on 'Virtual Internships' written by three experienced Nordic professors, Kristensen, Källström and Svenkerud provides a detailed account of how to prepare students, faculty members and business communities for cross-cultural work placements. Unique to this internship experience is how the authors integrated the use of technology (e.g., Blackboard, software programs) to promote understanding across cultures, to raise awareness of stereotyping and to promote understanding of cultural beliefs and values inherent in a multicultural workforce. The authors are generous in sharing multicultural problem-solving strategies and in providing a list of recommendations to create successful cross-cultural internships.

The last chapter 'Teaching Bioinformatics' is reserved for Niall Palfreyman, who has an interesting and very relevant perspective on promoting cultural competence in the classroom. He presents a strong argument for the need to bridge disciplines (in his case technical biosciences) where there is a historical cultural divide. In a fascinating narrative, he describes how students from the biological and technical sciences have their own distinctive sets of problem solving and communication styles. He interweaves cognitive psychology and constructivist theory to deepen the rationale as to why each discipline needs to understand and appreciate the strengths of other disciplines' 'cultures'. Similar to most of the chapters in the second half of this book, Palfreyman designs a course where the two distinct cultural groups have to work together to solve a series of problems, to learn how each perspective is valuable, but more so when different views of the problem are interconnected. This chapter contains ample material on how to run a course where two areas of study are merged into one cross-disciplinary unit. It is a good read and promotes an opportunity to expand the definition of culture within the higher education classroom.

8
One Size Fits All? Faculty Professional Development Workshops in a Multicultural Context
Lois Smith

This chapter looks at the influence of national and ethnic culture on educational development (professional development for those teaching in higher education). An introductory teaching programme for faculty in a Middle Eastern (United Arab Emirates) offshore campus of an Australian university is described as a means of exploring the effects of culture on training faculty in a multicultural context. I discuss my experience during the implementation of the teaching programme in relation to my own cultural background, which is different from that of most of the participants in the programme, as well as to the cultural setting of the institution. Some of the issues raised include dealing with differing concepts of teaching and learning, power distance, gender, and appreciation of student diversity. Although these issues relate to the specific context of the programme, they have significance for the kind of multicultural settings that are increasingly becoming part of modern transnational higher education.

Introduction

The cultural context of the educational development programme discussed in this chapter is quite complex, so the first section provides a necessarily detailed description of the somewhat unique, multicultural setting. The following sections outline the definitions and descriptions of culture used and the objectives of the programme; these serve to introduce the discussion of the programme's implementation, which is structured around the programme objectives and the cultural considerations necessary to achieve them. Some practical advice and suggestions are given, and the chapter concludes with some reflection and observation regarding the wider implications of culture for educational development.

Context

The Middle East, in particular the countries around the Arabian Gulf such as Qatar, the United Arab Emirates (UAE) and Oman, is experiencing a rapid phase of economic development. This is largely due to the production of oil, but in recent years some countries in the region have diversified into other sectors in order to develop a sustainable rate of economic and social development. A major part of this kind of development has been a focus on higher education, and there has been a huge amount of government and private investment in establishing a viable higher education sector.

At a global level, the recent trend towards transnational higher education has meant that western countries are not only looking to attract international students to their home institutions, they are aggressively expanding into foreign countries by offering degrees in partnership with local institutions, or by establishing their own offshore campuses. This move towards transnational education provides the home campus with a rich source of revenue and offers the local students the chance to get a 'western' degree without having to leave their own country (Altbach, 2004). In addition, the local university often gets the opportunity to develop a sense of autonomy and contribute to the economic and social development of the host country. The Arabian Gulf is a prime example of the development of transnational education, with North American, British and Australian universities, among others, rapidly expanding their operations in the region. The project described in this chapter is situated in an offshore campus of an Australian university.

As a western expatriate living and working in the UAE for over a decade I have witnessed, and had an active part in, the growth in higher education in this part of the world, and have become aware of the various cultural and social issues raised. As in other parts of the world, higher education in this region has become subject to quality assurance, with some countries requiring a rigorous accreditation process, as in the UAE (United Arab Emirates Ministry for Higher Education and Scientific Research, 2006). This in turn has led to a growing interest in the quality of teaching. In my role as an educational developer I have been involved with developing and running introductory teaching programmes and staff development workshops for faculty. It is the cultural complexity characteristic of this context which will be discussed in this chapter.

Students' cultural background

Third culture

In order to understand the cultural issues facing academics, and therefore educational developers, in the UAE it is necessary to first take a brief look at the cultural background of students and the effect this has on their approaches to teaching and learning. We are in an unusual position in the Gulf region in that we not only have host country, or 'domestic' students and visiting international students, but also a significant number of 'third culture' students (Pollock & Van Reken, 1999). These are expatriate students who hold passports of their country of origin and are not eligible for citizenship of the host country, but have spent little or none of their life in the country of origin, instead having been educated and brought up in the host country. Pollock and Van Reken (1999) discuss the phenomenon of a unique 'third culture' which develops in this kind of setting, and many students in the UAE are prime examples of 'third culture kids'. The impact of this on teaching and learning in higher education can be significant, as 'third culture kids' often develop their own cultural norms which differ from those of both the host country and the country of origin. This affects their attitudes to teaching and learning and makes them almost a separate cultural group from their compatriots.

Public versus private institutions

In the Gulf region there is a marked difference in the student population between public and private institutions. Public institutions are almost exclusively reserved for nationals of the country in which they are situated, and they usually provide free education. In these institutions therefore students are mainly from the same cultural group; that is the host country. Students in such public institutions are generally separated by gender, so that there are different campuses for men and women. In contrast, private institutions usually have a considerable cultural mix in their student bodies. This is due to the large number of expatriates living in the region, with some countries having up to 75 per cent of their population made up of expatriates (Middle East Online, 2004). The majority of that expatriate population tends in most Gulf countries to be from the Indian sub-continent, which is reflected in the

Table 8.1: Most frequently occurring nationalities among students at a private university in the UAE, 2004

Country	% of students
India	32
Iran	14
UAE	11
Pakistan	9
Jordan	4
Lebanon	3
Australia	2
Other	25

student population. An example of the multicultural nature of higher education can be seen in Table 8.1, which shows the nationalities found amongst students at a private university in the UAE with a total of approximately 1,700 students.

The 25 per cent of other nationalities mentioned in Table 8.1 includes one or more students from the following countries: Armenia, Bulgaria, Canada, China, Czech Republic, Egypt, Ethiopia, Germany, Indonesia, Iraq, Italy, Japan, Kenya, Morocco, Nigeria, Philippines, Russian Federation, Saudi Arabia, South Africa, Sri Lanka, Syria, Taiwan, Tajikistan, Tanzania, Thailand, Turkey, UK, USA and Yemen.

Just looking at the breakdown of nationalities, however, does not necessarily give an accurate picture of the cultural complexities involved in teaching students in these institutions. The educational and social background of students must also be taken into consideration. As stated above, there are a large number of 'third culture kids' among students in the UAE. This is especially true of students from the Indian sub-continental cultures and some Arab countries. In these cases students may have experienced a variety of different schooling. Many students attend schools which follow the educational system in their home countries, and which have students and teachers primarily from that same country of origin. On the other hand, many students attend international schools which may follow any number of educational systems, and which have students and teachers from a wide range of nationalities and cultures. Whatever their educational background, on entering higher education, the majority of students who have been educated in the host country will have had single-sex education, as there are few schools within the region which are truly co-educational.

In addition to students who have been educated wholly or mainly in the host country, there is a growing body of international students who are new to the region, either moving there with their families for work-related reasons, or on their own for the specific purpose of gaining an education. These students come from almost anywhere in the world, as is demonstrated in Table 8.1. Unlike their fellow students who have been brought up in the host country, these students often have little awareness of the host culture, or any culture other than their own.

Faculty's cultural background

In developing and preparing professional development programmes for faculty, as well as studying the cultural complexities of students, it is essential to be aware of the cultural background of the academics who will be participants on those programmes. It is common in most universities around the world for faculty to represent a range of cultural and educational backgrounds; indeed, this is one of the main contributors to the richness of academic life. In the Arabian Gulf region this is also the case, but the cultural diversity seen in other parts of the world is often more pronounced, with a wider range of academics represented within smaller institutions. For instance, at the UAE university mentioned above there is a wide cultural mix among the relatively small number of faculty, as can be seen in Table 8.2 below.

As is the nature of the region, there is a large transitory population, with many expatriates only spending three to five years in the host country before moving on elsewhere. This is reflected in institutions of

Table 8.2: Nationalities of academic faculty at a private UAE university, 2005

Country	No. of faculty	% of faculty
India	15	30
Iran	5	10
Pakistan, UK	4 (from both countries)	8 (× 2)
Algeria, Ireland, Palestine, Australia, Iraq, South Africa	2 (from each country)	4 (× 6)
Bosnia, Turkey, US, Canada, Lebanon, Syria, Jordan, Bangladesh, Egypt, Mauritania	1 (from each country)	2 (× 10)
TOTAL	50	

higher education, which often have a higher turnover of staff than in similar institutions in other parts of the world. Another factor in the changing nature of academic staff is the fact that most institutions in the region, whether public or private, are relatively new, and so are undergoing phases of expansion and development. As they grow, so their faculty increases. All this means that educational developers are often faced with an ever-changing body of participants in their programmes.

Educational development and cultural influences

When discussing the implementation of an educational development programme, it is important to consider teachers' conceptions of and attitudes towards teaching and learning. Prosser and Trigwell (1999) identify six qualitatively different, hierarchical categories of conceptions of teaching among teachers in higher education, ranging from 'teaching as transmitting concepts of the syllabus' to 'teaching as helping students change conceptions' (pp. 145–7). The range of these conceptions of teaching goes from a fundamentally teacher-centred, or didactic approach to a student-centred approach. Similarly, Samuelowicz and Bain (2001), revising their earlier work, identified nine belief dimensions ranging from 'imparting knowledge' to 'encouraging knowledge creation'. Kember (1997) conducted a significant analysis of the various independent studies into perceptions of teaching and learning, and found a high degree of consistency among the categories described, despite differing terminology. In my own small study of conceptions of teaching and learning in the present context I found a range of such conceptions, albeit with a tendency towards the teacher-centred end of the continuum (Smith, 2006). So, for the purposes of this chapter I will refer to a *teacher-centred* or *student-centred* approach to indicate conceptions held by participants loosely positioned towards either end of the continuum, or hierarchy. Both Samuelowicz and Bain (2001) and Kember (1997) highlight the importance of perceptions of teaching when planning teacher development programmes.

As well as considering conceptions of teaching and learning, it is also necessary to take cultural influences into account when planning teacher development programmes, especially in culturally complex situations such as my institution. Intercultural research over the years has sought to define and describe 'culture' (for example, Hall, 1976; Hofstede, 2001; Trompenaars & Hampden-Turner, 1997). In his review of the current state of intercultural research, Dahl (2004) describes culture as 'a shared set of basic assumptions and values, with resultant behavioural norms, attitudes and beliefs which manifest themselves in systems and institutions as well as behavioural patterns and non-behavioural items' (p. 6). In this chapter I will attempt to describe the implementation of an educational development programme in a multi-cultural setting with this definition in mind, while using the frameworks described below.

Hofstede (2001) describes five dimensions of culture, all of which played a part in the implementation of the programme which I will describe. First, he discusses the notion of *power distance*. This relates to the acceptance of unequal distributions of power within society or an organization. In cultures with a high power index, such as Arab countries and India there is an emphasis on hierarchical structure, with respect and deference paid to those at the high end of the scale. There is an acceptance of, even a desire for, inequalities among people. Alternatively, cultures which have low power distance orientation, such as Ireland, find inequality less acceptable. The power distance dimension of culture played an important role in the implementation of the educational development programme, especially when group work was involved.

Secondly, Hofstede (2001) talks about *uncertainty avoidance*, which he describes as the intolerance of ambiguity and uncertainty. People from cultures with a low uncertainty avoidance index, such as some European countries suffer less anxiety in ambiguous situations, tend to have a greater tolerance of diversity and are generally more open to change and innovation than people from cultures with a high uncertainty avoidance index. When it comes to the *individualism/collectivism* dimension which Hofstede describes, those from cultures which focus on the individual, such as the USA and UK (p. 262), tend to favour self-reliance and independence, whereas those from a collective culture, such as that of the UAE and other Arab and Asian countries, tend to value group needs over those of the individual, and to have strong group loyalties. Trompenaars and Hampden-Turner (1997) describe a very similar cultural orientation, communitarianism/individualism, in their 'seven cultural values' model. This particular dimension of culture had quite a strong influence on the implementation of our educational development programme, in particular in relation to reflection and feedback.

Hofstede's (2001) 'masculinity' index indicates degree of gender differentiation: those cultures having a high index display strong differentiation of 'the dominant gender role patterns in the vast majority of traditional and modern societies . . . the patterns of male assertiveness and female nurturance' (p. 284); those with a low index have a more nurturing attitude in both genders. This cultural dimension was also an important consideration in implementing the educational development programme, especially as many participants came from cultures with high 'masculinity' indices.

Hofstede's (2001) final cultural dimension is *long-term* versus *short-term* orientation. Societies with a long-term orientation, such as China, and to some extent, India typically value persistence, thrift and a sense of shame as well as ordering relationships by status. A society with short-term orientation, such as Pakistan, values, among other things, the receiving and giving of gifts and favours, and the protection of 'face', both for the individual and the group (Hofstede). Indeed, 'face-saving', or protecting dignity, self-respect and prestige links this cultural dimension to the collectivist culture, and was a significant influence on the implementation of the educational development programme, especially in relation to feedback on teaching.

As well as using Hofstede's (2001) cultural dimensions to examine the implementation of the educational development programme, I will also refer to the work of Hall (1976) to describe the cultural influences which affected the implementation of the programme. Specifically, Hall's two major cultural dimensions are *high-context* versus *low-context* cultures, and *polychronic* versus *monochronic* cultures. 'High context' and 'low context' refer mainly to communication. Hall (1976) describes low-context communication thus: 'most of the information must be in the transmitted message in order to make up for what is missing in the context' (p. 101); high-context communication on the other hand features 'preprogrammed information that is in the receiver and in the setting, with only minimal information in the transmitted message' (p. 101). In a culturally mixed group such as the participants in the educational development programme, a mix of high and low context cultures is usually found.

In relation to time, people from polychronic cultures have a synchronous, flexible approach to time. A polychronic culture often tends to be also high context, and people often carry on multiple conversations and tasks simultaneously. On the other hand, to someone from a monochronic culture schedules and deadlines are all important, and tasks and conversations are carried out in a sequential order (O'Hara-Devereaux & Johansen, 1994). During the implementation of the educational development programme I became acutely aware of the cultural differences in approaches to time and context, and indeed, realized that I come from a firmly monochronic, low-context culture, which made it hard at times for me to deal with people from different cultural backgrounds.

Objectives

The remainder of this chapter focuses on a mandatory introductory teaching programme for all faculty at a university in the UAE. This university is an offshore campus of the Australian university which is featured in Table 8.1 and Table 8.2, and the introductory teaching programme (ITP) had been successfully run at the main campus for at least ten years before it was introduced at the UAE campus. All faculty on the UAE campus, except full professors, were required to participate in the programme, regardless of their previous teaching experience, with an exemption process in place for those who had completed similar teaching qualifications elsewhere. The programme consists of two units. Unit One is a series of compulsory workshops covering topics such as assessment, teaching, learning, policy and evaluation, amounting to around 30 hours of participation. This unit culminates in a peer teaching session in which participants are split into small groups to teach a simple concept or theory from their area of specialization to a group of their peers from a range of disciplines. They then receive feedback from their peers and the group facilitator. Unit One is assessed by means of a written assignment consisting of a teaching plan, outline and reflection on the peer teaching, as well as participation in an online discussion of assessment, which follows the workshops. Unit Two of the programme is an individual 'Learning Through Teaching Programme', which follows three cycles of teaching observations by a colleague, written reflection, and observation of a colleague's teaching. Assessment is by a portfolio documenting the teaching cycles and the development of a personal theory of teaching and learning. The main focus of this chapter is on Unit One, as this was the first part to be introduced and currently only this data is available.

The objectives of the ITP are that through active participation in the introductory teaching programme participants will be able to:

- value the diversity of student experiences and backgrounds and appreciate the ways in which students learn;
- value and share their own and their colleagues' experiences and knowledge of teaching;
- design effective learning experiences for students;
- use appropriate presentation and communication technologies;

- choose and justify appropriate strategies for assessing student learning;
- use and justify appropriate strategies for evaluating teaching and subjects;
- reflect upon feedback from students and colleagues in order to evaluate and improve their own teaching practice.

Implementation

The programme objectives will be used to structure the following discussion of the implementation of the ITP in the UAE context. The cultural background of participants can be seen in Table 8.2 above; their disciplinary backgrounds were in Commerce and Information Technology. I was part of the initial introduction of the programme to the UAE campus and have been involved with its implementation since then. As well as being a facilitator for the workshops, I have acted as a liaison between the Australian Coordinator of the programme and the Executive at the UAE campus, and have worked closely with the Australian campus in the implementation of the programme. I have also taken part in the programme in Australia, where the majority of the participants are Australian, but a range of other cultures are also represented.

Diversity of student experience and cultural background
As higher education becomes global in the sense that students are no longer from predominantly homogenous cultural groups, teachers need to be able to facilitate learning in students with a wide range of values and attitudes, which are often very different from their own. Recognition of these differences can go a long way in avoiding some of the conflicts and misunderstandings in the classroom often associated with international students, such as the perception that Chinese learners adopt a surface approach to learning because of their propensity for memorization (Watkins & Biggs, 2001). To encourage participants to value the diversity of student experiences and cultural background, the topic of one of the workshops in the ITP ITT is *Teaching International Students and Cultural Diversity*. In the UAE context this is especially important, given the cultural complexities described above. The ability to communicate across cultures is essential, and it is important that educational developers help academic faculty to achieve this. One way to introduce the workshop on this issue is to discuss the barriers to communication amongst cultures, which include assuming similarity instead of difference, misunderstandings of non-verbal behaviour, stereotypes, high anxiety, language differences, and a tendency to

evaluate as well as to form preconceptions (Barna, cited in Fowler, 2006). An introductory activity to confront stereotypes, which works well in multicultural groups, begins with asking everyone to write down a selection of words or phrases which they feel describe their own national stereotype. These papers can then be displayed on the walls of the room (without names) for everyone in the group to read and discuss. If the activity is facilitated well it can be light-hearted fun, but the important point is that stereotypes should not define the people we work with.

When discussing diversity among students however, it should not be assumed that academics working in this kind of multicultural environment are automatically aware of the importance of recognizing cultural differences among their students. Indeed, on occasion, participants have questioned whether it is something we really need to be concerned about. I have found very few academics who give more than passing attention to the cultural complexities in their classrooms, yet students often have negative reactions when teachers fail to recognize cultural differences (Barmeyer, 2004). In practice, the sessions on cultural diversity have been very well received and have provided a useful platform for discussion about the different cultures within the group of participants as well as among students. In fact, on one occasion a participant requested that the session be extended because he had not had the chance to discuss culture and religion with all his fellow participants in the workshop.

Valuing and sharing each others' experiences

Valuing and sharing each others' experiences and knowledge of teaching involves participants' taking part in whole group and small group discussions. When introducing the programme in the UAE campus there were a number of cultural issues to consider. Power distance in relation to hierarchy is an important cultural factor to take into account when planning and preparing educational development programmes which involve a lot of group work, as this programme does. I have found that there is often a greater awareness of power distance in UAE institutions, which tend to have a greater cultural mix, than might be expected in similar instances in western countries. For example, this can be manifested through a reluctance to make eye contact or to directly address another person. The influence of power distance can affect interactions within a group, especially in small-group activities. In a culturally mixed group it is important to remember this and to be sensitive to the fact that some participants may feel uncomfortable talking openly with someone they deem to be higher or lower in the institutional hierarchy than themselves. A lot of thought also needs to go into setting up and monitoring group work: sometimes it is necessary to model a group discussion when participants are not used to interacting with their colleagues in such an informal setting.

It is important for a facilitator to be aware of the attitudes of participants towards power distance from the outset. A simple way to do this is to either ask participants to introduce themselves or to write their own name badges, if they are used. On one occasion I asked participants to write their name as they would like to be addressed during the programme and one participant wrote his name as 'Dr . . . '. Coming from a culture where first names are the norm amongst colleagues, I found this surprising, but I realized that I would have caused offence by referring to him without his title. It is also a good idea to ask participants what they would like to be called when issues of pronunciation or name-order are involved: names are an important part of identity in many cultures, and mispronunciation or using the wrong part of the name can be annoying and disrespectful.

Another cultural issue to consider in the context of group work is attitudes towards the opposite gender. While it would be unusual to find extreme sexist attitudes, many academics in the UAE come from cultures with a high masculinity index, where they may not be used to interacting with the opposite sex on terms of professional equality, especially on an informal basis. Based on my years of teaching in the UAE, I have noticed that, while women are generally accepted as teachers in higher education, their opinions and ideas are sometimes not valued as much as those of their male colleagues, particularly in relation to institutional matters such as policy. Malik (1995) discusses this 'gender gap' in higher education within the Islamic world and concludes that cultural factors rather than structural factors are responsible for it. When observing group interactions among participants on the programme I have been intrigued at times to see that male and female members sometimes assume the traditional masculine/feminine roles of 'master' and 'pupil', regardless of their position within the organization. I have also noticed that participants often find it harder to disagree or argue with members of the opposite gender than they do when the programme is run in Australia.

Designing effective learning experiences

When encouraging participants to design effective learning experiences for their students, culture has an important role to play. Although faculty and students at my institution come from a wide range of cultural and educational backgrounds, I have found a predominance of didactic or teacher-centred approaches to teaching and learning among faculty (Smith, 2006). Although this is certainly not unique to the UAE (for example Gow & Kember, 1993; Watkins & Biggs, 2001), I feel that there is a greater tendency to this 'traditional' approach to teaching and learning than in some other countries. The ITP strongly encourages a student-centred approach to teaching and learning, so getting participants to consider this approach when designing learning experiences was a challenge. One way in which I tried to encourage participants to think more about a student-centred approach was to use video clips of lectures and tutorials. During the playing of the video I asked half the participants to watch what the students were doing and half to watch what the lecturer was doing. Then we compared the two and discussed when the most student activity occurred, and how that influenced the learning which was taking place.

Another point to consider when discussing the design of learning experiences in a multicultural context is the use of language and specific terminology. Terms such as 'student-centred learning' are widely interpreted around the world, and I have found a huge range of meanings attributed to this term in the UAE context. There tends to be a greater variety of meanings in this region due to the greater range of cultures and educational backgrounds represented among faculty. For example, on one occasion I was told that a lecturer was using a student-centred approach because the students were actively answering his questions, which is very far from my own interpretation of the term 'student-centred approach'. Similar problems with terminology can occur with common terms such as 'tutorial', which can mean anything from a group of three or four students discussing selected questions with their professor in his/her office, to thirty or forty students in a classroom with a tutor receiving instruction on a particular problem. Therefore, it is vital that such terms are discussed and explored rather than just assumed to mean the same to all participants.

Using appropriate presentation and communication technologies

Linked to the design of learning experiences is the use of appropriate presentation and communication technologies. Part of the teacher-centred approach to teaching and learning is an emphasis on course content. Again, this is certainly not unique to faculty in the UAE campus, but it is an important issue which needed to be considered when implementing the ITP, because language considerations often influence lecturers' choice of presentation and communication. I have found that participants often feel the need to focus almost exclusively on 'covering' the course content or syllabus because they are aware that many of their students have limited abilities in English and so require a lot more assistance than their native-speaking counterparts. This leads to a dependence on Powerpoint slides and detailed verbal explanations.

Appropriate strategies for assessing student learning and evaluating teaching

Choosing, using and justifying appropriate strategies for assessing student learning and evaluating teaching and subjects forms a substantial part of Unit One of the ITP. When implementing the programme in the UAE context it was important to bear in mind the diverse educational backgrounds of the participants because of the great influence previous experience has on present practice. While most academic institutions around the world will have faculty from a range of previous experiences, in the UAE this phenomenon can be exaggerated, as seen in Table 8.2 above. Uncertainty avoidance is certainly a cultural component when looking at strategies for assessing and evaluating. At the testing level, this may result in a preference for closed questions in tests, so as to reduce the interpretation involved in marking. More generally, participants from cultures with a high uncertainty avoidance index are often reluctant to accept change and innovation, which can make it difficult to introduce new ideas about assessment and evaluation. At times I have experienced considerable resistance to the concept of peer and self-assessment during workshops on methods of assessment.

Reflecting on feedback

When it comes to reflection and evaluation of teaching practice as a means to improving teaching, Unit One addresses this objective through the peer teaching component towards the end of the workshops. This part of the programme needs careful consideration in the multicultural UAE context, and culture is an important issue in its implementation. As previously stated, there is often a high power distance awareness among participants, which makes it difficult or inappropriate to give constructive feedback in certain circumstances. For example, participants are often reluctant to appear 'critical' of someone in a senior position to themselves, and so feedback becomes noncommittal, with phrases such as 'very good' or 'it was OK'. In addition, for some participants from cultures with short-term orientations giving and receiving criticism is uncomfortable, as issues of 'loss of face' come into play. I have been acutely aware of this in some cases when participants have become very defensive towards what I would consider fairly innocuous comments. I have also observed a tendency towards feeling the need to counter or justify any slightly negative criticism. On one occasion a participant in a culturally mixed group complained in the written feedback after the teaching practice workshop that the group facilitator was not effective because she allowed people to be too critical, although other members of that group said they found the criticism to be valuable and constructive. When taking part in the teaching practice workshops in Australia I generally found a greater acceptance of criticism, and indeed, sometimes a more critical analysis of others' teaching. Thus, when implementing the teaching practice workshop in the UAE attention needs to be paid to cultural sensitivities.

Another issue to consider in relation to reflection and evaluation in a culturally mixed group is that of language. It may well be the case that English is not the first language for some or most of the participants, and indeed, some may not have used English for academic purposes before. A large part of the programme involves written personal reflection, and participants who are not using their first language may have difficulty expressing themselves accurately in English, either verbally, or in writing. This can lead to misunderstandings and false assumptions. The idea of reflection and self-analysis places an emphasis on the individual in a way which may be new or alien to participants from a collectivist background, so the concept needs to be introduced thoughtfully with perhaps an initial one-to-one discussion and questioning (Bell, 2005), as is the case in Unit Two. I have found that providing a structure for reflection, such as the *Describe, Analyse, Theorize, Act* process described by Peters (1991) helps participants to focus their reflective process, which can often appear to be a rather vague or overly introspective process at first.

Reflections and recommendations

Through my facilitation of the ITP over five years in the UAE campus I have experienced a range of reactions to it. However, the reaction of participants towards such teaching programmes can vary greatly for a number of reasons, irrespective of culture, as has been found in other regions of the world (Trowler & Cooper, 2002). It is also notoriously difficult to change teachers' perceptions of teaching (Ho, Watkins & Kelly, 2001). Having said that, the response to the programme has been overwhelmingly favourable and enthusiastic, both in informal feedback and in evaluation questionnaires.

Although I tried to anticipate some of the necessary cultural issues related to the introduction and method of delivery of the programme as mentioned above, there have been some unforeseen issues related to the cultural complexity of the situation. The first of these are the practical considerations of organizing such a programme in an offshore campus. Not only do have time differences have to be taken into consideration, but different working weeks as well, because the UAE has Friday and Saturday (or until recently Thursday and Friday) as the weekend, unlike Australia. The facilitation of the workshops involved educational developers coming from Australia so there was the added complication of different term times to consider when planning when to run the workshops. Another practical issue related to culture which I failed to anticipate relates to perceptions of time. As with some students in the UAE campus, some academics have a polychronic view of time, which means that they do not necessarily arrive at the specified start time, nor take the '10 minute break' as literally as I intended with my monochronic cultural view of time. I have been in the situation where I have found only one or two out of the enrolled number of participants to be present at the designated start time, which has caused me some consternation. This means that in practice the timing of sessions sometimes becomes fluid, a fact that some participants from cultures like my own with a more monochronic interpretation of time can find hard to deal with. In comparison, when I took part in the programme in Australia I was a little surprised to find that when I arrived at the designated start time that nearly all the participants were present and ready to begin. I realized my own cultural drift in matters of punctuality due to my years spent living in the Middle East.

Related to the polychronic/monochronic cultural dimension, I have found high and low context issues affecting my facilitation of the programme. I have noticed that during whole group discussions participants often 'talk over' each other so that there are sometimes two or three people talking at once, and often side conversations going on at the same time as the main discussion. When this happens I am aware that participants from more monochronic, low-context cultures sometimes become frustrated and irritated. It can be difficult to keep some kind of control of the situation at times, so I usually try to make sure everyone has the chance to speak and be heard whilst I attempt to draw out the main points from the various discussions and write them on the board. Providing this kind of summary helps to keep discussions focused while respecting the various cultural norms of communication.

As anticipated, power distance issues have arisen in relation to group work and giving criticism, In addition, I have experienced power distance related issues in approaches to teaching and learning. Consistent with a teacher-centred approach, I have often interacted with academics who exhibit attitudes and practices indicative of a high power distance index, such as seeing teaching as transmitting information and themselves as the holders of knowledge. Faculty who hold these views see themselves in an authoritative role and expect a certain amount of distance and respect from students. They do not generally encourage students to question them. This high power distance is often mirrored and reinforced by students within higher education in the UAE, who generally prefer to call lecturers either 'sir' or 'miss', or to use the lecturers' title and first name. I have found very few students in the UAE, especially undergraduates, who are comfortable with addressing academics by their first names. Sometimes a didactic approach to teaching and learning has been applied to the ITP itself, and I have found the expectation that I will provide the 'right' answer or approach, which is at odds with my role as a facilitator, as I see it.

As other chapters in this book show, there are clearly problems associated with delivering a programme designed in one cultural and educational context to a very different cultural context. Educational developers around the world are familiar with the cries of 'that's all very well, but it wouldn't work in my subject' from participants on teaching programmes, but I also heard the additional cry of 'that's all very good for Australian / western students, but it wouldn't work here'. Although I tried to adapt materials to the local context, out of necessity video clips and examples were Australian. In one particular video the subject being taught was mathematics (a fairly universal subject), and a majority of the students present were Chinese or from other East Asian countries, yet some participants were still not convinced the teaching methods demonstrated were possible for their students. Another culture-related issue I experienced using videos from Australia was the difficulty some participants had with the accent and the pace of speech.

Conclusion

Being involved in educational development in a cultural context which is different from my own and which includes academics from a wide range of cultures has taught me a lot about intercultural communication and awareness. I have had to examine my own cultural beliefs and values, and have found them tested at times. I have found that I need to be acutely aware of my own tendency to assume that all people have similar fundamental values, similar ways of interpreting behaviour, dealing with time and space, and showing respect (Fowler, 2006). When dealing with students it is easier to be on guard against these assumptions, but it is more difficult in an educational development situation when it is all too easy to assume that as academics we all have the same values and beliefs. This is probably the most important lesson I have learned during my facilitation of the ITP. By extension, this awareness of cultural diversity needs to be made an explicit part of educational development in a context such as the UAE.

As I have discovered, it is wrong to assume that because people live and work in a multicultural environment they are aware of the impact of culture on behaviour, or that they recognize the need for openly addressing cultural diversity in their classrooms. Bodycott and Walker (2000) claim that the challenges of increasing transnational higher education can severely test the beliefs and attitudes of teachers, particularly in relation to their own role and approach to an increasingly diverse student body. However, they argue that 'the development of inter-cultural understandings and related teaching practices must begin with the teacher's attitude, and the scaffolds created to support student learning' (p. 81). Given the cultural context within higher education in the UAE, it is vital that faculty learn to recognize and value different perspectives in order to learn the skills for dealing with, and building on, the differences among their students. I strongly believe that educational development programmes should be aimed at developing such skills, which will ultimately support student learning in the kind of multicultural environment which is becoming a reality in higher education around the world.

Reflection questions

1. How familiar are you with the cultural background of your colleagues?
2. How far do you think culture influences attitudes to teaching and learning?
3. What support does your institution provide to help faculty work in a multicultural environment?
4. What further support could your institution provide for faculty?

Resources

Bell, M. (2005). *Peer observation partnerships in higher education*. Milpera, Australia: Higher Education Research and Development Society of Australasia.
An excellent HERDSA Guide to developing peer observation as part of educational development which I used for the teaching practice part of Unit One, and extensively for Unit Two of the ITP. It contains lots of very useful tips and examples.

Hofstede, G., & Hofstede, G. J. (2005). *Cultures and organizations: Software of the mind* (2nd edn). USA: McGraw-Hill.
Updated version of Hofstede's ideas about cultures and their relation to the development of organizational culture and learning.

ITIM international: http://www.geert-hofstede.com
This website is run by Hofstede and contains an enormous amount of information about his work on cultural dimensions.

Rosinski, P. (2003). *Coaching across cultures: New tools for leveraging national, corporate and professional differences*. London: Nicholas Brearley.
This book contains some very useful examples of ways to introduce the concept of culture and activities which are useful in an educational development setting when dealing with participants from different cultures.

Society for Intercultural Education, Training and Research [SIETAR]: http://www.sietar-europa.org
This organization promotes the formation of intercultural groups among students and professionals working in intercultural communication.

University of Melbourne: http://www.unimelb.edu.au/diversity/inclusive.html
This webpage contains a range of links to useful information about cultural diversity in the classroom. The self-audit would be particularly useful as part of an educational development programme, both for individual use, and for group discussion.

Ziegahn, L. (2001). Considering culture in the selection of teaching approaches for adults. ERIC Digest. No. 231. Retrieved 12 September 2006 from http://www.ericdigests.org/2002-3/culture.htm
This short article gives a useful summary of the main cultural dimensions and is a useful starting point for an educational development workshop on cultural diversity among students.

9
Intercultural Competence: Examples of Internationalizing the Curriculum through Students' Interactions

Susana Eisenchlas and Susan Trevaskes

In our increasingly globalized societies, there is a growing need for us, as educators, to perceive ourselves as 'citizens of the world who are comfortable with diverse peoples' (Harrigan & Vicenti, 2004, p. 119). Thus the development of intercultural communication is recognized as one of the key competences required of future graduates, and has become enshrined in all Australian Universities' Mission Statements. Despite this recognition, there has been no comprehensive blueprint to explain how this imperative translates into the classroom situation. If universities are to prepare graduates that can communicate appropriately in a number of contexts and settings, then it may be more efficient to create situations where students can develop this competence through meaningful interactions. This chapter discusses three such approaches that use the international student population and the local migrant community to introduce, practice and negotiate cultural understandings in the target language.

Introduction

This chapter explores some of the ways in which, as educators, we can translate the concept of 'internationalizing the curriculum' into concrete practice. It reviews and discusses three educational programmes and initiatives that we developed and implemented, which illustrate concrete models of internationalization. Each of these case studies draws on students and the local community as a resource for teaching and learning. While each programme has been designed to address a discrete communicative context, they all emphasize some common principles and rationales. The first is the importance and implications of translating the concept of internationalization into academic practice. The second is the aim of promoting interaction between groups as an effective way of developing intercultural competence, and the third is the common view of culture that underlies the three programmes. Before describing the programmes, then, it is useful to reflect on these principles and rationales. We turn first to the conceptualization of internationalization in Australian universities, and the problem of translating 'internationalization' into classroom practice.

Context

One of the key consequences of globalization for universities in Western Europe, North America and other Anglo-Saxon regions over the last two decades has been the introduction of policies aimed at internationalization. In Australia, perhaps the most visible aspect of this process has been the proliferation of foreign, mainly Asian, students on campus. Universities in Australia have become increasingly dependent on this population of students to supplement their income.[1] Yet, beyond purely economic interests, Australian universities have now begun to recognize the need to respond to the educational imperatives of globalization and to identify and develop the skills students require to function effectively in a globalized environment. Hence, the rhetoric of 'internationalizing the curriculum' has become firmly entrenched in educational discourse and in the consciousness of educators and higher education policy makers alike.

Since the 1970s, Australian government policy on international education has sought to integrate the objectives of the nation's foreign policy into education policy. Evidence of this is the shift of policy focus from 'educational aid' post-war, to 'educational trade' in the 1970s and 1980s, and to the current promotion of internationalization starting in the early 1990s. Presently, due to reduced government funding to higher education institutions, universities have been driven to generate their own income sources. Thus, internationalization of Australia's university education policy has been mainly driven by profit considerations. This is what Appadurai may call a 'weak' manifestation of internationalization. Appadurai (2001) distinguishes between 'weak' and 'strong' internationalization, the former being essentially a 'superficial engagement with the issues whilst the latter is a (laborious, even contentious) deeper, more sophisticated and genuine desire to explore what it means to become internationalised' (Sanderson, 2002, p. 144). For many scholars and educators the benefits of 'strong' internationalization in higher education seem self-evident: international education is at once a counter hegemonic response to parochialism in scholarship; a foundation for developing and stimulating 'critical thinking and enquiry about the complexity of issues and interests that bear on the relations among nations, regions and interest groups' (Yang, 2002, p. 86); and a way of acquiring a certain 'cultural versatility' in understanding and communicating with people of diverse backgrounds (Pittaway et al., 1998, p. 62). Strong internationalization 'involves a journey or movement of people, minds or ideas across political and cultural frontiers' (Fraser and Brackman as cited in Hayden and Thompson, 1995, p. 17).

Strong internationalization can impact on all aspects of academic life. Yet, despite attempts to define internationalization in the literature, at the coalface of the classroom the core idea remains elusive. Key policy documents commonly employ Knight's (1999) definition of internationalization as a process of integrating international dimensions into teaching, research and service. However, this definition offers little tangible assistance to individual academics. While promising in its acknowledgement of interculturality as an important aspect of internationalization, Knight's definition does not go far enough towards a clear explication of *how* internationalization is to be achieved. The realisation of 'strong' internationalization at the grassroots level of teaching and learning in Australia is therefore hamstrung by a lack of conceptual models for its execution and implementation in the daily activities of teaching and learning. In this regard, Yang (2002) suggests that 'theoretical studies lag far behind practice' (p. 81). We would add that practical guidelines lag far behind universities' rhetoric.

Underpinning the call to internationalize the curriculum is the view, expressed in university mission statements across Australia, that the development of intercultural competence is a key goal of internationalization and that *all* students, i.e., local and international, need to obtain at least a minimal level of intercultural competence in order to operate effectively in an increasingly diverse society and globalized economy. Despite the acknowledgement of the importance of intercultural competence, there is little reflection on what it entails, and on how intercultural learning can be fostered at university level. Intercultural learning is rather taken for granted as 'an automatic outcome and benefit of intercultural contact' (Leask, 2005, p. 5).

But intercultural contact in itself is a problematic issue on the Australian university campus. It would be expected that the proliferation of international students in Australian campuses would help in the process of developing an understanding of, and tolerance for, other cultural practices and would enhance intercultural communication skills. However, a number of studies have cast doubts on the degree of intercultural contact at university, indicating that there is little interaction and high levels of disinterest between local and international students (Eisenchlas & Trevaskes, 2003; The University of Western Australia, 1999).

Emerging from the discussion above are two issues that we wish to address in what follows. The first raises the question of what aspects of 'cultural' learning might promote intercultural competence and, related to this, which programmes and practices might best promote intercultural competence. The second concerns how we might best promote intercultural contact between disparate groups.

Definitions of culture

'Culture' discussed in the context of national boundaries, as seen in many intercultural communication textbooks, remains for students a vague concept somewhat removed from their own tangible realities. We propose that a more effective access to an appreciation of intercultural and intergroup interaction is through these personal realities. The experience of everyday living involves culture as 'both something you perform and something you learn about' (Kramsch, 1991, p. 228): through their own experience, students can more readily learn to identify and understand the nature of culture. We share with Barro et al. the view that culture is not 'something prone, waiting to be discovered but an active meaning-making system of experiences which enters into and is constructed within every act of communication' (1998, p. 83). Our approach challenges stolid, isolated interpretations of culture, instead presenting a view that focuses on its fluid, situational and heterogeneous nature. Furthermore, through this immediate environment, internalized cultural norms, which seem 'invisible' to our awareness, can more readily be acknowledged. In order to become explicit, these taken-for-granted norms need to be questioned, a process that Barro et al. (1998) describe as 'making the familiar strange' (p. 83).

The acquisition of intercultural competence, defined as 'the ability to mediate between one's own culture and that of others' (Buttjes as cited in Dlaska, 2000, p. 249), is the first crucial step towards becoming able to reflect on one's own cultural norms and values, and also on how these norms and values shape the social identities of individuals and groups. We suggest that programmes should embody this ethos of interculturality, enacting the communicative agenda of internationalization through a learning process which enables individuals or groups to communicate their values, attitudes and aspirations better in intergroup situations, and to appreciate more the values, attitudes and aspirations of others.

Facilitating intergroup interaction

Both local and international students need to become competent intercultural communicators, within their learning environment and beyond. However, different challenges need to be recognized and addressed for each context. For international students, difficulties can be specifically language-related, or related more to their educational, cultural and social adaptation to Australian campus life. Harman (2004) acknowledges international students' dissatisfaction with their lack of social integration, citing a report which presents this problem as an image of 'two parallel streams of students'

> . . . proceeding through university – the Australian and the international – within close proximity but, in the majority of cases, with little or only superficial contact and interaction. A variety of exit and other surveys confirms this fairly common experience and records repeated expressions of disappointed expectations by international students who had hoped to meet and form close friendships with Australian students, visit Australian homes and experience local culture first hand. (Smart, Volet, & Ang as cited in Harman, 2004 pp. 115–16)

That these two 'parallel streams' exist has negative consequences for local students as well, since they also miss valuable opportunities to engage in meaningful cross-cultural communication, both in class and elsewhere. This lack of social engagement between international and local students can be seen to hinder in-class interaction, create resentment and reinforce stereotypical views: local students feel – and at times openly express the idea – that international students contribute little to classroom discussions and debates, while international students feel their opinions are not valued by their Australian classmates.

Rather than create separate programmes for issues specific to either local or international students, we propose effective programmes to internationalize the curriculum through group work and cooperation between the two groups. In terms of teaching content, we propose programmes that explicitly address the intellectual, social and cultural challenges and concerns that face international and local students alike at university.

To develop intercultural communication as a real life skill requires the *practice* of intergroup communication: This is/must be the means through which students can become competent communicators, developing the skills and attitudes to complement the theories they are exposed to in other classes such as languages, liberal arts or business subjects.

Three programmes to promote internationalizing students' experiences

We view culture as a dynamic construct, and we regard intercultural communication as a process of negotiation across individuals and groups; therefore we argue that internationalizing students' experiences is, by its very nature, a process which can occur only in specific 'instances' of interaction between individuals and/or groups within the very context of their own curriculum content and assessment practices. From this it follows that internationalization of the curriculum should be seen as contextual, like the concept of culture itself, taking on different meanings and significance in different contexts.

Within the student-centred pedagogy promoted in our courses, we aim to optimize student learning outcomes by preparing students for intercultural engagement, both in their immediate social environment and community and in their future professional fields. To this end, we have developed several programmes and activities that assume a definition of internationalization as essentially a process of communication and interculturality. Our main purpose is twofold: to prepare students for intercultural engagement in their immediate social environment, and to create opportunities for interaction and exchange of ideas between individuals and groups of diverse cultural backgrounds. In what follows, we describe three of these programmes, located in three different settings, starting in the more controlled classroom environment, moving through the university setting, and extending into the wider community. These programmes are situated within the broad spectrum of culture, languages and cross-cultural communication studies. However, similar approaches could be implemented on a smaller scale to introduce intercultural elements into courses in other areas such as business, education and health sciences.

Programme 1: Internationalizing the culture experience using research activities

Interactions between local and international students in Australian universities have been well observed and documented (Eisenchlas &

Trevaskes, 2003; The University of Western Australia, 1999). This research has shown a high level of disinterest between the local and the international student populations. This lack of interest, we suggest, may originate at least in part from a perception of the cultural 'Other' as relatively homogenous in behaviour and disposition. Studies of social categorization and perception show that people readily perceive diversity in their own culture, but fail to notice it in other cultural or ethnic groups (Berreby, 2005). Moreover, people readily recognize the fluidity of their own identity as a balancing act between a number of groupings to which we belong simultaneously, but tend to classify members of other ethnic groups in frozen, exclusive identities (Berreby, op. cit.). To address this phenomenon, we devised a course assessment item – a group research essay – that focused on the topics of internationalization, enculturation and intergroup contact. This assessment item required students to work together, to discuss their own experiences and to perform empirical research using the student international student population as their objects of inquiry. This process of engendering cooperative learning into the curriculum has been found to be an effective way of promoting academic achievement and reducing prejudice in intergroup contact (Harrison, 2001; Slavin, 1995).

Students were firstly asked to form groups and to include at least one student from a different cultural and/or linguistic background. Next, they selected a particular topic in the area of intercultural studies (e.g., intercultural adaptation) and were asked to explore the topic by examining how it is reflected in as many different cultures as participants were in the group. Although individuals were responsible for the section of their essay related to the language or culture of their choice, it was the group's responsibility to choose the content and style of the essay.

Students thus needed to exchange ideas and consider cultural practices perhaps previously unknown to them, combine them with their own perspectives and agree on the formal structure of the essay. Participation in small groups enabled international students, perhaps lacking the confidence to join fully in bigger class discussions due to linguistic limitations, to make significant contributions to the debates.

Designing and writing the research essay was, however, only a small part of the assignment. Since the essay was data-driven, students were required to undertake extensive research to gather their own data by accessing authentic media sources and conducting interviews or surveys, obtaining the participation of international and local peers. This necessarily brought students into further contact with members of different ethnic or linguistic groups and, since they were collecting data mainly from people of similar ages and interests, exposed them to attitudes and opinions that go beyond the usual cultural stereotypes portrayed in intercultural communication textbooks.

An example of a group essay was a comparative study of the perceptions and experiences of cultural adaptation of South Korean, Taiwanese and Thai international students in Australia. The study conducted by these undergraduate researchers focused on the following research questions: (1) What are the main differences of views on cultural adaptation into Australian society between South Koreans, Taiwanese and Thai international students? (2) What are the varying factors that might cause these differences? The study involved 42 international students and the data was collected through surveys. Some of their finding were perhaps unsurprising, but nonetheless new to the students: that levels of language proficiency and intended length of say could influence views and patterns of cultural adaptation. They also found that the South Korean students surveyed found it comparatively more difficult to adapt culturally and to interact with Australians.

Another project compared the levels of directness in Korean, Japanese and Australian English. Students collected the data by transcribing all the directives uttered in three films (specifically, comedies) produced in these countries, and classifying these directives according to standard taxonomies. The main finding of this study was that Korean patterned with Australian English in this respect, rather than with Japanese. This was surprising, as intercultural communication textbooks typically classify all Asian cultures as being indirect.[2]

These examples show how students gained a first-hand experience of the fluidity of cultural mores, that can be found even in societies often classified in intercultural communication texts as static and resistant to change. Furthermore, Australian students came to the realization that many of the generalizations they hold regarding, for example, 'Asian cultures' are untenable, as they became aware of the great diversity that exists within each culture. Equally importantly, students began to understand that the similarities they shared with young people from different ethnic and/or cultural backgrounds were greater than their differences. This is a first step to recognizing the above mentioned fluidity of identity across groups which, despite their ethnically diverse backgrounds, share common interests and experiences, the most obvious being their status as young university students. Among the skills to be gained from such activities are students' ability to recognize similarities as well as differences between individuals in ethnically diverse groups, to employ their own and others' experiences as objects of inquiry and to negotiate common goals.

Programme 2: Exploring culture and internationalization through interviews

Training students to be competent and confident intercultural communicators requires two key ingredients for success. Students need firstly opportunities for meaningful face-to-face interaction and secondly an understanding that manifestations of cultural norms in the behaviour of individuals need to be interpreted as 'situational' and 'contextual', rather than universal to all those who share a common ethnic background. As discussed above, it is incumbent upon universities (at least for those whose rhetoric involves 'internationalizing the curriculum') to provide opportunities for students to interact. International students in Australia face a range of confronting situations when settling into a new academic environment. Some universities have introduced mentoring programmes where local students guide international students through the transition phase; such programmes are certainly useful but they seem limited in scope, with few obvious benefits to the local students. Moreover, these types of programmes can cast international students into a dependent role rather than promoting meaningful interactions between participants on an equal footing.

Below, we discuss a pilot project that we developed to promote interaction between students in an informal face-to-face situation. The programme comprised structured weekly exchanges between Masters degree students from China, and Australian students learning Chinese. We named this pilot programme, *Culture in Everyday Life*, because its key rationale was to promote an awareness that individuals' expression of cultural norms are manifest in everyday practices such as making requests, accepting apologies and making complaints. The emphasis was on discussion and reflection on everyday practices and behaviours in specific settings in university life. For international students, these everyday practices and interactions are among the most relevant but often the least accessible aspect of Australian culture in general and of the academic culture of Australian universities in particular. Furthermore, these are not practices owned by one particular cultural group, so this allowed for the creation of a 'common ground' between the two populations, allowing students to create a non-threatening 'cultural space' from which to explore and reflect on their own and others' cultural mores and values.

Students met with their partners once a week for a period of six weeks, and each week they were given a different topic. They spoke to each other about the weekly topic, first in Chinese and then in English. Each participant received a weekly worksheet written in both English and Chinese, which was used as a springboard for discussion and as a record of the interaction. The worksheet presented scenarios focused on concrete situations (such as asking for advice, meeting someone at a party, negotiating in the academic setting, and so on). The six topics were: establishing first contacts, developing friendships, expectations in academic settings, what is negotiable in academic settings, seeking help and dealing with conflicting motivations. An example of a worksheet on the topic: 'What is negotiable in academic settings' is given below.

SCENARIO: An undergraduate student does not agree with the mark that the lecturer has given him/her.

1. What?
What would an Australian student do to solve this situation?
What would a Chinese student do if s/he faced a similar situation in China?
What are the main differences?

2. Why?
Try to discover the reasons or values underlying the behaviours or strategies adopted by the Australian and Chinese students trying to solve the problem.

3. How?
What are the phrases you need to use in these situations? List as many as you can think of, in English and Chinese.

4. When and where?
If you encounter a similar problem in a very different situation (with your boss at work, for instance), could you use the same solutions? Why/why not?

We structured the worksheet activities to stimulate reflection not only on what is typically done in a specific social situation, but also on the values that underpin behaviours. For example, on the topic of compliments and apologizing, we asked both parties to discuss the following question: 'What sort of compliments would you accept without feeling embarrassed?' We then gave students the following scenario: You've met someone for the first time and would like to become friends with that person. We asked: How would you compliment others on the following: the clothes they wear; their looks (hairstyle, general appearance); academic achievements; meals they make for guests; meals they make for family; and weight loss. Students were asked to write down both the

Australian and Chinese responses, and to compare them. We further asked them to reflect on whether the noted differences between Australia and China/Taiwan were related to underlying cultural values, and, if so, what values these differences reflect. This is important as a first step in recognizing that cultures are systems of interrelated values rather than collections of unprincipled behaviours.

A crucial aspect of the interactions involved students reflecting on the human variables (such as age, socioeconomic status, gender, religion) that play a significant role in modifying expected behaviours. For instance, in relation to the above topic we asked students whether they thought that there are differences between the way men and women accept compliments. (For example, some women don't respond to a compliment about their looks.) To reiterate here, we wanted to problematize the idea of culture as a monolithic construct and to help students become more aware of the heterogeneous nature of groups and societies in an increasingly globalized world. Hence, the focus of the interactions was on developing interpretation rather than enculturation.

For the Chinese students, we organized a focus group discussion following the conclusion of the pilot study. The focus session yielded mixed results. Opinions conveyed during the discussion indicate that the cognitive skills and aims were largely met. Students expressed increased confidence in their ability to understand aspects of Australian culture through a reflection on the university system. Those who had previous experience with the intercultural communication literature seemed to benefit the most, being able to articulate their observations and relate them to previous knowledge and experience. This suggests that preparation activities prior to the meetings would be instrumental in facilitating the exchanges by giving students a clearer understanding of the range of issues involved in culture and communication. Students' opinions indicate clearly that the affective aims were not met to the degree that we hoped, and that the interactions did little to modify entrenched attitudes. For instance, the majority of the Chinese students met with partners who were very interested in the interactions, but the discussion in the focus groups indicated that students came away with similar stereotypes of Australians that they had when they began the programme. Most of the Chinese students showed little ability to avoid generalizations about their partners' cultural norms and behaviours, still viewing them as members of 'the other group' rather than as individuals. This is hardly surprising since students only met for a total of six sessions, too brief a time to get to know their partners on a more personal level. Regardless of this outcome, most students regarded the experience positively.

Programme 3: An exchange programme in the local community

In the third and last case to be addressed in this chapter, we examine 'Spanish in the community', an exchange programme developed for an undergraduate advanced level Spanish language course. The aim of the project was to develop students' skills of interaction with members of the target culture(s) in the community, to enhance their cultural awareness in a way that bridges 'the distance between text and experience, between the cognitive and palpable, between reading about and living, which no amount of textual analysis can close' (Barro, Jordan & Roberts, 1998, p. 83). Moreover, this programme required students to be responsible for their own language learning, undertaking their own research and becoming, as Barro et al. describe, 'ethnographers', combining 'the experience of the ethnographer in the field and a set conceptual framework for cultural analysis with the best practice from communicative and immersion language learning' (p. 80). In this way, cross-cultural communication skills were targeted in addition to cognitive and affective aspects.

Although this programme shared similarities with the mechanics outlined in assignment 2, it differs in several important respects. As this was part of a university course, students' participation in the interactions was mandatory. Volunteer native speakers of Spanish, either individuals or families, were enlisted to work with students on a one-to-one basis, and weekly meetings between students and volunteers were arranged over a period of eight weeks. High priority was given to matching students with volunteers who had common interests, in order to maximize their level of motivation for participating in the programme. Each week the students received a topic to be discussed with the host families, that addressed features of the daily home life of Spanish speaking migrants in Australia and that also elicited memories of their former homeland. A list of the topics explored is given in Table 9.1.

The topics were designed to encourage comparisons between the Australian and Hispanic cultures, and to highlight the cultural similarities as well as the differences that existed, and how these were reflected in language. By exploring these topics with their Spanish-speaking partners, students would thus gain insights into life experiences hitherto unknown to them, such as the migration process,

Table 9.1: Topics in 'Spanish in the community'

Week	Topic
1	Writing letters of introduction to the families (Preparation stage)
2	Making phone calls and organizing meeting (Preparation stage)
3	First contact: Visit and description of hosts
4	The Hispanic family: continuity and change
5	The migration experience
6	National and cultural identity
7	Cultural values
8	Friendships and romance
9	Linguistic varieties of Spanish
10	Non-verbal communication

the reality of life as a member of a cultural minority, or the inter-generational conflict that can arise in migrant families with children born and raised in Australia.

In preparation for the meetings, students were given weekly readings in Spanish for class discussion. The readings took the form of, for example, newspaper articles, poems, short stories or diary entries. Based on these readings, students then devised surveys or questionnaires that they would use as the basis for intensive discussions with the volunteers. Findings from these interactions were then collated and discussed in class the following week. Particular attention was given to the similarities and differences that existed between Spanish speaking people and Australians. These de-briefing sessions were considered to be crucial to avoid possible misunderstandings and, in analysing and interpreting the intercultural communications, helped students gain an understanding of the 'bigger picture'. As a result, a survey conducted at the end of the semester revealed that students were highly positive about the programme. Not only did they welcome the opportunity to interact with native speakers other than their university lecturers and tutors, they also noted that the informal context was less intimidating than their language classes.

The topics selected provided students with a wide range of opportunities to reflect on and compare the conventions operating in their own and other cultures. This understanding enabled them to recognize commonly held stereotypical views and to develop a tolerance of other cultural practices. From classroom discussions it was obvious to instructors that students had gained a more reflexive view of their own culture and were eager to acquire a deeper understanding of Spanish-speaking people in their community. Interestingly, some students reported the initial stage of cultural adaptation, which scholars describe as evoking feelings of euphoria, excitement and satisfaction towards the 'new' culture (Dodd, 1995). Moreover, students became severely critical of Australian cultural practices and demonstrated over-valuation of what they identified as typically Hispanic customs such as the strength of family ties, the centrality of food and hospitality.

From a cognitive perspective, as revealed by responses and class discussions, students were seen to have developed a deeper understanding of the diversity that exists in Hispanic societies and co-cultures. Of greater significance, students were positively surprised to recognize the many similarities that Australian and some Hispanic societies share with regard to cultural values and life experiences. The positive outcome from this realization was that students acquired a perspective that does not rely on exotic or folkloric customs commonly illustrated by textbooks and other instructional materials, and, instead of focusing on the experience of 'Otherness', came to recognize the common elements that make up the human experience in its many guises.

Conclusion

In Australia today, attempts to progress from 'weak' to 'strong' internationalization are often frustrated not only by the problem of resources but also by the culture of 'monocultural chauvinism' that continues to pervade universities. Despite the recognized benefits of internationalizing the university, there are, to date, very few concrete models outlining how to integrate the values of cultural literacy and the skills of intercultural competence into educational experiences. In this chapter, we have argued that in terms of desirable outcomes, internationalization can and should be essentially about providing students prospects for 'transformative encounters' (Sanderson, 2002, p. 145) with international dimensions of social, academic and cultural life. Internationalization, in this sense, involves a more mutually engaging and interculturally inclusive dimension to grassroots learning and teaching. It entails providing learners with the tools for acquiring *competences* in managing their social, academic, cultural and work life in a globalized and internationalized world. This study has argued that we need to address these issues by improving opportunities for students from disparate cultural background to interact by exploring their own, and others', cultural identity and the cultural values that underlie behaviours.

Interaction, we have stressed, needs to be mutually and interculturally engaging of various communities within and around the university. Through programmes and practices that combine the imperative of developing intercultural competence and the imperative of providing opportunity for interactions between and among local and international students, our programmes have aimed to create spaces for student discussion and reflection on interculturality in the university setting. Hence, the focus is on the university's commitment to internationalize the academic international experience, both for those local students who are unable to enjoy the benefits of study-abroad programmes and for international fee-paying students who might normally have limited opportunities to explore issues of interculturality with local students (and so end up having an 'international' rather than an 'intercultural' experience).

We acknowledge that our own attempts are indeed 'piecemeal' and are certainly not a panacea for all the problems and limitations that accompany the internationalizing of the curriculum. Nevertheless, we hope that these models stimulate others to share their methods in this vital area of higher education. We would suggest that this view of the importance of developing intercultural competence as the key focus of internationalizing the curriculum, should be implemented comprehensively across academic structures, not in the existing piecemeal way we find today.

Reflection questions

1. To what extent are the experiences and problems of 'internationalizing the curriculum' in your context similar to the ones described in this chapter?
2. How might the case studies described in this chapter be modified to fit your context and your discipline?
3. What are some further ways in which we can encourage meaningful contacts between students of different cultural backgrounds?

Notes

1. The top ten source countries from 2002 to 2005 were (in order): China, India, Korea, Hong Kong, Malaysia, Japan, Thailand, Indonesia, USA and Singapore.

In 2005, 344,815 full-fee paying students were enrolled in Australian higher education. (http:// www.aei.dest.gov.au).

2. Some other examples of group essay topics include the following: Politeness strategies: why are Chinese students perceived to be impolite?; A comparative study of international students reactions to touch; Culture shock and international students; The factors that impact on homestay students' ability to culturally adapt to a new environment; and a cross-cultural comparison of lying and non-verbal communication.

Resources

Dlaska, A. (2000). Integrating culture and language learning in institution-wide language programmes. *Language, Culture and Curriculum, 13*(3), 247–63.
This paper is an interesting and thoughtful examination of some of the key issues involved in integrating intercultural skills into the university curriculum.

Knight, J. (1999). Internationalisation of higher education. In J. Knight & H. de Wit (eds). *Quality and internationalisation in higher education* (pp. 13–28). Paris: OECD.
This book presents a good overview of the issues that universities faced in the attempt to respond to the challenges of internationalization.

Kramsch, C. (1991). Culture in language learning: A view from the United States. In K. de Bot, R. B. Ginsberg & C. Kramsch (eds), *Foreign language research in cross-cultural perspective* (pp. 217–40). Amsterdam: Benjamins.
This book is perhaps the most cited work to date on the relationship between language and intercultural competence.

Yang, R. (2002). University internationalisation: Its meanings, rationales and implications. *Intercultural Education, 13*(1), 81–95.
This is a comprehensive exploration of the manifestation of the concept of 'internationalization' in the university setting.

10
Afrikaners and Arabs: Negotiating Course Delivery in a Blended Learning Context

Johannes C. Cronjé

This chapter tells what was learnt when three instructors from the University of Pretoria were involved in the design, development and presentation of eighteen months of coursework for a Master's degree programme in ICT for Education at the Sudan University of Science and Technology in Khartoum; and adapted a programme presented in one country to deal with the challenges of teaching at an institution thousands of kilometres away, where technological infrastructure, time, policy, language, religion and even the weather played an often disruptive role. Examples are shared to demonstrate how the instructors and students negotiated shared understanding of issues of teaching and learning, as well as the nature of learning tasks and assessment criteria in cross-cultural situations.

Introduction

From 2002 to 2004 Johannes Cronjé, Dolf Steyn and Seugnet Blignaut from the University of Pretoria, South Africa designed, developed and presented a tutored Master's degree in ICT for Education for twelve selected students of the Sudan University of Science and Technology (SUST), Khartoum. This chapter will show how seven assumptions from the literature on online learning were used to design the course, and Hofstede's (2001) dimensions of culture were used in interpreting the experiences of the instructors and students. The chapter reflects on the cross-cultural communicative experiences of professors and students as they negotiated shared understanding of issues of teaching and learning, as well as on the nature of learning tasks and assessment criteria in cross-cultural situations. The lessons learnt are related to the seven assumptions, and recommendations follow about presenting Internet-supported courses across cultural boundaries.

Context

The participating institutions are at opposite extremes in cultural and geographical terms. Pretoria is a predominantly Christian city, in a relatively wealthy emerging economy; Khartoum is a predominantly Muslim city in a relatively poor, war-torn developing economy. Geographically, Sudan is in the north of Africa, while South Africa lies at the southern tip of the continent.

The course described here was an adapted version of the University of Pretoria's Masters' degree programme in Computer-Integrated Education, which had been presented for ten years as blended contact/online distance qualification. The stated objective of the UP Masters' programme is to develop students to become consultants in the field of computers in education and training. Graduates should be able to analyse learning needs and develop a solution; they should be able to work at micro-level in a classroom, or at macro-level in a district, both in the school system and in adult learning. Thus the course combines ICT skills with management skills and teaching skills. SUST wanted to produce graduates to pioneer the successful integration of computers in the school system in Sudan, while making their students competent in English in order to be internationally competitive.

For the duration of the Khartoum course Professor Iskander, a US expatriate English professor, provided support in Sudan; a team of three South African lecturers took turns to travel to Khartoum for short periods of face-to-face teaching, with online contact in between. Two Sudanese Masters' students in computer science trained the students in computer literacy and provided technical support.

Theoretical background

We had to recognize that our 'white middle-class' approach was not culturally neutral (Bowers & Flinders, 1990) and develop shared meaning with the students. Bonham et al. (1995) propose constructivism as a useful worldview for approaching cultural problems in distance education: 'A teacher who wishes to have a useful, comfortable climate for interaction and learning will do well to remember that all culture is created by group negotiation and not by authority's fiat' (Bonham et al., 1995). This echoes Holliday's (1994) call for sustainability through sensitivity to local circumstances and the parameters of local institutions. The design and development of the programme was based on an integration of Merrill's (1991) six guidelines for instructional design, five principles of constructivism suggested by Brooks and Brooks (1993), and key suggestions about teaching across national borders from Daniels (1999), as synthesized by Cronjé (2006, pp. 285–6):

1. The curriculum should be designed in such a way that it provides relevant experiences from which students can construct their own learning.
2. Interpretation is personal and the student's point of view must be valued, but not at the expense of primary concepts.
3. Active learning tasks should incorporate assessment strategies that determine the extent to which experience has been converted into skills.
4. Multiple collaborative perspectives should be focused on primary concepts.
5. The curriculum should be adapted 'on the fly' if the real-life situation demands it.
6. Testing should be unobtrusive and focused on determining areas where the student should improve.
7. Administrative flexibility should be designed into the system from the outset.

Our pedagogical approach integrated constructivism and objectivism (Jonassen, 1991). Constructivism holds that learners construct meaning in their minds, while objectivism argues that objective reality exists outside the learner and must be taught. We believe that the two are not exclusive but complementary, and should be integrated, as is shown in *Figure* 10.1. Plotting the two complementary approaches at right angles produces four quadrants. One quadrant, *construction*, is high in constructivist features, where learners are encouraged to construct their own meaning with support, rather than instructions, from the facilitator. If learners are taught using the 'classical' lesson format, the instructor seems to '*inject*' direct instruction to the learner with minimum interference. This is the domain of rote learning. If there is little evidence either of direct instruction, or of planned scaffolding then learners learn by trial-and-error through *immersion* in the 'deep end' in the quadrant of serendipitous experience. We placed our design in the quadrant of *integration*, where, based on a specific desired outcome we would use either direct instruction in the form of a lecture, or we would allow the learners to construct their own meaning in the form of a learning task.

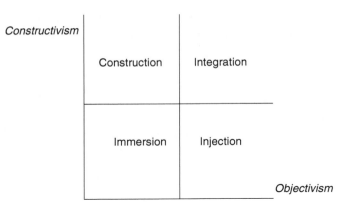

Figure 10.1: An integration of constructivism and objectivism
Source: (Cronjé, 2006)

Table 10.1: Hofstede's (2001) dimensions of culture for Sudan, South Africa and the USA

Dimension	Description (Hofstede, 2001, pp. xix–xx)	SA	ARA	US
Power distance	*'the extent to which the less powerful members of organizations and institutions accept and expect that power is distributed unequally'*	49	80	40
Uncertainty avoidance	*'the extent to which a culture programs its members to feel . . . uncomfortable . . . in unstructured situations'*	49	68	46
Individualism	*'the degree to which individuals are supposed to look after themselves* (In contrast, people in a collectivist culture *'remain integrated into groups, usually around the family')*	65	38	91
Masculinity	*'refers to the distribution of emotional roles between the genders . . . it opposes "tough" masculine to "tender" feminine societies'*	63	53	62

For the interpretation of our multicultural experience we reviewed the work of Hofstede (2001), who analysed the attitudes and values of workers of the IBM Corporation in 72 countries. Four of Hofstede's (2001) cultural dimensions are listed in Table 10.1; these guided us in interpreting the cross-cultural aspect of the programme. The figures in Table 10.1 are for South Africa, the Arabic-speaking region (which includes Sudan) and the USA (for comparison). The table suggests that compared to South Africa, Sudanese culture is high in power distance and uncertainty avoidance, collectivist rather than individualist, and 'tender' rather than 'tough'.

While Hofstede's work focuses on cultural differences and a static model of culture, this chapter uncovers the *commonalities* which were *constructed* as we negotiated the delivery of this course. Despite strong cultural differences, values and beliefs both students and instructors actively engaged to reach out across them.

Methods

Planning the course

Six months before the project started SUST recruited and selected a group of their strongest education finalists in various subject areas – five men and seven women, all unmarried, ranging in age from 23 to 27 – and put them through an intensive English language and end-user computing course. The author visited Khartoum to meet with the students, inspect the facilities and plan the presentation of the courses for the next year. The idea was to work in a way very similar to what was done in Pretoria, with contact sessions roughly every eight weeks. Contact sessions would last four or five days – the few days were spent examining work of the current course, and the last day focused on briefing students for the next course. The original programme schedule is shown

Table 10.2: An early version of the programme schedule

Date	Course (* = optional, select any 3)
9 Jan to 16 Feb	Evaluation of software and its effect on learning
11 Feb ongoing	Research methodology
28 Feb to 12 Apr	Learning theory for computers in education
23 Mar to 1 May	Tutorials, drills, simulations, games
24 May to 1 June	Instructional design
2 June to 15 July	*Authorware* (Systems and tools for authors)*
August	Project management and implementation of CIE*
September	Advanced use of databases
October	Computers in the classroom
Nov, Dec, Jan	Research project
Feb	ICT for schools and universities*
March	Computers in distance education (e-learning)
April	Computer-based testing*
May/June	Catch up

in Table 10.2. The students were enthusiastic, but concerned about their lack of English language skills. SUST had the necessary infrastructure to allow the course, but the Internet connection was painfully slow so most of the digital material was via CD-ROM, while Internet use was predominantly e-mail based.

Researching the course

Although the main objective of this course was educational, the process of negotiating and evaluating the delivery of the course involved gathering and analysing (mainly qualitative) data from the experience of the author; field notes and preparation material; the project diary; informal discussion, interviews and e-mail exchange with students, local facilitators, local administrators and co-presenters from Pretoria; and electronic artefacts produced by the students in the form of essays, term papers, websites, PowerPoint presentations, Authorware materials and Excel spreadsheets. The analysis (Ryan & Bernard 2000) involved scrutinizing all the products to determine emerging patterns, and relating them to the assumptions derived from the literature. While it is relatively easy to recognize the characteristics of Hofstede's dimensions through observable behaviour, interviews and an analysis of written texts, it is more difficult to see them in artefacts. In this respect Marcus (2000) presents a refinement of Hofstede's dimensions in terms of elements of web interface design. He suggests, for instance, that websites in high power distance countries are characterized by highly structured information, controlled access to information and vertical hierarchies in mental models. Marcus's descriptions of what can be expected for each dimension were used in the interpretation of visual artefacts such as PowerPoint slideshows and Websites.

Outcomes

Getting to know you – the first visit

The scheduled flight into Khartoum for the first contact session landed on a Thursday evening, and brought with it the first intercultural problem: the influence of religion on timetabling. Friday is the Sudanese day of rest – equivalent to a South African Sunday. We had to violate the day of rest, but we also worked on Sunday, as the return flight was at 03:40 on Wednesday morning; thus both parties gave up their religious holidays in mutual compromise.

The second problem was administrative. South African lectures start at 08:00; in Khartoum it is 09:00 and Friday transport is unreliable. Thus the course could only start at 10:30 on the first morning. At 11:00 breakfast was served, again interrupting proceedings. The fast Internet connection on the Friday (because businesses were closed) allowed us to register all students on a Yahoogroups mailing list – our main communication between contact sessions. At 13:00 we broke for lunch, and upon reassembly at 14:00 some did not return, as they were in prayer. We had to redesign a Sudan-friendly timetable for each day.

On day two we started at 09:00, working on the first project: evaluating a piece of educational software, selected at random from various international titles, for its suitability in a Sudanese setting. Students worked in groups of three, taking turns to be the principal evaluator, the supporter and the critic. Thus, every student did a close evaluation of one title, but actually engaged with three titles. A day was set for students to give individual talks, supported by PowerPoint presentations, about the results of their software evaluations.

As expected in a high power-distance context, students sat down obediently and worked methodically through the software. However, by lunchtime they showed discomfort with something. After a discussion among themselves they approached me and mentioned that it was disconcerting that someone with no knowledge of Sudan expected them to evaluate foreign software and then intended to assess their evaluations. They did not really trust their local English-speaking facilitator to speak on their behalf, and preferred to speak to me alone. They interpreted my words to one another, but struggled to express their own opinions. After much discussion among them, one or two of them would translate it into broken English. I would rephrase and ask if that was what they meant. They would discuss my version and make adjustments, until we were happy that we understood each other's concerns.

After some discussion it became evident that this was not a power-distance issue. The main reason for their discomfort was not so much that they did not trust my integrity or ability as evaluator; it was more a question of uncertainty avoidance. They had never before been assessed by a foreigner, and thus found it difficult to know how they were to prepare for such an evaluation. This problem was solved when the students and I sat down to draw up an assessment rubric together. It was also agreed that the whole class would assign the grades, and I would provide input, but would respect the final peer grade. In Pretoria I often asked for peer assessment, but I usually constructed the rubric myself. From what I learnt here I have subsequently moved to using negotiated rubrics in Pretoria too, if at all feasible.

We also decided to modify the schedule of the contact session so that there would not be class on the third day. Part of the support I received from SUST was the provision of a full-time driver with a sixteen-seat minibus. We therefore appointed a committee of students to design an itinerary to take me on a trip of the greater Khartoum area so that I could get a good idea of local conditions. The Sunday trip included visits to the University of Khartoum music department and a typical boys' school and a typical girls' school. Figure 10.2 shows computer laboratories from the boys' and girls' schools. We also visited the private homes of two students, one in a very wealthy area and the other in a less wealthy area. In keeping with the constructivist nature of the programme, the trip made me the learner and the students the teachers. I felt that I had developed a much better sense of what was happening and would, indeed, be better able to assess the students' evaluations, and to help them to understand what to look for in an evaluation of educational software for its appropriateness in a given situation.

The students' discomfort with their local facilitator is hard to understand in terms of power-distance. Were they more intimidated by a local professor, or less? As the year progressed it turned out that it had little to do with culture, but more with their dissatisfaction with the support that they were getting from SUST at that stage. As a SUST employee the local facilitator was not trusted, although as the programme progressed students' confidence in their own institution was restored.

The students spent Monday morning presenting mini-workshops on general topics they received on Friday, and the afternoon evaluating software for their feedback sessions on Tuesday. They had been divided into groups of three: each one facilitated an evaluation of one piece of software, supported by two peers. Peer support allowed them to formulate their English better, while rubrics allayed their uncertainty. My abstention from assigning grades challenged their high power-distance

Figure 10.2: School computer laboratories in Khartoum, Sudan

by forcing them to take responsibility: paradoxically it seems that one has to use power to give power. My abstention led to long periods of silence as students formulated their comments in English, and then gathered the courage to voice them in front of their peers; although their confidence increased considerably as they received affirmative feedback on their workshop presentations. A problem that I had anticipated was that the peer grades tended to run in a very small range of 'satisfactory', 'good' and 'very good' with the group tending to self-moderate away from the high and low extremes. Also, because the students had worked together in groups to prepare their individual projects their slideshows tended to be very similar in form and content and only the pre-set themes of PowerPoint varied.

Students were reluctant to select any of the Sudanese programmes on the market, or those made by the SUST multimedia section. Instead they chose commercial titles from the Davidson, Dorling Kindersley and Jumpstart stables, as well as a few titles produced by UP students: discussion with the students revealed that they already knew the local stuff and wanted to see what was out there. Two students independently evaluating *Reader Rabbit* found it motivational and useful for Sudanese learners. Both commented that the pictures should be more carefully matched to the text, but had no problem with the ethnic biases of the pictures.

At this point students' body language indicated great unease, and it became clear that they required very clear instructions and a very detailed examination rubric. Because communication was difficult and bandwidth was limited, it would have to be presented to them before I left, as the exams would be term papers on evaluations of the software with real learners. I constructed a rubric and an essay template, and we calibrated by working through an essay by a UP student, assessing it point-by-point and adjusting where necessary. I divided the students into support groups of three to evaluate one another's work using the rubric, before the author would have a last chance to improve the essay and submit it together with a self-assessment.

As it turned out, although the students were slightly more generous with their grades than I was, in only two cases did the discrepancy exceed 5 per cent. In both cases the students under-evaluated themselves, which is typical of the self-assessment of high achievers. The high correlation of grades was probably because the rubric had 54 items on a Likert scale, adding up to 200, with little room for flexibility. Combined with the template it restricted creativity; thus, the students felt more comfortable about the assessment, but I felt less comfortable with the spread of the grades, and the 'mechanical' quality of the resultant essays. Students adhered rigidly to the the example and worked directly to the rubric with little creativity.

Nevertheless, the essays provided valuable insights into the students' interpretation of a multicultural situation. The target populations of the research were Sudanese Arab, yet no student commented on any cultural factors: students had no problems with the appearance of snow in winter scenes, or with the Easter Bunny or Santa Claus as characters in the children's programmes. Not even intensive questioning during a focus group in a subsequent session raised any comment on the appropriateness of the symbolism and iconography of the programmes under evaluation. The students appeared to be concerned with the pedagogy and subject content, rather than with the superficial cultural features of the programmes.

Cool KAT – the second visit

Technical difficulties in the interim period meant that much of the student preparation for the second course was not done. Because of infrastructure constraints at the SUST campus the second contact session took place at the recently completed Khartoum Academy of Technology (KAT). At this point the students were anxious and frustrated because their work had not been completed, and they were unhappy about having disappointed me. We therefore adjusted the curriculum so that much of what the students should have read as homework would be presented as workshops or lectures. The high bandwidth of KAT allowed students to access materials and prepare mini-workshops more easily. Class was extended from 09:00 to 21:00, and I sent my full-time driver to pick students up from their homes in the 16-seater minibus to avoid late arrivals due to transport problems.

The KAT facility had an open-plan kiosk and Internet café in its foyer, where much communication took place between the students and me. Representatives from the Education Faculty visited us and showed much interest. It became clear that what the students saw as lack of support from SUST was simply the administrative lag that happens at any large institution. For example, they were promised a computer laboratory, but it had not materialized: the money was available and earmarked, but the builders were still working on another project.

It became very clear that the language barrier was greater than had been expected. From observing the students working in the Internet café and on the other computers, I could see that they were bright, enthusiastic, hard-working and dedicated. It was just difficult, without knowing

Arabic, to obtain verbal information from them, and using written tests and spoken presentations to assess their learning would disadvantage them unfairly. A way had to be found to measure directly what they were doing and learning, instead of using essays and tests. Since English was hard for them to understand, a way also had to be found to allow them more time to digest what they heard. This was overcome by putting students in groups to support one another. Frequent breakout group sessions ensured that students could support each other's understanding.

Another way in which common understanding was facilitated was through cooperative prototyping. Students were asked to produce prototypes of any tasks that they would have to complete during the time when I was away, so that any discrepancies between that which was required, and that which the student had in mind, could be ironed out at an early stage. I passed this information on when I briefed the other two instructors before their visits, and I also implemented the same strategy later in Pretoria. Work for two courses was covered in the second contact session. One was on *Tutorials, Drills, Simulations and Games*, and the other on *Learning Theory for Computers In Education*.

The course on *Tutorials, Drills, Simulations and Games* was based entirely on the textbook, and the challenge was for students to show mastery of the content, without resorting to an essay, which would simply summarize the chapters. Since the programme was about computers in education I also had to attend to their computer application skills. There were two learning tasks. For the first, students worked in groups of three to produce macro-enabled spreadsheets with questions and tick boxes, that would produce a graph suggesting the extent to which a given situation would best be served by a tutorial, drill, simulation or game. Students were divided into expert groups to study a chapter on each of these types of activitiy, and discuss the content. Each group then had to formulate a set of questions that would indicate their specific modality as a solution. Then home groups were formed with one member from each expert group to integrate these questions into a single spreadsheet. The advantage of this group work was that students could once again assist one another in understanding the English, and could help in the acquisition of spreadsheet skills. For individual tasks students had to produce PowerPoint slideshows called *Tutorials, Drills, Simulations and Games*. The slideshows had to contain the essential information about each type, and also provide an example. Students could use branching, linking and macros to make small examples of each type. Students produced small prototypes during the contact sessions and submitted the full individual project via e-mail.

The use of home groups and expert groups meant that the questions used on the spreadsheets were nearly identical. The home groups, however, showed some originality in the design of the sheets. Discussions with the students, as well as observation of the groups at work, showed that they had indeed mastered the subject matter. Evidence from the individual students' PowerPoint slideshows also indicated that all the theory had been adequately explored.

For the learning theory course, the students were to design a lesson using Gagne's (1985) 'events of instruction' as a basis (an essentially instructivist exercise). Then they were to turn it into a constructivist learning event, present it to a target population and record the event on video. From the video they had to extract clips for a PowerPoint presentation explaining what they had learnt. Finally they had to write a 3,000 word essay giving the learning theory rationale for their design and evaluation and presenting their findings.

Much time was spent discussing appropriate subject areas, topics and presentation styles. They then completed a 'learning event protocol template' and discussed it in their groups. We used the term 'learning event protocol' to distinguish it from the traditional 'lesson plan', and to emphasize the constructivist nature of the task. Finally each student presented the learning event protocol for feedback from all of us. The first set of protocols tended to be very instructivist and I suggested more constructivist angles. Then a second round followed: students would work on the protocols for three more weeks before submitting them via e-mail. A typical learning event protocol would contain the subject area, and the expected outcomes. Then it would have a table containing running time in minutes, learner activity, facilitator activity, resources and the rationale for what occurs in that time slot.

The learning event protocol ensured that we got a good idea of the lesson before it was presented; thus the students' high level of uncertainty avoidance was accommodated. The final e-mail submission was critiqued via a return e-mail sent to the entire group, so that they could learn from one another. In subsequent courses students came to expect collective, rather than individual feedback, which seems to fit Hofstede's classification of the Arab-speaking region as collectivist rather than individualistic.

The students submitted their final essays via e-mail as Word documents. The essays were reasonable, but the literature survey components of the essays contained severe 'cut-and-paste' plagiarism (which

I found to be a frequent escape route also for UP students with language problems). This had to be dealt with sensitively, but firmly.

Nevertheless, the findings, conclusions and recommendations were very good, and students made excellent use of tables, graphs and photographs to illustrate what they were saying. Once again it allowed me to gain some insight into what happens in Sudanese schools. I got to know aspects concerning school financing in Sudanese schools, their physical setup, their timetables, and their subjects. This was particularly useful to me in preparation for the penultimate course on the implementation of computers in schools.

The third visit – KAT under a hot tin roof

The students' PowerPoint-assisted feedback sessions took place during the third contact visit – once again conducted at KAT. The slideshows showed that the students had mastered the essential tenets of instructivist learning and of constructivism. The videos themselves showed that the students had developed some visual literacy – were able to use long, establishing shots, medium shots and close-ups to good effect, and were able to add appropriate sub-titles to specific scenes, as can be seen from the screen shots in Figure 10.3.

The *Instructional Design* course was to prepare students for the *Authoring Course* that would follow. The visit was characterized by extreme heat and power-cuts as a result of over-use of air conditioners throughout the city. Computers and data projectors could hardly be used. Consequently the practical component on instructional design was conducted on large flip-chart paper with wax crayons: students would submit the electronic copies via e-mail later. Initially I sent the comments to each individual using the 'reply' feature of my e-mail

Figure 10.3: Screenshots from a student video

program. Once again students spontaneously asked via an e-mail to the Yahoogroups list to have the critiques of their documents sent to all, so that they could learn from my comments on the work of their peers.

We had to adjust the time-table once again to make the best use of electricity when it came on. Whenever there was any electricity we would stop everything to listen to a PowerPoint and feedback session on the learning theory course; when the power went off, we continued with instructional design.

New faces – visits four and five

The *Authoring* course, using *Macromedia Authorware*, was presented in Khartoum by a Canadian facilitator not connected to the UP project. He had been contracted by SUST to teach their staff and other students *Authorware*, so it made sense to use him for the Masters' students as well. I set the task, and he taught them *Authorware* so that they could complete it according to my specification. The task was to build a prototype of the course that they had designed during the instructional design course. The students formed part of a larger group and did not receive the individual attention to which they had become accustomed, which may account for their high level of dissatisfaction with the training, and for the fact that they did not complete the assignments for the particular course satisfactorily by the deadline I had set.

To compensate for the shortcomings of the *Authorware* course a second *Authorware* project was added to the *Project Management* course, which followed upon it. Dr Dolf Steyn, who has extensive experience in project management and in *Authorware*, presented the course. He divided the twelve students into two groups of six, who had to run an authoring project that would culminate in a tutorial written in *Authorware*. They had to go through the entire instructional design and authoring process, but this time concentrating on the project-management aspects, identifying at the same time what had gone wrong in their previous *Authorware* projects. Dr Steyn also helped them to complete the abortive individual projects, and negotiated new submission dates on my behalf. I briefed him very carefully before his departure, as he had not been to Khartoum before, and he made a point of getting to know the students and their environment as intimately as time would allow. On my suggestion he accepted their invitations to sleep over in their private homes rather than in the hotels provided, and thus gained their trust very quickly, leading to requests from the students that he should present the course on the use of databases for education as well. By this time a pattern had developed: students would discuss their learning among themselves in the times between contact sessions, and then decide who would e-mail me with various requests (cc to Dr Steyn).

The learning task for the *Database* course was for learners to construct a database that would provide information about the appropriate use of computers in constructivist and instructivist settings. The task was designed specifically to cover some of the information that may have been missed during the course dedicated to objectivism and constructivism, as that course had been disrupted by technical difficulties.

While Dr Steyn was negotiating with the students about the submission dates for his project, the students informed him that the time of the next visit would be inappropriate as it would coincide with the month of Ramadan. We therefore agreed to postpone the visit and to present the next course (on Internet-based distance education) entirely online. This was not unusual and we did the same in Pretoria, as it makes sense to teach about distance education via distance education. However, the low bandwidth of SUST made it difficult for the students to do their projects there. Most of them opted either to arrange to work at KAT, or to work at commercial Internet cafés close to their homes, which was sometimes cheaper than travelling to the University where they would find it hard to work anyway.

Two for the price of one – the penultimate visit

The penultimate course, *Computers in Schools*, took the form of a public workshop, attended by decision-makers in the Sudanese education system, as well as principals of schools in the greater Khartoum area. The workshop took delegates through the process of strategic planning for computers in schools. At various points in the workshop students presented examples of their best work produced during the year, discussing the implications of the work that they had created, and its suitability in a Sudanese context. The students had very little practical teaching experience. Since I was completely unfamiliar with the Sudanese situation it made much sense for me to stick to 'academic' issues concerning strategy, and then to allow the principals and decision-makers to fill in the details about local policy issues. I presented the course, accompanied for the first time by a female professor, Professor Seugnet Blignaut.

Farewell – the last visit

Seugnet stayed on a few days more to present the last course, *Computers in the Classroom*, and returned to Khartoum again eight weeks later to assess it and present an introduction to thesis writing. She also acted as examiner for the course on computers in schools that I had started. She was very well accepted by the students. She remarked, however, that, whenever she walked in the streets of Khartoum she was stared at to such an extent that she thought that it was the inhabitants, not she, who were the tourists learning of foreign things. Once again this highlights the fact that in a constructivist intercultural environment both teacher and students learn from each other. The seven female students in the class found it a particular treat to have a female teacher, and shared with her many of their feelings about the course, and about their forthcoming marriages, their husbands, and the role of women in Sudanese society generally. It was she, perhaps, who came closest to the students in terms of crossing the barrier between the professor and the student. This could be explained by Hofstede's putting Sudan closer to the femininity side of his masculinity–femininity scale than South Africa or the United States; or it could simply be that she is the only woman professor with whom the students had had any contact during the programme. Also, by this time, more than a year into the course, students' self-confidence and language skills had also improved dramatically.

Discussion

From the narrative above we will now address some key questions concerning this intercultural experience.

What are the design issues to consider when presenting a blended learning programme across barriers of distance, language, religion and culture?

Students' comments on the second day showed that it would be inappropriate for outsiders to enforce rigid behaviours on them. Thus the curriculum should be designed in such a way that it provides relevant experiences from which students can construct their own learning.

The process of iterative design and prototyping of assignments during contact sessions, with students completing work for submission via e-mail, showed that it was necessary for students to be helped initially, to prevent them from misinterpreting the work, and then spending three or four weeks doing work that would be unacceptable. When students were left to their own devices for the *Authorware* course, they found that there was too little guidance. Thus it becomes clear that interpretation is personal and the student's point of view must be valued.

The spreadsheet tasks and the movies, in particular, showed that one could evaluate student performance adequately without using term papers and tests. These methods of evaluation proved so successful in Sudan that they have subsequently been incorporated in the Pretoria course. Active learning tasks should incorporate assessment strategies that determine the extent to which experience has been converted into skills. Testing should be unobtrusive and focused on determining areas where the student should improve.

The spreadsheet tasks, and the workshops with the school principals and decision-makers, showed that multiple collaborative perspectives should be focused on primary concepts. The instructors provided the primary concepts; the students, and the senior educators provided the collaborative perspectives.

The curriculum had to be re-adjusted frequently: to catch up work that was not done, to prevent possible misunderstandings, and to reinforce important concepts.

Constant mismatches between University timetables, technological considerations, and even the weather (with its consequent power-cuts) mean that administrative flexibility should be designed into the system from the outset.

The most important consideration, however, is that the main aim, when designing a blended learning programme across barriers of distance, language, religion and culture, should be to create an atmosphere of mutual trust.

To what extent does Hofstede's theory of cultural dimensions help understand the experiences of the participants?

Hofstede's dimension of *power distance* explained students' lack of self-confidence and their reluctance in taking initiative, letting the apparently more powerful professor take the responsibility. The *Authorware* course, where students were expected to work outside the clearly defined parameters of the Masters' course underscored their need for strong guidance. There seems to be a link between high power distance and *uncertainty avoidance*, which would explain why students required much guidance in terms of requirements and assessment rubrics, and why the student products tended to be very similar in the early stages of the programme.

The constant challenge that the professors made to the students to take initiative and to take risks led students to rely on one another, which was to be expected in a highly *collective* cultural context (c.f. Coleman, 1987; Holliday and Zikri, 1988). It could be that the absence of the anticipated autocratic leadership and the high levels of uncertainty also forced the students to rely upon one another, also to help with translation and negotiation.

The two cultures were closest together on the *masculinity/femininity* dimension and both almost in the middle of the range, which explains why not much was observed in terms of constructing new common understanding in terms of this dimension. However, I believe that bringing Seugnet on board helped us contact the female population better. Dolf and I stayed with the male students in their homes. Sudanese homes are clearly divided into male, female and common areas, which meant that we saw only the male and the common areas. Seugnet, on the other hand, visited students at their homes and saw the female and common areas. There may have been cultural issues of which we were not consciously aware, that are shared by men on the one hand, and by women on the other, and that were therefore covered fully because the presenters were representative of both sexes, supporting a more holistic understanding.

How does a constructivist presentation format contribute to the creation of shared meaning?

The constructivist approach allowed students a large degree of flexibility and forced them to explore their own situation. The products that they created allowed the professors to gain insight not only into the meaning that the students constructed, but also into the context within which the students operated. Video clips, photographs and descriptive essays became valuable artifacts for us to understand what the students were working with, and constructing them enabled the students to gain first-hand experience of the practical implications of what they were learning. The learning that the professors did was essential in allowing us to adjust the curriculum constantly to make it sensitive to local needs. The students also learnt how to alert us in time to aspects of concern, such as the implications of Ramadan. The most common mechanism that developed was the one of students huddling together, discussing, and then coming forward with an individual doing the talking, supported by the rest.

How does one assess in this situation?

Fair assessment using traditional tests and term papers was impossible. Portfolio assessment became the obvious choice, because of the rich data it provides, and the broad basis of negotiation it allows. The purpose of the assessment was not to exclude students (in other words to let them fail) but to understand their progress, and to determine what skills needed refining (Johnston, 2004). Our brief was to assist SUST to develop Masters' students who could develop the implementation of computers in schools in Sudan. Our end product was not just graduates, but people with a clearly defined set of consultation skills. We had to be sure that they would be competent to train more teachers to work with computers in schools. Instead of standardized, quantitative testing we did continuous qualitative evaluation. We did not need a binary answer or a percentage. We needed to know what skills students had acquired, and what skills they still needed. Thus holistic, qualitative assessment allowed more sensitivity to cross cultural issues.

Reflection questions

1. To what extent is the success or failure of a cross-cultural course dependent on the people who presented it? In our case, the three presenters knew each other well, deliberately dovetailed their presentations and briefed and debriefed one another before and after each contact visit. Would the same result have been obtained if they had been from different home institutions?
2. Should one design explicitly for Hofstede's dimensions of culture? For example, should one design much more comprehensive rubrics in order to avoid stressing students who are uncomfortable with uncertainty? Or should one deliberately give vague instructions to challenge students in high uncertainty avoidance cultures? In our case we did a combination of both. How would you design for cultural diversity?
3. How much scaffolding is required for constructivist learning in multicultural environments? Sometimes it seemed that too much scaffolding led to identical products; yet too little scaffolding led to panic, under-achievement and non-completion. Can you think of examples where students in your context have been over- or under-scaffolded? To what extent do you think scaffolding is dependent on culture, as opposed to being a pedagogical issue that depends on existing knowledge?

Resources

The textbook for the programme was:
Alessi, S. M. & Trollip, S. (2001). *Multimedia for learning: Methods and development*, 3rd edn. Boston: Allyn and Bacon.

This resource formed the textbook for the ICT master programme. http://www. geert-hofstede.com/
This website explains Hofstede's cultural dimensions.
The basis of our four-quadrant model of integrating constructivism with objectivism can be viewed at http://it.coe.uga.edu/itforum/paper48/paper48.htm
A number of examples of courses presented in South Africa can be seen at http://hagar.up.ac.za/catts/abchome.html

Acknowledgements

The work of Professor Seugnet Blignaut, Dr Dolf Steyn and the twelve students from Sudan is acknowledged with deep gratitude; as is the financial support of UNESCO-IICBA

11
Assessing Intercultural Dialogue: the German 'Wald' and the Canadian 'Forest'

Ulf Schuetze

This chapter presents a matrix of assessment criteria based on the praxis of an online second language course (German/English) that used WebCT to create a virtual learning environment fostering cross-cultural student–student dialogue. The analysis of the dialogue shows that students who asked wh-questions, drew on personal experience, argued emotionally, gave examples and brought new material to the course discussed the complexity of the themes to the fullest. In reference to studies in intercultural communication, these types of assessment criteria can be seen as part of an intercultural communicative competence.

Introduction

This chapter outlines an attempt to assess online intercultural dialogue – a rather daunting task, as pointed out by Belz and Müller-Hartmann (2003), who studied online interaction between a German and a US university by comparing requirements for teachers and students at those institutions, e.g., teacher's training, student workloads, systems of learning assessment. They examined patterns of communication using Agar's (1994) notion of 'rich points': points of opportunity when speakers misunderstand each other. These points are an opportunity to learn about and to glimpse into the world of culture; and it was this view of culture as difference that was the premise for my study.

After briefly introducing my teaching context, I will discuss the literature on intercultural communication and on assessment. I will focus on *intercultural communicative competence* as outlined by Byram (1997) and discussed by Alred, Byram and Fleming (2003); and I will distinguish between dimensions of intercultural communicative competence and evidence of that competence. I will then describe a matrix of assessment criteria founded in intercultural communication theory (Schuetze, 2005a, 2005b), that was developed during the course discussed. The aim of the matrix was to find additional evidence of intercultural communicative competence in order to give direct feedback to students. The results of the analysis, that is the application of the matrix to the dialogue of that course, are presented, showing that the use of wh-questions, reference to personal experience or emotion, and use of examples and new material seem to play an important role for students when grasping the complexity of the cultural themes discussed. In the light of online intercultural dialogue, a suggestion is made to include these five criteria as evidence of 'intercultural communicative competence'.

Context

The dialogue discussed in this chapter was generated by students engaging in an online intercultural exchange between second language learners at the University of British Columbia, Canada (German as a second language) and the University of Kiel, Germany (English as a second language). The course was taught in the Fall terms of 2003 and 2004, and the participants at both universities were third-year students. During the first six weeks of the term, from the beginning of September to mid-October, students at the University of British Columbia improved their German language skills in face-to-face classroom meetings with the instructor; students at the University of Kiel had taken English in high school, therefore their second language skills were presumably already well developed. The online portion of the course took place during the second six weeks: due to variation in term schedules between Canada and Germany, the exchange took place in the overlapping period from mid-October to the beginning of December.

For this period, all course material was uploaded to WebCT, using Macromedia Dreamweaver to create content pages. A typical content page included a number of files (short videos, pictures, audio recordings, and texts from newspapers), and the content pages were grouped around three themes: Selbstbild/identity; Natur/nature, and Multikulti/multiculturalism. The material could be accessed by students twenty-four hours a day for the duration of the exchange. Communication among students and with instructors also took place via WebCT, using the mail and discussion tools. The mail tool was used to post the weekly assignments, which told students what material to work on and what questions to answer; students used the discussion tool to discuss key issues and concepts and engage in a dialogue. The languages used were German and English: if the course material was in German, the language of communication was German; if it was in English, the language of communication was English. Each student was paired with a student at the other university to work on the assignments together.

This type of course is part of a trend to adopt innovations in information technology for the classroom. Among the advantages of this type of course is a student-centred approach that allows students to critically reflect on cultural differences (Merryfield, 2003; Ziegahn, 2005) and to interact with members of another culture in a virtual environment (Carey, 1999, 2001). Among the difficulties is to find means of assessment (Byram, 1997).

Theoretical background

The premise for this study was to view culture as difference: being intercultural involves experiencing and understanding the conventions, beliefs, values and behaviours of other groups (Alred et al., 2003). Often learners perceive other individuals or groups in terms of assumptions and stereotypes (Byram, Nichols & Stevens, 2001; Garner & Gillingham, 1996; LePage & Tabouret-Keller, 1985); an intercultural speaker is faced with the difficult task of negotiating between his/her own conventions, beliefs, values and behaviours and those of the group with which s/he associates her/himself (Weber, 2003): it becomes a question of social identity. Tajfel (1978, 1981) and Ivanic (1998) point out two overlapping layers of cultural membership: firstly, the relation of the self to a group; secondly, the relation of one group to another group. In second language intercultural communication a third layer is added: the relation between languages, and between cultures expressed in particular words and linguistic forms. In other words, learning and speaking a second language means investigating many forms of social identities, those of other groups as well as one's own.

In the context of acquiring a second or foreign language, Kramsch (1993) argues that the intercultural is a process in which the language learner acquires literacy in the L2 by:

> expressing personal meanings that may put in question those of the speech community. The language that is being learned can be used both to maintain traditional social practices, and to bring about change in the very practices that brought about this learning. (p. 233)

Applying this process to intercultural communication in general, the intercultural speaker becomes an intercultural mediator (Alred et. al., 2003).

The question remains how to assess intercultural dialogue generated by students in an online course. Studies on assessment have focused on the development of an intercultural communicative competence (Byram, 1997). Byram defines intercultural competence as the intercultural speaker's ability to interact with speakers of another culture; to accept that speaker's perspectives and perceptions of the world; to mediate between different perspectives; and to be conscious of these processes. In his work, Byram attributes five dimensions to an intercultural communicative competence:

1. knowledge: 'knowledge of social groups and their products and practices . . . and of the general processes of societal and individual interaction' (p. 94);
2. skills of interpreting and relating: 'ability to mediate between conflicting interpretations of phenomena' (p. 98);
3. skills of discovery and interaction: 'to identify significant references within and across cultures' (p. 99);
4. attitudes: 'willingness . . . to engage with otherness' (p. 91);
5. critical cultural awareness: 'an ability to evaluate perspectives, practices and products . . . to interact and mediate in intercultural exchanges' (p. 101).

One of the challenges for researchers is to find evidence of intercultural communicative competence. Byram (1997) provides three types of evidence for his five dimensions: the learner's factual knowledge about culture; questioning techniques the learner uses when interpreting, relating, discovering, interacting, and mediating; and choices made. The criteria of choice is particularly interesting as it refers to choices made by the learner as to what represents his or the other culture in terms of values, beliefs, customs and conventions. In that sense, it gives evidence to the dimension of critical cultural awareness. One dimension that is very difficult to measure is attitudes. This is particularly interesting in an online course where students are expected to engage in a dialogue with other students. Little (2001) and Littlemore (2001) researched online courses involving e-mail exchanges between students of two different first languages who communicate in their respective second languages. They emphasized two important steps for the success of such exchanges. Firstly, students have to take the initiative to engage in a dialogue and to expand on the number of messages sent, that is, to continue sending messages; secondly, students have to display skills of navigating through messages, that is, to select messages they consider important. These two steps of initiating/expanding and navigating/selecting can assist when measuring students' 'willingness . . . to engage with otherness' (Byram, 1997, p. 91).

In summary, the literature on intercultural communication suggests five kinds of evidence of Byram's (1997) intercultural communicative competence:

1. factual knowledge
2. questioning techniques
3. choices
4. initiative/expansion
5. navigation/selection.

These five points were used as reference points for the assessment matrix. Initially, they were used to assess students in the online course described in this chapter. Although students and instructors found these five points very helpful, the online character of this particular course necessitated additional criteria. Students were given weekly assignments and therefore they relied on direct feedback regarding the dialogues they had generated. Telling them to show more initiative or to ask different questions was just a start.

Objectives

The objective of this study was to assess online intercultural dialogue generated in a virtual learning environment for a second language course. The innovative aspect of this course was its exchange component, which emphasized student–student learning by means of a written exchange (Schuetze, 2005a, 2005b). One of the aims of second language learning is to further the understanding of our own culture as well as that of other countries and regions of the world (Kramsch, 1993, 1998), and intercultural exchange is one means of achieving this goal (Alred et. al, 2003; Byram, 1997; Byram & Buttjes, 1991; Byram et. al., 2001).

In order to assess online intercultural dialogue, a matrix of assessment criteria was developed. Based on five reference points provided by the literature on this topic, the assessment criteria were developed by students and instructors of the course described. They were first drawn up by students, then refined by instructors and discussed with colleagues. Once the list of criteria was completed, it was applied to the dialogue which students generated in the exchange component of the course.

Method

The design of the course was that of an interactive, international course in Canadian/German cultural comparisons, analysing theoretical texts, authentic video, audio and print material reflecting modern German and Canadian culture. For example, students viewed paintings by nineteenth-century German painter Caspar David Friedrich, and their assignment was to describe the function of colour and light in the paintings, and the position of individuals; to discuss the relation between man and nature depicted in the painting in relation to the German context at that time; and to relate this theme to the Canadian context at that time.

Students used the online discussion tool to discuss key issues and concepts and to engage in a dialogue. The messages students generated were monitored by the instructors, and at the end of each week students were given feedback on their dialogues. During the exchange in the Fall of 2003 the instructors of the course noticed that students often made reference to personal experiences rather than analysing the course material in detail. As a result, the instructors sometimes added additional questions to the assignments to guide the students towards a dialogue in which they would discuss the themes in a more analytic way, that is, by drawing on the material provided in the course. At this point, instructors regarded personal comments by students as a distraction. However, students continued to draw on personal experiences in the dialogue, and the evaluations at the end of the term showed that students would have liked a more open discussion. Instructors took up this idea to use personal experiences by students in the course, regarding this as an opportunity to glimpse into culture as difference.

The question arose of how to assess the students' performance in such a scenario. In the Fall of the following year, 2004, students were asked to write a short self-evaluation after each assignment. At the end of the term, students compiled a list of criteria they would have liked to be assessed on. After the course had been completed, the list was discussed among the instructors and was also given to other university teachers for comments and suggestions. This process led to a list of fourteen assessment criteria and four control mechanisms. A positive answer to each of these questions means a higher assessment. The criteria were:

1. Did the speaker listen to the other speaker's argument?
2. Did the speaker ask a yes/no question?
3. Did the speaker ask a wh-question?

4. Did the speaker bring in a new argument?
5. Is the speaker in disagreement?
6. Are the speaker's comments based on emotion?
7. Are the speaker's comments based on rational thought?
8. Did the speaker give an example?
9. Did the speaker draw on personal experience?
10. Did the speaker bring new material to the discussion?
11. Did the speaker suggest an activity?
12. Did the speaker appeal to the other speaker's sense of logic?
13. Did the speaker appeal to the other speaker's five senses?
14. Did the speaker engage in a discussion outside the course?

The criteria interact in multiple ways forming a model for assessment criteria (see Figure 11.1, discussed further in Schuetze, 2005b). At the centre of the list is the student. Applying the reference points in linear order, the question is what choices he or she makes, in what ways he or she takes the initiative, expands, navigates and selects messages.

Applying the criteria in linear order, some of the examples are: 1) Did the student listen to an argument and asked a question? What kind of question? (e.g yes/no question: 'is there much logging in Canada?'; wh-question: 'how much logging is there in Canada?'); 2) Did the student bring in a new argument, was it in disagreement and based on emotion? (e.g., 'I felt embarrassed and sad seeing those clear cuts'); 3) Did the student give an example by bringing in new material? (e.g., 'I found the following website: www.focs.ca'); 4) Did the student suggest an activity outside the course based on one of the five senses? (e.g., 'I will send you a CD I compiled with my favourite meditating songs').

Applying the criteria in circular order (indicated by the solid black circular lines), some of the examples are: Did the student asked a question in disagreement based on personal experience referring to one of the five senses? (e.g: 'I don't think you can say that. In Spain the landscape was deforested to build ships for Karl the Great. The land is barren. Something you have to see with your own eyes because not a thousand words can explain that. I was there last summer. Where, if you don't mind, is the difference to Canada?').

Applying the criteria in spiral order (indicated by the various dotted lines), some of the examples are: 1) Did the student listen and show agreement in his or her response by drawing on familiar material? (e.g., 'Die Schwarzwaldtour ist toll, nicht wahr? Man weiss nie was man als naechstes entdeckt. Wir sollten noch ein bisschen damit spielen. [*The [virtual] tour of the Black Forest is awesome. You never know what you discover next. Let's play more.*]; 2) Did the student bring in a new argument using material within the course? (e.g., 'Märchen gibt es nicht nur im Schwarzwald sondern auch im Erzgebirge.' [*Fairy tales originate not only in the Black Forest but also in the ore mountains*]; 3) Did the student give an example referring to the mind based on thought? (e.g., 'The pine beetle devastates the forest. Studies have shown that it can only be stopped by killing it off. It is the logical thing to do'); 4) Did the student suggest an activity that provoked a reaction, was successful, accountable and feasible? This last example refers to the four control mechanisms on the outside of Figure 11.1.

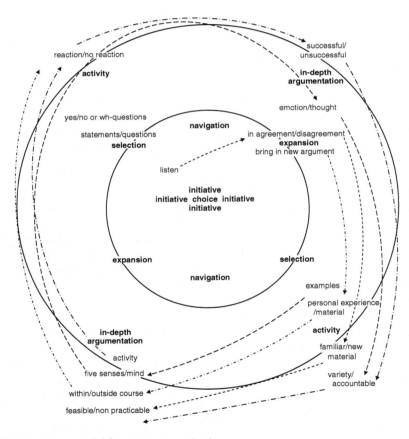

Figure 11.1: Model for assessment criteria

The control mechanisms served as a tool for instructors to ensure that dialogues would stay focused on the topic and the assignment. The four control mechanisms were:

1. Does the speaker react to statements/questions/arguments/examples/activities? (If there was no reaction, instructors reminded students that they are engaged in a dialogue and not a monologue.)
2. Is the speaker using a variety of materials? Is the material accountable? (Students usually asked if they were allowed to bring other material to the discussion. Instructors then told them that it has to be referenced appropriately and to make sure that it is not repetitive.)
3. Are activities feasible or non-practical?
4. Is the speaker successfully engaging in the dialogue? (This mechanism has to be seen in relation to the assignments. Students had to write a minimum number of messages on each assignment. If they terminated their dialogue prematurely, it was considered to be unsuccessful.)

The overall question was in what time frame did the learner achieve what kind of learning through direct exchange with other students. How can this learning be assessed?

The matrix was then applied to the messages generated by students at the University of British Columbia (UBC), Canada and at the University of Kiel (UKiel), Germany in their dialogue with one another. Note that the dialogue was asynchronous, for two reasons. Firstly, there is a nine-hour time difference between the West Coast of Canada and Germany; secondly, the courses at the two universities met on different days. Therefore students had 48 hours to reply to a message.

Outcomes

One of the sub-themes of Natur/nature in the course was 'Mythos Deutscher Wald [the myth of the German forest]/Canadian wilderness'. Students at both universities viewed the paintings 'Kreidefelsen auf Rügen' (1818a) and 'Wanderer über dem Morgennebel' (1818b) by Caspar David Friedrich, which show man in harmony with nature; viewed a short news clip on acid rain entitled 'Waldsterben in Deutschland' (Westdeutscher Rundfunk, 1995); engaged in a virtual tour of the romantic representations of 'Der Schwarzwald' (Tourism Office, 2003); read an excerpt of Catharine Parr Traill's *The backwoods of Canada* (1836) where man/woman struggles with nature; viewed pictures of logging on Vancouver Island in British Columbia (David Suzuki Foundation, 1993); and viewed an advert by the government of British Columbia to promote tourism outlining the endless possibilities to explore the wilderness by canoe, kayak or hiking (Tourism British Columbia, 2003).

The analysis is based on the course in the Fall of 2004. Students were put in pairs (one student from each university) to work on the material and to carry out their assignments together. Dialogue 1 is the beginning of a dialogue generated by students after viewing pictures of logging on Vancouver Island. The assignment was to discuss why forests are logged in British Columbia; why forests are logged/not logged in Germany; and what other purposes the forest serves in Canada as well as Germany. The underlying aim of the assignment was to bring out differences in notions about the forest as it is seen as a 'retreat' in Germany and as it is seen as a 'resource' in Canada.

Dialogue 1

UKiel student: My first thoughts about this topic were that the forest does not mean as much to Canadians as it does to Germans because they [the Canadians] have more of it and maybe that's why they don't appreciate it as much. The pictures about logging on
5 Vancouver Island are shocking. How important is the forest as a resource for Canada?

UBC student: The forest is used as industry here, a big part of the export of British Columbia. I found an article on Clayqout Sound: www.focs.ca. It is about people who fight for keeping the forest as it
10 is and to stop logging on Vancouver Island.

UKiel student: Read the article. If this continues you will be soon in the same situation we are. I mean you won't have much forest left.

UBC student: Yes. However, many jobs and much money will be lost if logging is stopped. We would need to create new industries, e.g., tourism. Then people could use our forest as a retreat. As they do
16 in Germany. Although most of my friends want the adventure. A week along the coast in a kayak.

UKiel student: I have heard that Canadians are tough. Although many Germans look for adventure in Canada as well.

At the beginning of the dialogue the two students talk about resources and the Canadian forest (lines 5–8). The UKiel student refers to emotions when seeing pictures of logging (lines 4–5), the UBC student brings in additional material that he/she found on the Internet (lines 8–10). Both students listen to each other (lines 7, 11, 13) and bring in arguments (lines 11, 13, 14). The dialogue moves on with both of them looking for a solution to using the forest as a resource. The UBC student suggests tourism and mentions the notion of retreat (line 14) using friends as examples (line 15). This reaction is based on personal experience, as is the response by the UKiel student.

This dialogue illustrates how the aspects of resource and retreat were discussed by asking a wh-question (lines 5–6); bringing in arguments (lines 2–4, 11–12, 13–15); adding new material (lines 8–9); drawing on emotions (lines 4/5, 9) and personal experience (line 15). It is the last two points I would like to emphasize as they seem to carry the dialogue. This is evident in another example. Dialogue 2 was generated by two students after engaging in an interactive virtual tour of 'Der Schwarzwald' [The Black Forest]. Again, the implicit aim of the assignment was to bring out differences between the notion of resource and retreat. The assignment was 'Wer und was begegnet dir im Wald? Würde das in einem Wald in British Columbia auch so sein oder wem oder was würdest du da begegnen?' (*Whom and what do you encounter in the forest? Would those encounters also happen in a forest in British Columbia? Whom or what would you encounter there?*) Despite the asynchronous set up of the course, these two students treated it as a synchronous conversation, that is, they reacted to the other student's message as if it had just been sent. The following is the beginning of the dialogue:

Dialogue 2

UKiel student: Was denkst du?

[*What do you think?*]

UBC student: Sehr mystisch. Oder mythisch? Ich weiss nicht. Wie bei Märchen. Hänsel und Gretel.

5   [*Very mystical. Or mythical? I don't know. Like in a fairy tale. Hänsel und Gretel.*]

UKiel student: Ja. Viele Märchen haben im Wald ihren Urpsrung. Hänsel und Gretel kommt allerdings aus dem Harz, dem nördlichsten Mittelgebirge Deutschlands, und nicht aus dem Schwarzwald.

10   Aber ich weiss, was du sagen willst. Es ist wie in einer anderen Welt.

[*Yes. The origins of many fairy tales are in the forest. Although Hänsel and Gretel is from the Harz mountains, the northernmost mountains in Germany, and not from the Black Forest. But I know what you mean. It's like being in a different world.*]

15 **UBC student:**   Hast du Lord of the Rings gesehen? Wie gefiel es dir?

[*Have you seen Lord of the Rings? What do you think?*]

UKiel student: Super! Die Flucht in ein andere Welt ist immer faszinierend. Das drückt die Sehnsucht nach etwas
20 anderem aus. So wie die Bilder von Caspar David Friedrich, die wir ansehen mussten. Typisch Deutsch. Romantik und Erholung im Wald. Allerdings ist er nicht gerade meine Lieblingsmaler.

[*Fantastic! The retreat into another world is always fascinating. It expresses the longing for something else. As do the pictures of Caspar*
25 *David Friedrich, which we had to view. Typically German. The forest as romance and retreat. Although he is not my favourite painter really.*]

UBC student: Ich weiss nicht, warum wir nicht die Group of Seven gesehen haben. Die haben viele Bilder von Kanada und Natur gemalt. Aber verschieden. Die Bilder sind wild und
30 bedrohlich. Friedrich ist viel Harmonie. Was ist dein Lieblingsmaler?

[*I am not sure why we didn't view pictures of the Group of Seven. They painted lots of pictures on Canada and nature. Different, though. The paintings are wild and threatening. Friedrich is all harmony. Who is*
35 *your favourite painter?*]

The dialogue starts with a wh-question (line 1) followed by an example given by the UBC student about Hänsel and Gretel (line 4). The UKiel student listens and responds with an explanation about the origin of Hänsel and Gretel (lines 8–9). The dialogue is kept alive by the UBC student's comparison with *Lord of the Rings* which is linked to another wh-question (line 15). In the response, the UKiel student draws on familiar material (lines 18–19) but also brings in his personal view on Caspar David Friedrich (lines 20–22). The UBC student carries on by bringing in the example of the Group of Seven (lines 27–9) and asking a wh-question (line 30). As in the first dialogue, talking about personal views, ideas or emotions in the comparison to *Lord of the Rings* and the opinion on Caspar David Friedrich plays an important role in the dialogue. It is at that point that the aspect of retreat is mentioned.

Twenty-eight students (fourteen at each university) participated in the dialogue. On the sub-theme of 'Mythos Deutscher Wald (*the myth of the German forest*)/Canadian wilderness' students generated 364 messages in 14 dialogues over a time period of two weeks. The average number of messages exchanged between a pair of students was 26.3; the minimum number was 10 (the instructions told them to write a least five messages each), the maximum number was 37.

The content of the exchanges was analysed in relation to three levels:

Level I: Neither the aspect of retreat nor the aspect of resource was brought out in the dialogue.

Level II: One of the aspects – retreat or resource – was brought out.

Level III: The aspect of retreat as well as the aspect of resource was brought out in the dialogue.

Most notable were the following differences (based on the 364 messages):

1. *Wh-questions*: Students asked twenty-six wh-questions (5.2 wh-questions per dialogue) when the aspects of resource and retreat were brought out (level III) but only seventeen (4.2 wh-questions per dialogue) or eighteen (3.6 wh-questions per dialogue) wh-questions when these aspects were not or only partially mentioned.

2. *Emotion* (statement, arguments, examples or activities based on emotion): Students referred to emotions thirty times (level II: 6 statements etc. based on emotion per dialogue) and thirty-five times (level III: 7 statements etc. based on emotion per dialogue) discussing the aspects of resource and retreat partially or fully but only nineteen times (level I: 4.75 statements etc. based on emotion per dialogue) when they did not discuss these aspects.

3. *Examples*: Students gave twenty-three (level III: 4.6 examples per dialogue) and nineteen (level II: 3.8 examples per dialogue) examples when the aspects of resource and/or retreat were brought out, but only ten examples (level I: 2.5 examples per dialogue) when these aspects were not mentioned.

4. *Personal experience* (statement, arguments, examples or activities based on personal experience): Students referred to personal experiences twelve times each (levels II and III: 2.4 statements based on personal experience per dialogue) discussing the aspects of resource and retreat fully or partially but only seven times (level I: 1.75 statements based on personal experience per dialogue) when they did not discuss these aspects.

5. *New material:* Students brought new material to the discussion nine times each (level II and III: 1.8 times per dialogue) when their discussion brought out one or both aspects of retreat and resource but only

five times (level I: 1.25 times per dialogue) when their discussion did not bring out those aspects.

In summary, the aspects of retreat and resource were discussed successfully when these five criteria were satisfied. These five criteria are unique to the learner. Every learner has different personal experiences and emotions; formulates wh-questions in relation to his/her own skills; gives examples s/he thought of; or brings to the discussion material s/he researched. In other words, the learner creates his or her personal voice, a point Kramsch (1993) made in talking about intercultural communication and second language acquisition. A similar point has been argued by Touraine (1997), who suggests that we rediscover the uniquely personal and creative sources of the free human 'Subjekt'. In the matrix, three of these five criteria are present in one of the four linear orders (examples, personal experience, new material) indicating that other linear orders such as arguing or activities did not have such an impact on the dialogues generated by students.

Discussion

The purpose of the described online course at the two universities was to engage learners in a virtual learning environment to generate intercultural dialogue. The next question was how to assess that dialogue. The analysis of the dialogue using a matrix of assessment criteria showed criteria that challenge the learner to use his or her personal voice are most helpful.

In studies on intercultural communication, Byram (1997) defined intercultural competence as the intercultural speaker's ability to interact with speakers of another culture. The assessment of intercultural communicative competence is based on five dimensions (Byram, 1997): knowledge; skills of interpreting and relating; skills of discovery and interaction; attitudes; and critical cultural awareness. The results of the study presented in this chapter suggest evidence for these five dimensions. The criteria of wh-questions, emotion, examples, personal experience and new material indicate that the student is developing and expanding the dialogue in the sense of being willing to engage in it. Apart from questioning techniques, the learner uses his or her personal voice also to interact, relate and mediate in the dialogue. When giving examples or introducing new material the learner chooses what he or she thinks is relevant and representative of the topic discussed; in other words, the learner shows that culture is difference.

With the current rapid progress of new technologies being applied to foreign language teaching, it is crucial to implement guidelines for assessing students in those courses. It is even more important that these guidelines are not theoretical but based on real data generated by students. The matrix of assessment criteria (see Figure 11.1) in its application to the data generated by students in the online exchange is a first step in this direction. It can be applied to courses other than language courses, and be used in institutions other than universities.

The organization of such a course is not an easy task; it was particularly difficult to fit it into the department's curriculum. In the first year the course was taught, students did not quite know what to expect, and some students were unwilling or unprepared to engage in an intercultural dialogue (although the course outline clearly stated the format of the course, including the exchange component and the expectation of students to participate). It seems that it takes some time for the word to spread among students of what this type of course is about. In the first year, there was also a problem with the number and length of messages being sent, because the instructors, wanting to have as much dialogue as possible, had not set any limitations. Consequently, some students wrote many messages of great length and others wrote hardly anything. This was clarified in the second year by giving and enforcing instructions about the number and length of messages.

Another point to note is that some students exchanged personal e-mail addresses and continued the dialogue once the course ended. It would be interesting to glimpse into these exchanges as they might provide more insight into the creativity of students. Naturally, ethical guidelines and the limitation of the analysis in the course prevent this. However, it is nice to know that the understanding of the intercultural continues beyond the classroom.

Reflection questions

1. The complex issue of cultures, languages, teaching and assessment calls for an interdisciplinary approach. In what ways could you imagine your department working together with instructors from different departments/faculties in your context collaborating to address intercultural competence?
2. What could be done to challenge students to use their personal voice in a course / programme in your context?

3. In my next project, I am planning to integrate an audio function into the online course so that students can hear each other's voices. In what way do you think this might change the dynamics of the student–student dialogue, student–instructor interaction and the matrix?

Resources

Alred, G., Byram, M., & Fleming, M. (eds). (2003). *Intercultural experience and education.* Clevedon: Multilingual Matters.
This volume is part of the 'Languages for Intercultural Communication and Education Series'. In thirteen chapters, researchers of different national, language, academic disciplinary groups and cultures identify key issues and present theories on intercultural communication. The book includes an amusing foreword by Peter Ustinov.
Byram, M. (1997). *Teaching and assessing intercultural communicative competence.* Clevedon: Multilingual Matters.
This book is on foreign language teaching and the development of an Intercultural Communicative Competence as an educational process. The book gives a framework for assessment which pays much attention to the classroom.
Byram, M., Nichols, A., & Stevens, D. (eds). (2001). *Developing intercultural competence in practice.* Clevedon: Mutlilingual Matters.
This volume is part of the 'Languages for Intercultural Communication and Education Series'. Seventeen educators from all over the world give examples of projects on language learning and teaching in the classroom (at a beginners, intermediate, and advanced level) and beyond the classroom (on new technologies, tandem courses, developing resources).
Government of Canada. <http://www.canadianheritage.gc.ca>
This government website provides much information on the themes of arts and culture, citizenship and identity, diversity and multiculturalism.
Material collection sponsored by the Government of Germany. <http://www.heimat-in-deutschland.de>
This website is a great resource on foreigners and Germans living in Germany, providing a large amount of data and materials including lesson plans. It is financed by the German government in liaison with the Goethe Institut and several publishers of German language materials.
Schuetze, U. (2006) *Speaking cultures.* (Available at: <http://germanfortravellers.com>)
This DVD displays short videos on Canadian and German contemporary culture in English as well as German and comes with an instruction manual for classroom use. It can be used as a linguistic and cultural trainer at an intermediate level of proficiency.

12

Virtual Internships for International Cooperation: Experiences of Learning, Teaching and Networking

Regitze Kristensen, Eija Källström and
Julie Ann Svenkerud

This chapter describes two virtual mobility post secondary cross-cultural projects which used Information and Communication Technologies (ICTs) in real life companies. Students, faculty, and business companies interacted with each other across geographical and cultural boundaries. The projects (INTERN & EUROCLASS) demonstrated the value of integrating ICT teaching, research, and in designing joint educational modules to promote cultural understanding. The chapter offers practical strategies for teachers on how to implement these type of projects in their classrooms.

Introduction

The chapter starts with an overview of the educational context of the two projects: INTERN and EUROCLASS, both of which were financed by the European Union. Thereafter the pedagogical model constructed for the projects is presented, which emphasizes the interplay between theory and practice, and suggests a variety of Information and Communication Technology (ICT) tools for different phases of the projects. Following this, some practical assignments are presented. The outcomes of the assignments are discussed with a focus on the role of culture in international projects. The chapter ends with some suggestions for teachers wanting to implement this type of learning environment, together with some suggested do's and don'ts.

Context

Since 1992, the authors have implemented a range of various cooperative endeavours, primarily student projects using information and communication technologies (ICTs). In all projects, the student groups were both cross-cultural and cross-disciplinary. The authors represent different academic disciplines and higher education institutions: Arcada Polytechnic (Finland) contributed with expertise in international business, Tietgen Business College, Odense (Denmark) with expertise in management and ICTs and Buskerud University College (Norway) with expertise in communication and language.

The basic idea of INTERN is to enable students to participate in *Virtual Internship* projects for international companies. The authors defined the concept of Virtual Internships as follows:

> A *Virtual Internship* involves the use of an Information and Communication Technology supported environment, where students interact with each other, and companies, independent of time and space and across traditional geographical boundaries. In this environment, effective communications are created between students, faculty and company representatives, in order to carry out a specific and meaningful work-based activity that fits within the student's compulsory educational curriculum. (INTERN Management Group, 2002a, p. 22)

INTERN provided the opportunity for close co-operation between companies and students as well as between faculty from higher educational institutions in different Northern European countries. The participating students were from different programmes in the respective institutions. The Danish students were first- and second-year students from the Market Economist programmes; the Norwegian students were first- to fourth-year students participating in a one-year course of English studies including business communication; and the Finnish students were third-year business students taking a course in Project Management.

The basic idea of EUROCLASS was to develop competent *faculty staff groups* using ICTs for projects, research and joint modules across national boundaries. A total of 31 teachers participated in the project, from Arcada Polytechnic, Tietgen Business College, Buskerud University College and EuroFaculty in Latvia, Estonia and Lithuania. Teachers interacted with each other during the first faculty training session that took place in Vilnius (Lithuania), and during the pilot projects where students were involved in virtual internships. Cross-border interaction among teachers and students was facilitated by using technologies, including WebCT, Blackboard, and videoconferencing. The national cultures included in these two projects therefore generally represented a Nordic-Baltic geographical area. The Nordic and Baltic countries are all small countries in the same region, but with very different histories and cultures. During the last decade of the twentieth century the Baltic countries witnessed drastic political and social changes; at the same time, the Nordic countries initiated several educational initiatives in the Baltic countries.

Theoretical background: the INTERN model

Nonaka et al. (1998) and other authors argue that knowledge creation results from the interplay between tacit and explicit knowledge. Tacit knowledge is personal and context-specific and sometimes hard to verbalize; it includes intuitions, unarticulated mental models and embodied technical skills. Explicit knowledge refers to knowledge that can be coded and verbally transmitted, such as a meaningful set of numbers or diagrams (e.g., Nonaka et al.). The interplay between tacit and explicit knowledge takes place within 'communities of interaction' that can cross intra- and inter-organizational levels and boundaries (Nonaka & Takeuchi, 1995; Nonaka et al.). The interaction of tacit with explicit knowledge is generally seen to lead to dynamic knowledge creation and timely development of new products and services. Based upon the concepts of tacit and explicit knowledge, and the interaction of theory and practice, a model of work-based learning at the individual level has also been developed (Raelin, 1997).

These sources were important for the pedagogical model developed by the authors for the implementation of the INTERN and EUROCLASS projects. The model (Figure 12.1) is called INTERN, after the project, and it shows how different learning processes operate through the interplay between theory and practice, and between tacit and explicit knowledge. For each phase of the learning process, ICT tools are suggested. It needs to be said that the authors do not propose any rigid approach with regard to the ICT infrastructure; they suggest ICT tools and support mechanisms for user-friendly, cost-efficient cross-border communication, collaboration and knowledge sharing.

The student's learning process in the virtual internship starts with theoretical *conceptualization* of the specific academic fields studied. Explicit theoretical concepts, provided by the faculty, give the students

	Explicit knowledge	**Tacit knowledge**

Theory

CONCEPTUALIZATION

- Planning of project
- Creating a theoretical basis for the individual pilot (developmental) project.

ICT tools:
- audio conference for project planning with remote participants.
- videoconference for guest lectures from partner institutions.
- use of electronic databases and web-search for articles and materials related to the topic studied.

EXPERIMENTATION

- Broadening the understanding of theories used in individual pilot project.

ICT tools:
- studying previous cases distributed on the Internet.
- informal and formal discussions on project's web-site related to material distributed.
- group-discussions using web-cams for smaller groups on specific topics.

REFLECTION

- Students analyse practical results of their research.
- Students report findings to partner companies and to students in other countries.
- Company representatives and students evaluate their learning experience.

Practice

ICT tools:
- multipoint videoconference facilitating feed-back from all participants.
- web-based questionnaire including software applications for analysing results.

EXPERIENCE

- Assignments to students in own country and abroad.
- Practical basis laid by company representatives.
- Students perform research according to the assignment.

ICT tools:
- videoconference with presentation by company representatives.
- discussions on projects web-site open also for company representatives.
- group-discussions using web-cams for smaller groups on specific topics.

Figure 12.1: The INTERN model

the means to tackle the forthcoming assignments. Guest lectures by professors from partner institutions are also transmitted through video-conferencing in order to further clarify the theories applied. In the *experimentation* stage of the learning process, the theoretical concepts are applied to the individual pilot projects. For example, students study previous cases in their specific field, participate in web-discussions, and are active on the project's web-site. All this allows for further theoretical discussions and modelling between participants situated in different countries. At this stage, students add new knowledge to their previous mental models and explicit knowledge can become practice.

First-hand knowledge from practical business life is thereafter introduced into the project, when company representatives share their experience and tacit knowledge with the students. This stage gives the students *practical experience* and deeper tacit knowledge through solving the assignments given to them by the company. Students learn both from the contact persons in the firms and through their own research contributions. The students' learning process is considerably strengthened by problem-solving in practice.

In the *reflection* stage, students report their findings to the company representatives, often through videoconferencing. The tacit knowledge that the students have gained is made explicit in verbal statements and written reports. During the videoconference, representatives from both the business and academic sector evaluate the students' project results. The learning process thereafter continues in a learning cycle, as the students utilize the knowledge and experience gained in the project in other courses and assignments.

Along with specific academic knowledge, students also gain experience of working in a multicultural environment in an academic as well as in a business context. The above stages helped students to develop their knowledge and experience in working with colleagues representing different national and organizational cultures.

Objectives

The primary objective in implementing the INTERN and EUROCLASS projects was to gain the necessary skills to make students and teachers successful in a 'Learning Society' (Edwards, 1997). In order to achieve this objective we knew that we would have to initiate learning strategies that would utilize ICT in cross-cultural settings, improve English language and communication skills and heighten student awareness regarding cross-cultural skills and their importance as an integral part of business. English was the lingua franca throughout the entire project because English is the language primarily used in international business. We have focused on the concept of the 'Learning Organisation', introduced by Senge (1990) in his book, *The fifth discipline*. In order to function as employees in the modern learning society, students and teachers must obtain skills that enable them to:

1. Collect knowledge from various academic areas in a conscious synergetic process;
2. Utilize this knowledge to generate new approaches to a problem;
3. Manage and complete a business task communicating in English;
4. Utilize ICT to coordinate business processes;

5. Adapt to and manage unpredictable situations (see examples of cross-cultural misunderstandings);
6. Be sensitive to and understand an entire spectrum of communicative indicators (signs, symbols, codes, diagrams etc);
7. Work in teams to communicate, co-operate and participate in a collective endeavour;
8. Work and succeed in a cross-cultural environment.

The EUROCLASS and INTERN projects, by their very nature, step into the minefield of European culture and language: taking students from one country and asking them to co-operate with a company operating in another opens up not only terrific opportunities for learning but also certain risks. While the college can prepare the student through extensive language preparation, there is currently less preparation to equip the student with all the skills he or she will need in order to understand the cultural differences which will occur. While it is our belief that a great deal of cultural clichés and myths exist in this area, there is no doubt that company cultures differ from country to country and region to region. Preparation in the form of intercultural awareness-raising and the provision of as much back-up as possible was necessary, and various sets of 'What If . . .' scenarios were discussed beforehand in order to try to predict the kinds of problems that may occur with regard not only to culture and language but in the execution of the overall projects. For example:

• what if key people taking part in the project have to withdraw?
• what if the students find difficulty in finding the right tone for communication purposes?
• what if the ICT infrastructure fails to perform as predicted?

Method

Action Learning was the overall pedagogical method applied in the projects (Senge, 1990). New knowledge was created when theory and practice were combined in real-life assignments, as described in the INTERN model (Figure 12.1). During INTERN we organized various Virtual Internships. For example:

1. Buskerud University College: Virtual Internship for the Norwegian company *Tronrud Engineering*, to research markets, exhibitions and

fairs for one of their products in other countries. This Internship took place from September until December 2001 and involved students in Denmark, Norway and Finland.

2. ARCADA: Virtual Internship for *ICL* (Nordic service provider and operator of advanced information systems). The objective of the Virtual Internship that ran from September until December 2001 was to find out more about the use of Information Technology in customer relationship management (CRM) in hotel chains in Finland and Norway; it involved students from Finland and Norway.

3. Tietgen Business College: Virtual Internship for the Danish *DFDS Transportation Group*, who wanted to have a logistic survey of track and trace systems in Finland. This Internship ran from September until December 2001 and involved students in Finland.

During the assignments, cross-border communication between students, faculty, and companies took place, and the various tools suggested above in the INTERN model were extensively used. In addition, some of the assignments involved travel to another country for actual field studies. In these assignments, the students interacted initially online using the electronic learning platforms. During the project development they met face-to-face, and continued their collaboration electronically after the 'business trip'. The real-world nature of this project and the desire to cooperate across cultural and geographical borders stimulated a higher degree of cultural awareness among the students, and any communication problems could also in most cases be solved directly by the students themselves.

The students and teachers involved had several course sessions to discuss the role of culture. These sessions included cross-cultural theory as well as a multicultural problem-solving simulation, Ecotonos (Nipporica Associates, 1997). In this simulation, students create their own imaginary society and culture, and then work together to solve a culturally-related problem in a multicultural environment. In the first stage of the simulation, the participants were divided into three monocultural groups and given 'cultural rule' cards. The groups then discussed and agreed on how they would enact their rules. Then they created a story about how their culture originated and practiced their cultural rules. In the second stage, each group is given a task (such as creating a community where all the members can live), which they complete according to their cultural rules. Finally, after completing the task, the participants discussed their experiences and observations.

In the written evaluation, participants were generally very positive to the experience; they commented that the simulation was very realistic, and that they were surprised that they identified with their new culture so quickly and easily. They learned the importance of listening skills, mutual respect, knowledge of self and others, the importance of clarification, the vast myriad of options available in multicultural problem solving, and the importance of balancing task and process.

During the EUROCLASS project, we especially addressed the problems related to culture during our introductory seminar for all the teachers involved. This seminar was an important step in teacher development, both in terms of cultural awareness and in terms of supporting faculty who wanted to introduce Virtual Internships in their own courses. The seminar focused on the setting-up of workshops, and other training activities, and familiarizing everyone with the tools that were to be used. For some teachers, the dependence on ICT support, and the very remoteness of the company taking part, can cause anxieties. During the seminar, there was time to practise with the chosen ICT infrastructure away from students, in order to allow faculty to build up competence before the Virtual Internship activity started. At this stage each project agreed upon the learning platform which they would use.

The introductory seminar highlighted the importance of cultural awareness and commitment to concepts like lifelong learning. Successful teachers seem to be those who have the necessary flexibility in working with colleagues in other countries and who believe in the essential link between ongoing learning and the workplace, where the concept of Virtual Internships can be applied, independent of time, schedule or distance constraints. Flexibility is necessary because there are always other methods, solutions or objectives that need to be considered and adopted when dealing with several cultures. The realities of current teaching practice, with increasing pressure on resources, a surplus of information, an emphasis upon collaboration and cross-curriculum learning, and an increasing dependence on ICT, have made many teachers less comfortable with this kind of work.

Outcomes

Virtual Internships offer an important learning opportunity for both students and academic/teaching staff. Using ICT in a real-life context will certainly improve competence and increase skills in an ICT environment. The level of basic ICT competence expected within the workforce is increasing, and a well-operated Virtual Internship can increase first-hand competence in this area. This was an important outcome of the Virtual Internship projects, as reported in the evaluations (INTERN Management Group, 2002b; EuroClass Management Group, 2004). In fact, students and staff alike appreciated the opportunity to increase their ICT competence through Virtual Internships.

We also found that the choice of ICT infrastructure to be used during a Virtual Internship is very important. A successful decision is based upon a realistic analysis of what the Virtual Internship requires regarding communication and activity support, in the light of what is in use and available within the organizations taking part. The role of ICTs within a Virtual Internship is important. We see ICT as playing a supportive role, being used to facilitate the kind of activity in which we are engaged. In other words, we replace traditional face-to-face activities with those supported by ICT. In practical terms, this means that we replace or complement traditional face-to-face meetings with synchronous video/audio conferencing and asynchronous meetings. Learning materials, reports and documents that are prepared either individually or collaboratively can be created and distributed using digital means. Research is conducted not only through traditional routes, but also through extensive web searches.

In INTERN and EUROCLASS, evaluations were led by an external evaluator assisted by an evaluation team from all of the participating institutions. Interviews and questionnaires were utilized as instruments of evaluation for faculty and students. The evaluations showed that students' motivation was enhanced because they were able to contribute to solving business tasks on a cross-cultural and real life basis. Through utilizing learning platforms such as Blackboard and WebCT the students had a common meeting place where they could exchange information.

Examples of cross-cultural interaction

Through long-term cooperation on various Nordic projects, the authors have observed and experienced several cross-cultural differences between Nordic countries. Students and teachers tend to assume that Nordic educational partners and businesses with their common Nordic background will communicate and interact in a very similar manner. However, the failure of a number of cooperative business endeavours between the Nordic countries illustrates the difficulties enterprises have in communicating and working together. During the project several cross-cultural misunderstandings were experienced between the Nordic partners. These experiences taught all the participants the necessity of clarifying the objectives of the project at the beginning and implementing it with cultural considerations in mind.

Two specific examples of Nordic cross-cultural misunderstanding that occurred were mentioned in the INTERN Norwegian student evaluation. The Norwegian students referred to the Finnish business manager in the video-conference as 'a man in a suit', which in Norwegian is a negative description meaning a much distanced figure of authority, unable to communicate in a motivating manner: They had not really listened to his message because of his dress and manner. The Finnish students on the other hand were very satisfied with this partner, because he was an expert and very knowledgeable: They had respect for his contribution, and expected a man of his position to dress and communicate in this manner. This illustrated a very basic difference between working cultures in two Nordic countries; and it gave an excellent learning opportunity where the students could discuss a first-hand business experience which they also might encounter in a real-life context. The Norwegian students learned from this discussion that their way of viewing the businessman was very different from the Finnish students' and that they must be cautious about stereotyping business situations involving other cultures.

Another cross-cultural misunderstanding occurred due to differences between learning methods. The Danish students were to research markets, exhibitions and fairs for one of the Norwegian company's products in other countries. During the video conference, the Norwegian manager praised and thanked the Danish students for their insight and work, and in her evaluation she compared their findings with company knowledge of potential markets. The Danish students were disappointed to learn that the company had done previous research regarding their markets, having assumed that their work was groundbreaking and unique. The Norwegian manager explained that their Danish viewpoint was invaluable and had provided the company with new insight. The students however felt that they had been 'cheated' because they had assumed that their work would be a real task, as if they were a professional marketing company, because they were used to working on real tasks from Danish business. The Norwegian viewpoint was that this task was to provide original insight from another cultural perspective but that it would also act as a check and balance to the information already known. In addition, it was viewed by the Norwegian teacher as a satisfactory task because the accuracy of the Danish student findings could be compared to previous knowledge. This type of misunderstanding might have been avoided if expectations had been more clearly defined to all participating parties at the beginning of the project.

Another marked difference was made apparent during the EURO-CLASS teacher seminar. This was between the Nordic countries participants and the Baltic participants. This concerned the concept of active learning. We learned through the process of defining student tasks, that there was a great difference regarding the perceived value of peer learning processes. In planning video-conferences the partners from the Baltic countries felt that only 'experts' (meaning teachers or business people) should give video-conference lectures, while partners from the Nordic countries felt that well-prepared students could also make worthwhile contributions. This difference of opinion was addressed by defining and providing a rationale for active learning processes and by organizing an active learning session, which utilized the cross-cultural simulation, *ECOTONOS*. During the final discussion between participants, the successful groups discovered that the simulation's task goal can only be attained when there is a creative synergy between all group members. In this manner, each group member owns the task and feels that he/she is personally responsible for the final outcome.

Evaluation of the projects

In the evaluation of the INTERN project, the 51 students generally emphasized the following learning aspects:

- 80 per cent felt that they had developed cross-cultural communication skills and improved their communication skills in a foreign language
- 78 per cent held the international environment to be the most motivating factor
- 77 per cent felt that they had gained substantial knowledge of e-learning networks
- 71 per cent regarded the practical work as a motivating factor
- 59 per cent reported increased reflection on learning processes.

Students generally found working in a multicultural atmosphere to be highly motivating. Therefore it was important to highlight this aspect as much as possible in the initial project descriptions for the Virtual Internships provided to later project participants.

In the EUROCLASS project the teachers generally reported to have learnt (Euroclass management group, 2004):

- new technical skills
- management responsibilities of international projects
- new pedagogical challenges with ICT
- networking with other universities/polytechnics.

Among the projects' *physical outcomes* for the project stakeholders (e.g., higher education institutions, companies, educational authorities) were a Best Practice Manual for the INTERN project and for the EUROCLASS Project, and a CD of learning materials used during the project. These materials were produced by the projects' management teams. The Best Practice Manual included:

- an introduction to the project
- a discussion of Virtual Internships and the case studies implemented
- best practice guidelines and recommendations.

The Learning Materials included:

- the Action Learning Seminar held in Vilnius in Lithuania for all the participants
- pedagogical aspects of ODL (Open and Distance Learning) projects
- technical aspects of ODL projects
- practical steps in implementing a successful ODL project.

Discussion and recommendations

Based upon our experience, we suggest Virtual Internships as a useful means of increasing cross-border cooperation in the educational arena. Throughout our projects, Virtual Internships have been used in a variety of disciplines including law, languages, economics, and business administration. We think that the INTERN model and Virtual Internships are applicable across disciplines, as long as the following guidelines are followed when designing student and faculty projects:

Choose assignments from companies that involve useful work, where the project is well defined and achievable within the given time schedule. Try to ensure there is a written and explicit working agreement with the company, which explains the roles and responsibilities of everyone taking part. Choose students who are independent and able to work on their own initiative. Involve academic and teaching staff who support the idea of action learning and who are dynamic and open to new ideas. They should believe in the essential link between learning and the workplace, independent of time, schedule or distance constraints.

Choose an ICT infrastructure carefully and try to select tools that are generic, fit-for-purpose and user-friendly. The ICT infrastructure is particularly important as it supports a range of communication and collaboration activities, and is also part of the learning experience.

Plan the internship carefully, allowing enough time for familiarization with the company, the commercial sector involved and the technology to be used. Make sure the task is shown to be serious work and is introduced by a senior representative of the commissioning company.

Right from the start, *make sure that students understand the culture of the company* and what it does. Company representatives should also be familiar with the characteristics of the students, what is needed for their success, how they perceive instruction and what they expect. Make sure that everyone is equipped with the appropriate language skills and that inter-cultural communication is well supported.

During the internship, *monitor progress carefully* to make sure everyone is meeting their responsibilities, including administrative staff in the educational institution(s) taking part. Virtual internships can significantly improve students' overall project management, language, cultural understanding and ICT skills, so try to ensure these aspects are highlighted and supported.

Finally, *evaluate and record* carefully. Not only does this provide necessary feedback about the current virtual internship, but it will also help you make improvements in the future.

Reflection questions

1. How (if at all) are the following recommendations in the box below, based on our experience, relevant to implementation of a virtual project, in your context? Whose responsibility is it to ensure that these recommendations are taken into consideration, and how can they be successfully carried out? What kind of cultures can play a part in this process?

Do	Don't
• Provide sufficient orientation on cross-cultural understanding and communication to students BEFORE they begin to collaborate on the project. • Be available to the students as a sounding board when any unpredictable cross-cultural misunderstandings occur. • Be explicit concerning the project structures and tasks for all participants • Allow for enough time for trust development between the participants. • Keep records, reports and evaluations for future demonstration and evaluation purposes.	• Assume that everyone understands because they communicate in English. • Expect the students to deal with the project with little assistance from faculty members. • Choose your ICT infrastructure before you know what is appropriate for the local context. • Underestimate the importance of having documentation as a part of the learning process and for further projects.

Resources

Bijnes, H., Boussemaere, M., & Petegrem, W. (2006). *Being mobile: European cooperation in education through virtual mobility*. www.being-mobile.net.
This handbook includes short summaries of innovate and model projects or initiatives with a specific focus on replicable outcomes.
Dodd, C. H. (1998). *Dynamics of intercultural communication*. New York: McGraw-Hill.
This book has been a success in defining culture's variability in the communication process due to its examples and user-friendly text.
Fowler, S., & Mumford, M. (1995). *Intercultural sourcebook: Cross-cultural training methods*. Yarmouth, Maine: Intercultural Press.
This sourcebook is useful due to its concrete examples and six categories of training methods including simulations.
Nipporica Associates (1997). *Ecotonos: A multicultural problem-solving simulation*. Yarmouth, Maine: Intercultural Press.
This simulation is designed to teach participants about multicultural decision making and problem solving. The simulation was a success due to the action learning format where participants experienced realistic reactions to monocultural and multicultural problem solving across differences.
Vanbuel, M. (2000). *Towards a learning organization*. Leuven: Leuven University Press.
This book gives companies' and organizations' perspectives in using ICT in developing and implementing new learning and training technologies.

13
Teaching Bioinformatics: Using Storytelling to Negotiate Cultural Divisions in the Sciences

Niall Palfreyman

In this chapter we address the situation of German students in the technical biosciences who are required to negotiate the divisions of disciplinary culture currently existing between the biological and technical sciences. Between the modes of thinking of biologists and technical scientists exists a major cultural divide which can cause problems for students of bioinformatics; a central aim of any bioinformatics course must therefore be to help students to recognize and learn the skills of both cultural groups. In this chapter we seek a rapprochement of these cultures through a social understanding of knowledge not as a commodity to be absorbed, but rather as a social praxis of problem-solving through the narration of 'stories' from experience. By taking this narrative account of problem-solving seriously, we arrive at a question of general educational relevance: How can we help students to learn new cultural narratives which empower them to solve problems, and to adapt these narratives in the light of experience?

Introduction

Biotechnology and bioinformatics are relatively new sciences, combining elements of biology, engineering and informatics; students of bioinformatics must therefore learn to speak to two different kinds of professionals: biologists and technical scientists. We shall see that each of these two groups operates within a very different frame of reference from the other, and bioinformatics students may feel more affinity to one frame or the other. As a result, these students may have difficulties not only in talking to professionals from the other frame, but also in talking to each other. In the first section of this chapter we shall look at how these communication problems may impact the success of bioinformatics students in the German tertiary education system. In the following section we then interpret this impact in terms of a particular distinction in thinking styles of the two disciplinary groups. We shall then relate this interpretation to models of learning and problem-solving behaviour in the psychological literature, and so arrive at several practical assertions regarding teaching in the technical biosciences, which are also of relevance to other 'bridging disciplines' such as business studies or sports science. Finally, we shall see how these assertions can be implemented in a bioinformatics foundation course, and will inspect the evidence so far for the success of this course structure.

Context

Bioinformatics is a *bridging discipline*: it fulfils an urgent need which arose particularly in the 1990s to analyse the huge quantities of data coming out of the Human Genome Project. On the one hand these data are biological in nature, while on the other hand they demand methods of analysis deriving mainly from the technical, or engineering, disciplines. The work of bioinformaticians therefore requires them both to grasp the biological relevance of the data with which they work, and also to interpret these data in terms of their significance for engineering systems. In short, the bioinformatician must speak two languages: biological and technical.

This situation is common to many disciplines which seek to combine knowledge from disparate subject areas. Other bridging disciplines which spring to mind are environmental science, linguistics and theatre studies. And we must also bear in mind that almost any subject makes use of insights from related areas which may nevertheless be rooted in very different cultural backgrounds: for example, all sciences draw on a common core of basic mathematics and physics, and any vocational course must combine the sometimes competing needs of theory and practice.

In this chapter we look at the problem of bridging the sometimes deep cultural divisions existing within a 'single' discipline by looking at the specific example of bioinformatics students at the Fachhochschule Weihenstephan (FHW) in Freising, Germany. This example will touch on both the biology/engineering division and also the ubiquitous division of theory and practice, and we shall be particularly interested in the extent to which our specific situation at FHW can teach us something of general applicability in further education.

The German *Fachhochschulen* (FH: *Universities of Applied Science*) are vocational educational institutions designed to provide students with both the theoretical knowledge *and* the practical skills required in a wide variety of professional areas. The effective professional bioinformatician must learn to marry efficiently the sometimes conflicting requirements of practical relevance (highly valued in the life sciences) and theoretical significance (highly valued in technical sciences). This problem of cultural division experienced by bioinformatics students is symptomatic of a more general issue relating to vocational and praxis-relevant education in many subjects whose aim is to bridge the divisions between conventional academic disciplines.

Unfortunately, the marriage of theory and practice is not always straightforward for students, as evidenced by the following general finding from Heublein, Schmelzer and Sommer (2005):

> *Observation (i)*: Over 50 per cent of German students entering tertiary study programmes in the technical disciplines Mathematics, Physics and Informatics in the coming year will terminate their studies without successfully completing their degree examinations. This fact exacts each year a huge economic and personal price.

According to Heublein, Spangenberg and Sommer (2003), many students become disenchanted with their degree course for two main reasons: they see the abstract theory and skills taught in their course as either irrelevant to their chosen profession or insuperably difficult to master. The practical and vocational nature of FH education means that FH students are typically motivated not so much by love of a *subject* as by aspiration to a *profession*. If these students are not given the opportunity to embed their learning within a practical context, they often find it difficult to maintain the enthusiasm which, let's face it, is essential for effective learning.

So how can we help students to make this crucial connection between the theory of their course and the practice of their chosen profession? The following observation of students entering the degree programme in bioinformatics at FHW suggests the existence of a distinction between students which mirrors the above divisions of engineering-biology and theory-practice, and in the process indicates a way of answering this question:

> *Observation (ii)*: Our experience at FHW suggests the existence of two very distinct thinking styles that I shall term technically (T) and biologically (B) oriented. Students oriented towards T-style thinking typically excel at subjects like mathematics and physics, while B-style

thinking is more appropriate to subjects like biology and organic chemistry. T-oriented students are good at solving problems, but see problems as having a single 'correct' answer; consequently they often reject social interaction as a valid means of constructing knowledge: indeed for them knowledge is not constructed, but acquired. B-oriented students on the other hand frequently lack the problem-solving skills required of them in a technical discipline, but perform well in classification and interpretation tasks. They also frequently engage in social interaction to negotiate with others the interpretation of an observed phenomenon.

While the terms 'T' and 'B' are new, the T/B distinction is not. Keller (2002) relates the story of the 1934 confrontation between mathematician Rashevsky and biologist Davenport concerning Rashevsky's mathematical model of an idealized spherical cell. Davenport's comment was: 'I think the biologist might find that whereas the explanation of the division of the spherical cell is very satisfactory, yet it doesn't help as a general solution because a spherical cell isn't the commonest form of cell' (Keller, p. 85), which elicited the following retort from Rashevsky: 'It would mean a misunderstanding of the spirit and methods of mathematical sciences should we attempt to investigate more complex cases without a preliminary study of the simple ones' (Keller, p. 85).

What we observe in this altercation is a division between the thinking of biologists and technical scientists which is of such deep-set nature that it can only be described as *cultural*, where, together with Jablonka and Lamb (2006), we define culture to be the set of shared values and practices which characterize a distinguishable social group. Biologists must learn early in their career that living systems are inherently too complex to hope to understand or explain them in every detail. They learn to base their world around classifications of what *is*, rather than what *ought* to be, and to treat with suspicion any theory which departs too far from a sensory underpinning. *Engineers* on the other hand develop during their training a confidence in their own ability to describe the world in terms of relatively simple theories which enable them to move beyond their senses and act on that world in novel ways. The result of this division is that a student of the technical biosciences is pulled in two conflicting directions: s/he is required on the one hand to develop a deep appreciation of the complexity of living systems, yet must simultaneously learn to abstract from this complexity tractable solutions with predictive power. In essence this student must straddle a cultural divide between the concrete, pragmatic culture of the biologist, and the abstract, activity-based culture of the engineer.

Now comes the catch. Viewed from a T-perspective it is easy to stigmatize B-oriented students as being simply weak in abstract thinking; however a number of observations belie this analysis:

Observation (iii): While T-oriented students are effective at comprehending and applying abstract rules, they often need to be told which rule is needed in a given situation, and in my experience may become upset and frustrated when unsure of the 'right' way of doing things.

Observation (iv): Since the inception of the bioinformatics degree course at FHW we have had a steady trickle of students who performed extremely weakly in areas requiring abstract thinking, yet who achieved excellent results when they switched to a biology degree course in which B-thinking is emphasized.

Observation (v): Those B-oriented students who remain on the bioinformatics course despite poor technical grades often receive glowing reports when they complete their practical industrial placement, *even when this placement is in a technical position*. It seems that even in technical professions, the social and pragmatic abilities of B-thinking are well appreciated by employers.

Observation (vi): A wide variety of mathematics examination questions specify a particular rule, and require the candidate to apply this rule to a given situation – a primarily T-oriented task. Such questions are prejudicial to the performance of B-oriented students, who perform better on questions requiring them to classify a specified situation in terms of rules applicable to it.

A pattern seems to emerge here. The abstract thinking which is so often taken as the hallmark of academic success (and of 'deep learning' – see Apfelthaler et al., this volume) consists in taking an internal story and 'running with it' in abstraction from the vagaries of any specific real situation: mathematical texts devote much effort to eliminating any specifics which might limit the scope of application of the text. Yet precisely this obsession with generality is a handicap when performing a chemical or phylogenetic analysis, or even when debugging a computer program. In these situations the practitioner must learn to set aside her inner intuitions in order to focus solely on the reality of the data presented by the situation under analysis. However this important skill is frequently not examined (or practised) in T-oriented subjects!

In the terms of Airey and Linder (2006), each discipline has its own 'disciplinary way of knowing' and while learning to use the discourse of a science, 'students need opportunities to use the representations, tools and activities of the discipline as an integral part of their science education' (p. 35). How, then, can we help students to learn this new 'way of knowing'?

I view the praxis of science as consisting essentially in the activity of solving problems, and in the remainder of this chapter I shall argue the following points:

- Scientific discourse has a particular structure which is based on viewing the world as a network of mutually co-dependent events in a coherent *narrative*. B- and T-thinking differ chiefly in their attitude to this narrative.
- Proficiency in scientific discourse involves competency in both B- and T-thinking: T-thinking involves the ability to apply specified narratives, while B-thinking involves the ability to recognize and question the relevance of narratives to a given problem.
- Students can gain proficiency in both aspects of scientific discourse by sharing and critiquing narratives relevant to carefully chosen problem situations.
- During this activity students also move towards an understanding of knowledge not as a commodity to be absorbed, but rather as a *social praxis of recognizing and applying abstract rules to solve novel, and often ill-defined, problems.*

Problem-solving and learning

Problem-solving behaviour is the central focus of cognitive psychology. Much of our behaviour as human beings centres around either adapting the environment to our purposes (*problem-solving*) or else adapting ourselves to our environment (*learning*) in order to improve our success in solving *future* problems. A crucial element of problem-solving is *narrative* (Bruner, 1990). Orr (1986) and Schön (1990) both note the narrative nature of diagnostic problem-solving in a variety of fields: by relating and recounting stories, problem-solving professionals make sense of their experience, and in the process they also reshape their knowledge about the problems they face, and about themselves as problem-solvers. The schemata we use to solve problems are simply the narratives we relate to ourselves and others about these problems, and a crucial aspect of such narratives is that they *empower*: we appear in our stories as more or less effective agents.

If we as educators take this narrative account of problem-solving seriously, we must answer the question: *How can we help students to learn narratives which empower them to solve problems, and to adapt these narratives in the light of experience?* In the remainder of this section we look at a variety of answers in the literature to this crucial question.

The *constructivist* position (Ormrod, 2005) is a useful starting-point. Since we construct our knowledge through interaction with the environment, that knowledge must be learned by trial-and-error within the context of social interaction. Watzlawick (1981) uses the simile of a ship's captain negotiating a narrow sea channel in the dark: only by wrecking his ship on the rocks can the captain learn something truly new about the channel, and all his theories can never match, but only fit, the true nature of the channel. The implication here is that we may learn most from situations where our narratives do *not* work.

Further clues come from semiotic analyses of meaning-creation, which suggest that we model the world at three hierarchical levels: iconically, extensionally and symbolically (Sebeok & Danesi, 2000). Developmentally, as children we first model the world at a very concrete, sensory level (*iconically*). Later on we then *extend* these iconic models into more general areas of application. Finally, *symbolic* modelling enables us to cast aside all sensory connection between model 'and referent. It also entails the ability to utilise forms creatively and resourcefully. [. . . W]e literally let our cultural symbols "do the thinking" for us most of the time. [. . . They allow us] to experiment with the real world, and even to alter it to fit specific needs' (Sebeok & Danesi, 2000, p. 129). We find here two important ideas: that modelling is a staged process of abstraction from the world; and that our ultimate (i.e., symbolic) representations are far from static, but are essentially *dynamic* in nature. These ideas are both central aspects of the difference between B- and T-thinking: the T-thinker revels in the freedom of flight of abstract thinking, and scorns the B-thinker's prosaic insistence on sensory groundedness; while the B-thinker is acutely aware of the novelty of all that happens in the world, and instinctively mistrusts the T-thinker's flighty disconnectedness from factual data. This distinction is akin to the Myers-Briggs attitudes of judging and perceiving: T-thinking tends to construct meaning by reference to accepted rules and procedures, while B-thinking instead leaves options open, and seeks meaning within the external data.

Kolb's (1983) work on experiential learning, prefigured 40 years earlier by Pólya (1945), similarly emphasizes a four-stage cycle by which we learn through engagement with the world. Engagement starts when I have concrete experience (i.e., *observe*) some regularity in the environment. I then **reflectively observe** this regularity, *interpreting* it as a postulated new rule in my model of the world. In the next stage of learning, I form an **abstract conceptualization** of this new rule, *relating* it to other internal rules to form a narrative with its own distinctive dynamic. Finally I engage in **active experimentation** by *asserting* my internal rule in tentative behaviours aimed at influencing the world, and then again seek concrete experience of evidence to check the domain of applicability of my new rule.

The stories told by Orr's (1986) engineering informants show that narratives serve another function: that of merging (relating) ideas. One informant recounts the story of a photocopier which failed its diagnostics test, and subsequently triggered a relay problem; this prompts another informant to relate a similar story in which the relay problem arose from a faulty power supply; together the two create a new model of reality in which emphasis is shifted from the diagnostics test to the power supply. This synthesis of relevant narratives is the essence of Kolb's abstract conceptualization. We need to see our internal representations of the world not as static schemata, but as *narratives* shaped by both experience and culture. Only narratives combine the ability to deliver conclusions which act upon the world with the ability to flexibly merge ideas from seemingly disparate situations to generate genuinely new behaviour.

When teaching students to solve problems, prove theorems, build mathematical models and design software, I have found it useful to adopt the following framework for problem-solving, which is crystallized from the foregoing discussion:

1. I *observe* my environment: I focus on some single, concrete aspect of the world which comes to my attention, and study it particularly closely. (E.g., I note my thirst and the presence of a mug of tea on my desk.)
2. I *interpret* this observation within the context of narratives familiar to me from past experience. (E.g., I interpret the tea as a potential solution to my thirst problem.)
3. I *relate* the narrative of which this interpretation is the central protagonist: I merge it with other related narratives into an archetypal myth, and follow through the plot of this myth to its fitting conclusion. (E.g., I play through the familiar narrative of reaching out and swigging the tea.)

4. I *assert* the outcome of this internal narrative in the form of actions and symbols which affect the world: I act on my environment. (E.g., I reach out for the tea.)
5. This action focuses my attention on that part of the world which I hope to affect, and I *observe* the evidence for my success, leading to reiteration of the cycle. (E.g., I note the new situation of having the mug in my hand.)

Objectives

I have tried in the previous sections to make two things clear:

- Bioinformatics students need to cross a wide cultural gap which involves accepting and assimilating a whole new attitude to learning and problem-solving as a *social* activity. This attitude is intrinsic to neither T- nor B-thinking.
- Learning and problem-solving are core components of social engagement: they are the key skills by which we narrow the gap between the stories we relate ourselves and the stories in which our physical and social world requires us to take part.

Phrased in this way, an interesting realization emerges. What seemed initially a somewhat abstruse concern of a small group of bioinformatics students now turns out to contain a general consequence. There is a key cognitive cycle in which we engage at every moment of our lives: observe-interpret-relate-assert; and the aim of this cycle is not just to solve problems or to model the world, but to bridge gaps, to cross cultures and to help us relate more fully to our environment. In other words, we use the same basic skill for both problem-solving *and* making social contact. Can we use this insight to design a course which helps both B- and T-oriented students to cross the gulf which divides them? To achieve this, a course should fulfil the following basic objective:

Objective: The nature of the cultural division between the B- and T-oriented groups lies in their mutual inability to recognize their respective strengths, so both groups need the opportunity to articulate the strengths of their own position and to recognize those of the opposite group. B-oriented students need to demonstrate and apply abstract rules, and T-oriented students need to learn to *question* such rules by observing and interpreting feedback from their environment.

Methods

The bioinformatics foundation course at FHW seeks to satisfy this objective by fulfilling the following criteria:

1. The problem-solving cycle discussed above plays a two-fold role in the course structure: it should form a framework within which B- and T-oriented students learn from each other, and it should also form a practical tool which students can use to solve problems in the course content.
2. This clearly implies that lessons should contain both concrete and abstract problems which students can solve; but it also implies that lessons should allow students to solve problems freely within this framework without being overly pre-programmed by specific lectured rules.
3. The course as a whole should also demonstrate the interconnectedness of different subject areas by showing how they address different aspects of the problem-solving cycle.
4. The course should be flexible: it should provide the teacher with clear guidelines on course content and the order in which this content can most fruitfully be presented, but should permit the creativity of moment-to-moment decisions on the manner of teaching.
5. The course should give students adequate opportunity to engage in and become proficient in scientific discourse with their fellow students by emphasizing discovery and group story-telling as essential to the scientific 'way of knowing'.

Table 13.1 illustrates how the FHW bioinformatics foundation course seeks to fulfil these criteria. Each week of the course is associated with a single narrative which runs through the week's lectures in mathematics, physics and informatics. These narratives are presented to the students as parables whose structure and plot form the basis for discussions of the particular skills being addressed that week in each of the three subjects. These subjects were specifically chosen because they respectively provide a firm grounding in the problem-solving activities of relating, interpreting and asserting. In the bioinformatics foundation course we simply frame them within a biological context.

Week 9 illustrates this idea. The theme of the week is 'Creating the future from the present', and is introduced by viewing a computer-simulation of the evolution of altruistic behaviour taken from Centola et al. (2000). Following this, Euler's method is introduced in mathematics – Euler's method is a procedure for predicting the dynamical unfolding of a narrative over a short period of time on the basis of an initial state

Table 13.1: Abbreviated structure of the FHW bioinformatics foundation course

Week	Narrative	Subject		
		Maths	Informatics	Physics
1	Modelling the world	Derivatives model change	Programming simple models	Exponential decay of blood alcohol
2	Divide and conquer	Vectors divide space into components	Mapping an action over components of a list	Reducing 2-D dynamics to components
3	Applying rules	Using formal rules	Defining functions as transformation rules	Equilibrium indicates a rule input = output
6	Playing on a roundabout	Exponential function rotates complex numbers	Plot complex functions	Rotating bodies
7	Building systems from simple rules	Proving theorems from axioms	Abstract data types defined by simple behaviours	Kinetic theory built from five simple axioms
9	Creating the future from the present	Euler's method builds future step by step	Animation as a sequence of time-steps	Vibrations propagate in a string to create waves

of the narrative. This ability to progress step-by-step into the future is the main process used in constructing computer simulations, so its relevance is immediately perceived in informatics when students programme a computer-simulation of oscillations in a biological system. The topic of oscillations is then given a basis in sensory experience in physics when students study the very tangible example of oscillations in a guitar string. Such cross-linkages provide many opportunities both to reduce course time and for students to approach the content simultaneously from several complementary perspectives and modalities.

Each lesson is based around a worksheet whose structure reiterates the cycle of observe-interpret-relate-assert. Indeed this cycle is explicitly covered in three different contexts: as a strategy for tackling exam questions, as a strategy for model-building, and as the structure of the software development cycle. Another aspect of the worksheet format is that it severely circumscribes the amount of content which can be covered in a single lesson. This is important since the perceived need for high throughput of factual content is a common reason given by lecturers for rejecting group-work in favour of purely frontal lecturing. The decision to address discursive fluency in the classroom necessarily involves a radical rethinking of the amount of explicit content necessary in a course, and the creation of a worksheet focuses this rethinking wonderfully. In general, it may be said that groupwork moves the emphasis of teaching away from providing 'whistle-stop' tours of a subject, and towards investigating the deeper structures underlying key topics.

An extremely important aspect of the worksheets is their mix of content with exercises which have been carefully chosen to encourage storytelling in which both B- and T-skills come into play. The exercises point to precisely those areas in which the student's intuitions do *not* work, and so encourage them to engage in social interaction with their fellow students in an attempt to resolve these paradoxes. One example might be the following physics question: 'The sum of all the external forces acting on an object are zero. What can you say about the movement of the object?' A common response to this question is to say that the object therefore cannot move. Telling students that this is not the case prompts an explosion of (small group) discussion in which students talk through their experience of what it means to apply a force to an object, and what effect it has. I find it particularly satisfying if they can talk themselves round to the situation of freewheeling down a hill at constant speed, since emphasizing the observed phenomenon of constant speed shows the contribution of B-thinking to the developing group narrative.

A consequence of this format is that lectured material may (but need not) be presented at the moment when it is needed, rather than as preprogramming to enable students to solve upcoming problems. The format enables the teacher to switch creatively between lecturing and groupwork according to the needs of the moment.

A format which I personally find fruitful is to first give a 10-minute introduction to a lesson, and then divide the students into 'expert' groups: one group for each topic to be covered in that lesson. In the expert groups, students then tackle a problem from the worksheet which is central to their own particular topic. During this phase the expert group starts to formulate the 'story' of their problem – homing in on a consensual storyline synthesized out of suggestions from all group members. It is often helpful to encourage students to formulate this storyline diagrammatically. Next the expert groups split up into learning groups comprising at least one member from each expert group, and the learning group members then swap stories from their respective expert groups. The result is a cacophony of activity which nevertheless with surprising regularity results in fun and learning. It is of course essential that the teacher remains constantly ready to pull strands together to ensure that all students assimilate the fundamental target skills of the lesson. A significant advantage of the expert-group format is that it can be adapted to almost arbitrarily large groups.

Outcomes

The bioinformatics foundation course presented here has now completed the first year of its introduction, so it is still a little early to be certain of results. However a number of interesting outcomes can definitely be noted, although it remains to be seen to what extent these are contingent upon this particular intake of students:

- One immediate observation is that these students display a quite remarkable willingness to form spontaneous learning groups, in which students meet in their own time to discuss and learn together. This was an unforeseen and extremely gratifying emergent bonus.
- The level of engagement of this class has been notably higher than in previous years, as measured in terms of optional attendance and the number of students volunteering questions and answers in class.
- The evidence from examination results is less clear. In previous years bioinformatics followed the pattern of many technical degree courses at German colleges of further education: about 10 per cent of students left before taking their first examinations, and 40 per cent– 50 per cent left during the following two years, after investing up to three years in unsuccessfully resitting examinations. This year the situation is much more polarized. Thirty per cent of this year's intake have terminated their studies before sitting their first examination – this seems from interviews to be due to the high intensity of participation required in the course. These students fall without exception into the category of those who might on the basis of past experience have been expected to leave, but this year their leaving was (a) much sooner than otherwise, and (b) accompanied by much more rancour than in the past.
- Of the students who remain, one thing is absolutely clear: their examination results are a marked improvement on previous years. About 10 per cent more have passed than in previous years, and about 20 per cent more have passed than in a control group which in

previous years has had comparable examination pass rates to those of bioinformatics. In addition the average mark of those who pass the examination has risen. The format of the examination has deliberately *not* been changed to reflect the new course structure, although this may be done in future years.

- This examination emphasizes components of both B- and T-styles of thinking, and the student's showing in the examinations reflect an improved ability to adopt both styles.
- The students who have passed seem subjectively more tired at the end of the academic year than students in previous years: the intensity of the course has also taken its toll on these students.
- Students taking this course perform noticeably better than previous years' students on 'open' questions requiring them to interpret a situation in terms of appropriate solution techniques.
- Some students at first sabotaged requests to discuss in groups; however after only 2–3 such sessions they responded very positively to this aspect of the course, and the 'smile level' during and after classes approached 100 per cent. On the other hand the following two comments made by students at the end of the course indicate the dangers of relying too heavily on pure discovery and negotiation as a means of learning:

'I enjoyed the group work, but I did not take away so much learning from the class as when you explained from the board.'
'I liked the transfer between topics from maths and physics. At first I didn't for example know why we need complex numbers – it was like that in many branches of maths. Only when we used them in physics did I understand their application. The only bummer was when we did group work and the "expert" in our group didn't have a clue.' (Translated from German)

On the basis of these and past observations I feel strongly encouraged to extend the storytelling format to other undergraduate courses, but increasing the flexibility of interweaving between lecturing and group work to ensure that negotiated information is formally summarized for the entire class. The fact that many students terminated their studies earlier than in the past may on the whole be viewed as a positive result; yet it will be necessary to pay close attention in the future to the level of stress on the course, since this appears to have been a major cause of their departure. There can be no doubt that the narrative approach advocated in this chapter makes high demands on the students participating in it!

Discussion

What implications do these ideas have for pedagogical practice in general? It seems to me that both problem-solving and social knowledge construction are essential elements of almost any course. The following check-list indicates those aspects of the bioinformatics foundation course which I have found most helpful in promoting these elements:

- Storytelling by the teacher can always be used as an initial motivation for a class topic. For example, relating the story of alcohol breakdown in my liver after three glasses of wine can motivate a discussion of the mathematics of exponential decay.
- Course materials can emphasize the problem-solving cycle by using it as the basic structure for presenting information.
- In addition the problem-solving cycle should be explicitly covered to provide a framework within which both B- and T-oriented thinkers can identify the usefulness of their respective contributions.
- Compressing the information in a single lesson onto a single sheet forces the teacher to sift out the irrelevant from the lesson content, and gives the students reference material which can more easily be processed within the space of one lecture (= 1.5 hours at FHW) than the sheaf of notes required for many science lectures.
- The materials should contain a constant mix of content and exercises to enable flexible integration of both frontal teaching and groupwork into the lesson format.
- (*Important*) Exercises should cover *all* of the following aspects: (a) practical exercises which focus the student's mind on the concrete application of techniques; (b) philosophical, or open, questions which stretch the students' minds to consider non-obvious ramifications of the material; and (c) non-intuitive exercises in which the students' intuitions let them down. Precisely this last category of question promotes the coming together of B- and T-thinkers into effective solving groups, and prompts them to exchange stories of past experiences in problem-solving. This work is time-consuming, but can in my experience be enormously fruitful in terms of students' ability to transfer learning into new situations.

Conclusion

Storytelling lies at the heart of what it means to be social, problem-solving beings, and we have seen in this chapter that we can make use of this storytelling aspect of problem-solving to support students in learning *both* problem-solving *and* competency in disciplinary discourse. It is essential that we allow students to tell stories to each other. In relating these stories, they also come to a recognition of each other's strengths: some have a keen eye for the details of a problem situation; some quickly make the connection from this problem to related ones; others excel in participating in a solution to carry it through to its logical conclusion; and yet others have the ability to organize a story into a specific decision as to what should be done. Every one of these abilities is crucial to the problem-solving endeavour.

Reflection questions

1. What disciplinary cultures are represented in the classes and subjects you teach, and what special contribution does each have to make?
2. Which components of a course/programme in your context involve the students primarily in (a) reality-checking, (b) reflecting, (c) relating or (d) asserting?
3. If some of these positions are not currently practised in the course programme, why not? Are these missing stages *really* irrelevant to the learning aims?
4. What do your students in your context really enjoy telling stories about: practical situations? philosophical questions? biology? car mechanics? romance?

Resources

Baker, A. C., Jensen P. J. & Kolb, D. A. (2002). *Conversational learning: An experiential approach to knowledge creation.* (Westport, CT: Quorum Books).
In this book the authors discuss creation of meaning through the medium of conversation. They show how everyday conversations can be viewed as social experiences through which we discover new perspectives on the world, so resolving conflicting systems of belief.
Fry, H., Ketteridge, S. & Marshall, S. (2001): *A handbook for teaching and learning in higher education.* (London: Kogan Page).
This book is packed with ideas for engaging students in their own learning. Particularly useful are the many suggestions in the book for small-group work.
www.clexchange.org
The Creative Learning Exchange is an excellent source of narrative-based teaching materials on assorted subjects from the physics of harmonic oscillators to a literary criticism of *Romeo and Juliet*. These materials typically use the Stella system dynamics software for visualization, but can easily be adapted to the more biologically motivated Narrator software mentioned below.

www.narrator-tool.org
Narrator is a freeware biological representation tool, developed by FHW students, which is used as part of the bioinformatics foundation course at FHW. Narrator provides a very general and very visual language for representing and 'running through' networks of narrative relationships in a wide range of scientific and non-scientific disciplines.

References

Adler, N. J., & Bartholomew, S. (1992). Managing globally competent people. *Academy of Management Executive, 6*, 52–65.

Agar, M. (1994). *Language shock: Understanding the culture of conversation.* New York: William Morrow.

Airey, J., & Linder, C. (2005). Looking for links between learning and the discursive practices of university science. Paper presented at EARLI 2005 11th Biennial conference, 23–27 August, Nicosia, Cyprus. Accessed 10 April 2007 at http://www2.hik.se/applikationer/forskning/publication.asp?id=2056

Ajzen, I. (1993). Attitude theory and the attitude–behavior relation. In D. Krebs & P. Schmidt (eds), *New directions in attitude measurement* (pp. 41–57). Berlin/New York: Walter de Gruyter.

Allport, G. W. (1954). *The nature of prejudice.* Reading, MA: Addison-Wesley.

Alred, G., Byram, M., & Fleming, M. (eds). (2003). *Intercultural experience and education.* Clevedon: Multilingual Matters.

Altbach, P. (2004). Higher education crosses borders. *Change, 36*(22), 18–26. Retrieved 26 April 2006, from Proquest 5000 database.

Ameny-Dixon, G. M. (2004). Why multicultural education is more important in higher education now than ever: A global perspective. *International Journal of Scholarly Academic Intellectual Diversity, 8*(1). Retrieved 30 September 2006, from: http://www.nationalforum.com/Electronic%20Journal%20Volumes/Ameny-Dixon,%20Gloria%20M.%20Why%20Multicultural%20Education%20is%20More%20Important%20in%20Higher%20Education%20Now%20than%20Ever.pdf

Angelo, T. A. (1995). Beginning the dialogue: thoughts on promoting critical thinking: Classroom assessment for critical thinking. *Teaching of Psychology, 22*(1), 6–7.

Appadurai, A. (ed.). (2001). *Globalization.* Durham: Duke University Press.

Aronowitz, S., & Giroux, H. (1991). *Postmodern education: Politics, culture and social criticism.* Minneapolis: University of Minnesota Press.

Aspland, T. (1999a). Struggling with ambivalence within supervisory relations. In A. Holbrook & S. Johnson (eds). *Supervision of postgraduate research in education* (pp. 95–111). Coldstream, Victoria: AARE.

Aspland, T. (1999b). You learn round and I learn square: Mei's story. In Y. Ryan & O. Zuber-Skerrit (eds), *Supervising postgraduates from non-English speaking backgrounds* (pp. 25–39). Buckingham: The Society for Research into Higher Education & Open University Press.

Avruch, K., & Black, P. W. (1991). *The culture question and conflict resolution.* Washington, DC: United States Institute of Peace Press.

Bakhtin, M. M. (1963/1984). *Problems of Dostoevsky's poetics* (Emerson, C., trans.). Minneapolis: University of Minnesota Press.

Ball, S. J. (1990). *Politics and policy making in education: Explorations in policy sociology.* London: Routledge.

Ballard, B. (1987). Academic adjustment: The other side of the export dollar. *Higher Education Research and Development, 6*(2), 109–19.

Ballard, B., & Clanchy, J. (1984). *Study abroad: A manual for Asian students*. Kuala Lumpur: Longman.

Ballard, B., & Clanchy, J. (1988). *Studying in Australia*. Melbourne: Longman Cheshire.

Ballard, B. & Clanchy, J. (1991). *Teaching students from overseas: A brief guide for lecturers and supervisors*. Melbourne: Longman Cheshire.

Ballard, B., & Clanchy, J. (1997). *Teaching international students: A brief guide for lecturers and supervisors*. Canberra: IDP Education Australia.

Barmeyer, C. (2004). Learning styles and their impact on cross-cultural training: An international comparison in France, Germany and Quebec. *International Journal of Intercultural Relations*, 28(6), 577–94. Retrieved 24 April 2006, from Science Direct database.

Barmeyer, C. I., & Bolten, J. (1998). *Interkulturelle personalorganisation*. Vorwort. Sternenfels: Verlag Wissenschaft und Praxis.

Barro, A., Jordan, S., & Roberts, C. (1998). Cultural practice in everyday life: The language learner as ethnographer. In M. Byram & M. Flemings (eds), *Language learning in intercultural perspective: Approaches through drama and ethnography* (pp. 76–97). Cambridge, UK/New York: Cambridge University Press.

Bauman, Z. (2000). *Liquid modernity*. Cambridge: Polity.

Becher, T. (1993). *Academic tribes and territories: Intellectual enquiry and the culture of disciplines*. Buckingham: The Society for Research into Education and Open University Press.

Beck, U. (1992). *Risk society: Towards a new modernity*. London: Sage.

Belenky, M. F., Clinchy, B. M., Goldberger, N. R., & Tarule, J. M. (1986). *Women's ways of knowing: The development of self, voice, and mind*. New York: Basic Books.

Belich, J. (1996). *Making peoples: A history of the New Zealanders*. Auckland, New Zealand: Penguin.

Bell, M. (2005). *Peer observation partnerships in higher education*. Milpera, Australia: Higher Education Research and Development Society of Australasia.

Belz, J. A., & Müller-Hartmann, A. (2003). Teachers as intercultural learners: Negotiating German–American telecollaboration along the institutional fault line. *Modern Language Journal*, 87, 71–89.

Bennett, C. I (2003). *Comprehensive multicultural education: Theory and practice*. Boston: Pearson Education.

Bernstein, B. (2000). *Pedagogy, symbolic control and identity* (Rev. edn.). New York and Oxford: Rowman & Littlefield.

Bernstein, B. (ed.). (1973). *Class, codes and control (Vol. 2): Theoretical studies towards a sociology of language*. London: Routledge & Kegan Paul.

Berreby, D. (2005). *Us and them: Understanding your tribal mind*. New York: Little, Brown and Company.

Bhabha, H. (1994). *The location of culture*. London & New York: Routledge.

Biggs, J. (1997). *Teaching across and within cultures: The issue of international students*. Paper presented at the Learning and Teaching in Higher Education Conference, Advancing International Perspectives. Adelaide, South Australia.

Biggs, J. B. (1987). *Student approaches to learning and studying*. Hawthorn, VIC: Australian Council for Educational Research.

Biggs, J. (1999). *Teaching for quality learning at university*. Maidenhead: Open University Press.

Biggs, J. B., Kember, D., & Leung, D. Y. P. (2001). The revised two-factor study process questionnaire: R-SPQ-2F. *British Journal of Educational Psychology*, *71*, 133–49.

Birkey, R. C., & Rodman, J. J. (1995). *Adult learning styles and preference for technology programs*. San Diego: National University Research Institute.

Bodycott, P., & Walker, A. (2000). Teaching abroad: Lessons learned about inter-cultural understanding for teachers in higher education. *Teaching in Higher Education*, *5*(1), 79–94.

Bogdan, R. C., & Biklen, S. K. (2003). *Qualitative research for education. An introduction to theories and methods* (4th edn). Boston: Allyn & Bacon.

Bohm, A., Fallari, M., Hewett, A., Jones, S., Kemp, N., Meares, D., Peare, D., & Van Cauter, K. (2004). *Vision 2020: Forecasting international student mobility, a UK perspective*. British Council: London.

Boisot, M., & Child, J. (1996). From fiefs to clans and network capitalism: Explaining China's emerging economic order. *Administrative Science Quarterly*, *41*(4), 600–628.

Bonham, L. A., Cifuentes, L., & Murphy, K. L. (1995). *Constructing cultures in distance education*. Retrieved 11 May 2006, from http:// it.coe.uga.edu/ itforum/paper4/paper4.htm

Bourdieu, P. (1986). The forms of capital. In J. Richardson (ed.), *Handbook of theory and research for the sociology of education* (pp. 241–58). New York: Greenwood Press.

Bourdieu, P. (2003). *Firing back: Against the tyranny of the market 2* (L. Wacquant, Trans.). London, New York: Verso.

Bourdieu, P., & Passeron, J.-C. (1965). Introduction: Language and relationship to language in the teaching situation. In P. Bourdieu, J.-C. Passeron & M. de Saint Martin (eds), *Academic discourse* (pp. 1–34). Stanford: Stanford University Press.

Bowen, W. G., & Bok, D. (1998) *The shape of the river: Long-term consequences of considering race in college and university admissions*. Princeton, NJ: Princeton University Press.

Bowers, C. A. & Flinders, D. J. (1990). *Responsive teaching: An ecological approach to classroom patterns of language, culture, and thought*. New York: Teachers College.

Boyer, E. (1990). *Scholarship reconsidered: Priorities of the professoriate*. San Francisco: Jossey-Bass.

Brady, P. (2004). Jocks, teckers, and nerds: The role of the adolescent peer group in the formation and maintenance of secondary school institutional culture. *Studies in Cultural Politics of Education*, *25*(3), 351–64.

Britzman, D. (1998). *Lost subjects, contested objects: Towards a psychoanalytic inquiry of learning*. Albany: State University of New York.

Brookfield, S. D. (1995). *Becoming a critically reflective teacher*. New York: John Wiley & Sons.

Brooks J. G., & Brooks M. G. (1993). *In search of understanding: The case for constructivist classroom*. Alexandria, VA: Association for Supervision and Curriculum Development.

Brown, A. L. (1978). Knowing when and how to remember: A problem of metacognition. In R. Glaser (ed.), *Advances in instructional psychology (Vol. 1)* (pp. 77–165). Hillsdale, NJ: Erlbaum.

Bruner, J. S. (1990). *Acts of meaning*. Cambridge, MA: Harvard University Press.

Budby, J. (2001). The academic quandary: An Aboriginal experience. In A. Bartlett & G. Mercer (eds), *Postgraduate research supervision: Transforming (R)elations* (pp. 247–54). New York: Peter Lang.

Bullen, E., & Kenway, J. (2003). Real or imagined women? Staff representations of international women postgraduate students. *Discourse: Studies in the Cultural Politics of Education, 24*(1), 36–50.

Burbules, N. C. (1993). *Dialogue in teaching: Theory and practice.* New York: Teachers College Press.

Burbules, N., & Bruce, B. (2001). Theory and research on teaching as dialogue. Retrieved 16 August 2006, from http://www.isrl.uiuc.edu/~chip/pubs/dialogue.html. Also in V. Richardson (ed.), *Handbook of research on teaching* (4th edn). Washington, DC: American Educational Research Association.

Buttjes, D. (1989). Landeskunde-Didaktik und landeskunliches Curriculum. In Bausch, K. H., Christ, H., Hüllen, W. and Krumm, H. J. (eds), *Handbuch Fremdsprachenunterricht* (pp. 112–19). Tübingen: Francke Verlag.

Byram, M. (1997). *Teaching and assessing intercultural communicative competence.* Clevedon: Multilingual Matters.

Byram, M., & Buttjes, D. (eds). (1991). *Mediating languages and cultures: Towards an intercultural theory of foreign language education.* Clevedon: Multilingual Matters.

Byram, M., Nichols, A., & Stevens, D. (eds). (2001). *Developing intercultural competence in practice.* Clevedon: Mutlilingual Matters.

Cadman, K., & Ha, H. T. (2001). Only connect: Transcultural supervision as the Rainbow Bridge. In A. Bartlett & G. Mercer (eds), *Postgraduate research supervision: Transforming (r)elations* (pp. 215–32). New York: Peter Lang.

Carey, S. (1999). The use of WebCT for a highly interactive virtual graduate seminar. *Computer Assisted Language Learning, 12*(1), 85–98.

Carey, S. (2001). Evaluating the success of ESL online communities. *Proceedings of the Tenth International Symposium of English Teaching.* Taiwan Normal University, Taipei.

Carroll, J. and Ryan, J. (eds) (2005). *Teaching international students: Improving learning for all.* Oxford: Routledge.

Castells, M. (1997). *The power of identity.* Oxford: Blackwell.

Cazden, C. B. (2001). *Classroom discourse: The language of teaching and learning* (2nd edn). Portsmouth, NH: Heinemann.

Centola, D., McKenzie, E., & Wilensky, U. (2000). Survival of the groupiest: Facilitating students' understanding of multi-level evolution through multi-agent modeling – The EACH project. *Fourth International Conference on Complex Systems.* New England Complex Systems Institute.

Chalmers, D., & Volet, S. (1997). Common misconceptions about students from South-East Asia studying in Australia. *Higher Education Research & Development, 16*, 87–98.

Chan, S. (1999). The Chinese learner – a question of style. *Education and Training, 41*(6/7), 294–304.

Chang, M. (ed.), (2003). *Compelling interest: Examining the evidence on racial dynamics in colleges and universities.* Palo Alto, CA: Stanford University Press.

Cheng, S. K. (1990). Understanding the culture and behaviour of East Asians – a Confucian perspective. *Aust N Z J Psychiatry, 24*(4), 510–15.

Coffield, F., Moseley, D. E., Hall, E., & Ecclestone, K. (2004). *Should we be using learning styles: What research has to say to practice.* London: The Learning and Skills Research Centre.

Coleman, D. (1998). The foundations of higher education: Do students make the grade? In D. Davis & A. Olsen (eds), *Outcomes of international education: Research findings* (pp. 19–33). Canberra: IDP Education Australia.

Coleman, H. (1987). Teaching spectacles and learning festivals. *ELT Journal*, *41*(2), 97–103.

Cortazzi, M., & Jin, L. (1996). Cultures of learning: Language classrooms in China. In H. Coleman (ed.), *Society and the language classroom* (pp. 169–206). Cambridge: Cambridge University Press.

Cowan, G. (2005). Interracial interactions at racially diverse university campuses. *Journal of Social Psychology*, *145*(1), 49–63.

Cowan, J. (1990). *Dance and the body politic in Greece*. Princeton: Princeton University Press.

Crawford, D. (2000). Chinese capitalism: Cultures, the Southeast Asian region and economic globalization. *Third World Quarterly*, *21*(1), 69–86.

Cronjé, J. C. (2006). Pretoria to Khartoum – how we taught an Internet-supported Masters' programme across national, religious, cultural and linguistic barriers. *Educational Technology & Society*, *9*(1), 276–88.

Dahl, S. (2004). Intercultural research: The current state of knowledge. *Middlesex University Discussion Paper No. 26*. Retrieved 5 June 2006, from Social Science Research Network: http://ssrn.com/abstract=658202

Daniel, J. (2004). Education across borders: What is appropriate? *The 1st UK International Education Conference, Going Global: The Internationalization of Education*. Edinburgh, UK.

Daniels, M. (1999). Reflections on international projects in undergraduate computer science education. *Computer Science Education*, *9*(3), 256–67.

Darder, A., Baltodano, M., & Torres, R. D. (2003). Critical pedagogy: An introduction. In A. Darder, M. Baltodano, & R. D. Torres (eds), *The critical pedagogy reader* (pp. 1–23). New York and London: Routledge Falmer.

David Suzuki Foundation (1993). *Forests*. Retrieved 8 August 2003, from www.davidsuzuki.org

De Bono, E. (1996). *Textbook of wisdom*. New York: Penguin & Putnam.

Department of Education, Science & Training (2005). *Students 2004 (full year): Selected higher education statistics*. Retrieved 18 October 2005, from http://www.dest.gov.au/sectors/higher_education/publications_resources/profiles/students_2004_selected_higher_education_statistics.htm

Dickerson, V. (2004). Young women struggling for an identity. *Family Process*, *43*(3), 337–48.

Dlaska, A. (2000). Integrating culture and language learning in institution-wide language programmes. *Language, Culture and Curriculum*, *13*(3), 247–63.

Dodd, C. H. (1995). *Dynamics of intercultural communication* (5th edn). Boston, MA: McGraw-Hill.

Doherty, C., & Singh, P. (2005). How the West is done: Simulating Western pedagogy in a curriculum for Asian international students. In P. Ninnes, & M. Hellsten (eds), *Internationalizing higher education: Critical explorations of pedagogy and policy* (pp. 53–73). Hong Kong: Comparative Education Research Centre, University of Hong Kong.

Dyson, A. H., & Genishi, C. (2005). *On the case*. New York: Teachers College Press.

Edwards, R. (1997). *Changing places? Flexibility, lifelong learning and a learning society*. London: Routledge.

Eisenchlas, S. A., & Trevaskes, S. (2003). Creating cultural spaces in the Australian university setting: A pilot study of structured cultural exchanges. *Australian Review of Applied Linguistics*, *26*(2), 84–100.

Ellis, C., & Bochner, A. P. (1996). Talking over ethnography. In C. Ellis & A. P. Bochner (eds), *Composing ethnography: Alternative forms of qualitative writing* (pp. 13–45). Walnut Creek, CA: AltaMira Press.

Ellsworth, E. (1989). Why doesn't this feel empowering? Working through the repressive myths of critical pedagogy. *Harvard Educational Review, 59*(3), 297–324.

Ellsworth, E. (1997) *Teaching positions: Difference, pedagogy, and the power of address*. New York: Teachers College Press.

Emerson, R. M., Fretz, R. I., & Shaw, L. L. (1995). *Writing ethnographic fieldnotes*. Chicago: University of Chicago Press.

Entwistle, N. J. (1992). *The impact of teaching on learning outcomes in higher education*. Sheffield: CVCP Staff Development Unit.

Entwistle, N. J. (2003). *University teaching-learning environments and their influences on student learning: An introduction to the ETL Project*. Paper presented at the British Educational Research Association (BERA) conference. Heriot-Watt University: Edinburgh.

Entwistle, N. J., & Ramsden, P. (1983). *Understanding student learning*. London: Croom Helm.

Entwistle, N. J., & Tait, H. (1994). *The revised approaches to study inventory*. Edinburgh: Centre for Research into Learning and Instruction, University of Edinburgh.

EuroClass Management Group (2004). *Evaluation report for EuroClass*. Odense: Tietgen Business College, Denmark.

Felder, R. M., & Silverman, L. K. (1988). Learning and teaching styles in engineering education. *Journal of Engineering Education, 78*(7), 674–81.

Felman, S. (1982) Psychoanalysis and education: Teaching the terminable and interminable. *Yale French Studies, 63*(1), 21–44.

Flavell, J. H. (1976). Metacognitive aspects of problem solving. In B. Resnick (ed.), *The nature of intelligence* (pp. 231–6). Hillsdale, NJ: Erlbaum.

Foucault, M. (1990). *The history of sexuality: An introduction (Vol 1)*. New York: Vintage Books.

Fowler, S. (2006). Training across cultures: What intercultural trainers bring to diversity training. *International Journal of Intercultural Relations, 30*(3), 401–11. Retrieved 24 April 2006, from Science Direct database.

Freire, P. (1972). *Pedagogy of the oppressed*. Harmondsworth: Penguin.

Friedman, M. (1970, 1 September). The social responsibility of business is to increase its profits. New York. Reprinted in T. L. Beauchamp, & N. B. Bowie (eds), *Ethical theory and business* (1993). Englewood Cliffs, NJ: Prentice-Hall.

Friedrich, C. (1818a). *Kreidefelsen auf Rügen*. Berlin: Nationalgallerie.

Friedrich, C. (1818b). *Wanderer über dem Morgennebel*. Berlin: Nationalgallerie.

Fukuyama, F. (1996). *Trust: The social virtues and creation of prosperity*. London: Penguin

Gadamer, H.-G. (1975). *Truth and method*. London: Sheed and Ward.

Gagne, R. M. (1985). *The conditions of learning and theory of instruction* (4th edn). New York: Holt, Rinehart and Winston.

Garner, R., & Gillingham, M. G. (1996). *Internet communication in six classrooms: Conversations across time, space and culture*. Mahwah, NJ: Lawrence Erlbaum.

Gass, L. (1998). *Teaching for creativity in science: An example, CDT Link*. Centre for Development of Teaching and Learning, National University of Singapore. Retrieved 19 April 2006, from www.cdtl.nus.edu. sg/link/jul1998/practice1.htm

Gay, G. (1994). A synthesis of scholarship in multicultural education. *Urban Education Monograph Series, NCREL Urban Education Program*. Retrieved 12 June 2006, from http://www.ncrel.org/sdrs/areas/issues/educatrs/leadrshp/le0gay.htm

Geake, J., & Maingard, C. (1999). NESB postgraduate students in a new university: *Plus ca change, plus c'est la même chose*. In Y. Ryan & O. Zuber-Skerritt (eds), *Supervising postgraduates from non-English speaking backgrounds* (pp. 48–60). Buckingham: SRHE & Open University Press.

Ghoshal, S. (2005). Bad management theories are destroying good management practices. *Academy of Management Learning and Education, 4*(1), 75–91.

Gollnick, D. M., & Chinn, P. C. (2002). *Multicultural education in a pluralistic society* (6th edn). Upper Saddle River, NJ: Pearson Education.

Goodnow, J. J., Miller, P. J., & Kessel, F. S. (1995). *Cultural practices as contexts for development*. San Francisco: Jossey-Bass.

Gow, L., & Kember, D. (1993). Conceptions of teaching and their relationship to student learning. *British Journal of Educational Psychology, 63*, 20–33.

Grant, B. (2003). Mapping the pleasures and risks of supervision. *Discourse: Studies in the Cultural Politics of Education, 24*(2), 175–90.

Green, B. (2005). Unfinished business: Subjectivity and supervision. *Higher Education Research & Development, 24*(2), 151–64.

Green, M. F. (1989). *Minorities on campus: A handbook for enhancing diversity*. Washington DC: American Council on Education.

Hall, E. (1976). *Beyond culture*. New York: Anchor Books.

Hall, S. (1991). Old and new identities, old and new ethnicities. In A. D. King (ed.), *Culture, globalization and the world system* (pp. 41–68). London: Macmillan.

Hall, S. (1996a). On Postmodernism and articulation: An interview with Stuart Hall. In D. Morley & K.-H. Chen (eds), *Critical dialogues in cultural studies* (pp. 131–50). London, New York: Routledge.

Hall, S. (1996b). Introduction: Who needs 'identity'? In S. Hall & P. du Gay (eds), *Questions of cultural identity* (pp. 1–17). London: Sage.

Harrigan, H., & Vincenti, V. (2004). Developing higher-order thinking through an intercultural assignment: A scholarship of teaching inquiry project. *College Teaching, 52*(2), 113–20.

Harrison, J. (2001). Developing intercultural communication and understanding through social studies in Israel. *Social Studies, 92*(6), 252–9.

Hartman, V. F. (1995). Teaching and learning style preferences: Transitions through technology. *VCCA Journal, 9*(2), 18–20.

Hativa, N., & Marincovich, M. (1995) (eds). Disciplinary differences in teaching and learning: Implications for practice. *New Directions for Teaching and Learning, 64*. San Francisco: Jossey-Bass.

Hayden, M., & Thompson, J. (1995). International education: The crossing of frontiers. *International Schools Journal, 15*(1), 13–20.

Heelas, P. (2002). Work ethics, soft capitalism and the 'Turn to Life'. In P. du Gay & M. Pryke (eds), *Cultural economy,* (pp. 78–96). London: Sage.

Heikkinen, A. (2004). Evaluation in the transnational management by projects policies. *European Educational Research, 3*(2), 486–500.

Harman, G. (2004). New directions in internationalizing higher education: Australia's development as an exporter of higher education services. *Higher Education Policy, 17*, 101–20.

Heublein, U., Schmelzer, R., & Sommer, D. (2005). Studienabbruchstudie 2005. *HIS-Kurzinformation*, A1/2005.

Heublein, U., Spangenberg, H., & Sommer, D. (2003). Ursachen des studienabbruchs. *HIS-Hochschulplanung*, 163.

Higher Education Statistics Agency (2006). 6.1 per cent increase in overseas students for 2004/05: Business and admin retains most popular subject status. *Press Release, PR97, 13* (March). Retrieved 15 August 2006, from http://www.hesa.ac.uk/press/pr97/pr97.htm

Hinkel, E. (2001). Building awareness and practical skills to facilitate cross-cultural communication. In M. Celce-Murcia (ed.), *Teaching English as a second or foreign language* (3rd edn, pp. 443–58). Boston, MA: Heinle & Heinle.

Ho, A., Watkins, D., & Kelly, M. (2001). The conceptual change approach to improving teaching and learning: An evaluation of a Hong Kong staff development programme. *Higher Education, 42,* 143–69.

Hofstede, G. (1986). Cultural differences in teaching and learning. *International Journal of Intercultural Relations, 10,* 301–20.

Hofstede, G. (2001). *Culture's consequences: Comparing values, behaviours, institutions and organizations across nations.* Thousand Oaks: Sage.

Holliday, A. (1994). *Appropriate methodology in social context.* Cambridge: Cambridge University Press.

Holliday, A. (2002). *Doing and writing qualitative research.* London: Sage.

Holliday, A. R. (2005). *The struggle to teach English as an international language.* Oxford: Oxford University Press.

Holliday, A. R., & Zikri, M. (1988). *Distance learning in large classes: Appropriate methodology.* Proceedings of the 7th National Symposium on English Teaching in Egypt. Cairo: Centre for Developing English Language Teaching, Ain Shams University (pp. 267–72).

Holliday, A. R., Hyde, M., & Kullman, J. (2004). *Intercultural communication: An advanced resource book.* London: Routledge.

Honey, P., & Mumford, A. (1992). *The manual of learning styles.* Maidenhead: Peter Honey.

House, R. J., Hanges, P. J., Javidan, M., Dorfman, P. W., & Gupta, V. (eds) (2004). *Culture, leadership, and organizations. The GLOBE study of 62 societies.* Thousand Oaks, London, New Delhi: Sage.

Hwang, K. (1987). Face and favour: The Chinese power game. *American Journal of Sociology, 92,* 944–74.

Hyundai Apologises (2006). Hyundai apologises amid scandal. *BBC News online.* Retrieved 25 April 2006, from http://news.bbc.co.uk/2/hi/business/4921350.stm.

In praise of rules: A survey of Asian economies (2001). *The Economist, 5.* Retrieved 15 August 2006, from www.economist.com/surveys/displaystory.cfm?story_id=E1_VVJPRJ.

Institute of International Education (ed.). (2003). *Atlas of student mobility.* Compiled by Todd M. Davis.

INTERN Management Group (2002a). *Virtual Internships: Real experience in a world: A best practice handbook for those interested in the concept of virtual internships in business education.* Odense: Tietgen Business College, Denmark.

INTERN Management Group (2002b). *INTERN evaluation report.* Odense: Tietgen Business College, Denmark.

Ivanic, R. (1998). *Writing and identity: The discoursal construction of identity.* Philadelphia: John Benjamins.

Jablonka, E., & Lamb, M. J. (2006). *Evolution in four dimensions: Genetic, epigenetic, behavioral, and symbolic variation in the history of life.* Cambridge, MA: MIT Press.

Johnson, C. (1995). Disinfecting dialogues. In J. Gallop (ed.), *Pedagogy: The question of impersonation* (pp. 129–37). Bloomington: Indiana University Press.

Johnson, L., Lee, A., & Green, B. (2000). The Ph.D. and the autonomous self: Gender, rationality and postgraduate pedagogy. *Studies in Higher Education, 25*(2), 135–47.

Johnston, B. (2004). Summative assessment of portfolios: An examination of different approaches to agreement over outcomes. *Studies in Higher Education, 29*(3), 395–412.

Jonassen, D. H. (1991). Objectivism versus constructivism: Do we need a new philosophical paradigm? *Educational Technology Research and Development, 39*(3), 5–14.

Jones, A. (1999). Desire at the pedagogical borders: Absolution and difference in the university classroom. *Educational Theory, 49*(3), 299–315.

Jones, A. (2001). Cross-cultural pedagogy and the passion for ignorance. *Feminism and Psychology, 11*(3), 279–92.

Jones, A. (2004) Talking cure: The desire for dialogue. In M. Boler (ed.), *Democratic dialogue in education: Troubling speech, disturbing silence* (pp. 59–71). New York: Peter Lang.

Jones, A., & Jenkins, K. (2004). Pedagogical events: Re-reading shared moments in educational history. *Journal of Intercultural Studies, 25*(2), 143–59.

Kachru, B. (1996). World Englishes. In S. McKay, & N. Hornberger (eds), *Sociolinguistics and language teaching* (pp. 71–102). Cambridge: Cambridge University Press.

Kağıtçıbaşı, Ç (1988). Diversity of socialization in cross-cultural perspective: A model of change. In P. R. Dasen, J. W. Berry, & N. Sartorius (eds), *Health and cross-cultural psychology.* Newbury Park, CA: Sage.

Keller, E. (2002). *Making sense of life.* Cambridge, MA: Harvard University Press.

Kember, D. (1997). A reconceptualisation of the research into academics' conceptions of teaching. *Learning and Instruction, 7*(3), 255–75.

Kember, D., & Gow, L. (1990). Cultural specificity of approaches to study. *British Journal of Educational Psychology, 60*, 356–63.

Kember, D., & Gow, L. (1991). A challenge to the anecdotal stereotype of the Asian student. *Studies in Higher Education, 16*(2), 117–28.

Kenway, J., & Bullen, E. (2003). Self-representations of international women postgraduate students in the global university 'contact zone'. *Gender and Education, 15*(1), 5–20.

Kim, K. C., & Kim, S. (1989). Kinship group and patrimonial executives in a developing nation: A case of Korea. *Journal of Developing Areas, 24*, 27–46.

Kimball, S. T. (1978). The transmission of culture. In J. I. Roberts & S. K. Akinsanya (eds), *Schooling in the cultural context: Anthropological studies of education* (pp. 257–71). New York: David McKay.

King, M. (2004). *A History of New Zealand.* Auckland: Penguin

Kirkwood T. F. (2002). Jamaican students of color in the American classroom: problems and possibilities in education, *Intercultural Education, 13*(3), 305–13.

Knight, J. (1999). Internationalisation of higher education. In J. Knight & H. de Wit (eds), *Quality and internationalisation in higher education* (pp. 13–28). Paris: OECD.

Knight, J. (2002). *Trade in higher education services*. Report to Observatory on Borderless Higher Education. Retrieved 2 April 2006, from www.unesco.org/education/studyingabroad/highlights/global_forum/gats_he/jk_trade_he_gats_implications.pdf

Kolb, D. (1976). *Learning style inventory technical manual*. Bosten: McBer.

Kolb, D. A. (1983). *Experiential learning: Experience as the source of learning and development*. New Jersey: Prentice-Hall.

Kramsch, C. (1991). Culture in language learning: A view from the United States. In K. de Bot, R. B. Ginsberg, & C. Kramsch (eds), *Foreign language research in cross-cultural perspective* (pp. 217–240). Amsterdam: Benjamins.

Kramsch, C. (1993). *Context and culture in language teaching*. Oxford: Oxford University Press.

Kramsch, C. (1998). *Language and culture*. Oxford: Oxford University Press.

Kramsch, C. (2002). In search of the intercultural. *Journal of Sociolinguistics, 6*(2), 275–85.

Kubota, R. (2001). Discursive construction of the images of US classrooms. *TESOL Quarterly, 35*(1), 9–38.

Lau, A., & Roffey, B. (2002). Management education and development in China: A research note. *Labour and Management Development Journal, 2*(10), 1–18

Lau, W. M., Chan Yan Y. A., Chong P. Y., & Siu Wai Chung, S. (1998). The needs and problems of postgraduate research students: Cultural and environmental influences. *HERDSA Conference Proceedings*, Vol. 21, University of Auckland.

Lave, J., & Wenger, E. (1991). *Situated learning: Legitimate peripheral participation*. Cambridge: Cambridge University Press.

Lawrence, G. (1979). *People types and tiger stripes. A practical guide to learning styles*. Center for Applications of Psychological Type.

Leask, B. (2005). *Internationalisation of the curriculum and intercultural engagement: A variety of Perspectives and Possibilities*. Paper presented at the Opportunities in a Challenging Environment: the Australian International Education Conference 2005, Sydney.

Lee, A., & Williams, C. (1999). Forged in fire. Narratives of trauma in PhD supervision pedagogy. *Southern Review, 32*(1), 6–26.

Lee, S. M., & Yoo, S. (1987). The K-Type management: A driving force of Korean prosperity. *Management International Review, 27*, 68–77.

Lenwartowicz, T., & Roth, K. (1999). A framework for culture assessment. *Journal of International Business Studies, 30*(4) 781–98.

LePage, R. B., & Tabouret-Keller, A. (1985). *Acts of identity: Creole-based approaches to language and identity*. Cambridge: Cambridge University Press.

Little, D. (2001). Learner autonomy and the challenge of tandem language learning via the internet. In A. Chambers & G. Davies (eds), *ICT and Language Learning: A European Perspective* (pp. 29–38). Lisse: Swets and Zeitlinger.

Littlemore, J. (2001). Learner autonomy, self-instruction and new technologies in language learning: Current theory and practice in higher education in Europe. In A. Chambers & G. Davies (eds), *ICT and language learning: A European perspective* (pp. 39–52). Lisse: Swets and Zeitlinger.

Luo, Y. (1997). Guanxi: Principles, philosophies and implications. *Human Systems Management,* 16(1), 43–52.

Malik, L. (1995). Social and cultural determinants of the gender gap in higher education in the Islamic world. *Journal of Asian and African Studies,* 30(3–4), 181–95. Retrieved 9 April 2006, from Expanded Academic ASAP database.

Manathunga, C. (2005a). The development of research supervision: Turning the light on a private space. *International Journal for Academic Development,* 10(1), 17–30.

Manathunga, C. (2005b). Early warning signs in postgraduate research education: A different approach to timely completions. *Teaching in Higher Education,* 10(2), 219–33.

Marcus, A. (2000). International and intercultural user-interface design. In S. Constantine (ed.), *User interfaces for all* (pp. 47–64). New York: Lawrence Erlbaum.

Marton, F., & Säljö, R. (1976). On qualitative differences in learning: Outcome and process. *British Journal of Educational Psychology,* 46, 4–11.

McClure, J. W. (2005). Preparing a laboratory-based thesis: Chinese international research students' experiences of supervision. *Teaching in Higher Education,* 10(1), 3–16.

McConaghy, C. (2000). *Rethinking indigenous education: Culturalism, colonialism and the politics of knowing.* Queensland, Australia; Post Pressed.

McGugan, I. (1995). Canada's hottest export-business professors. *Canadian Business,* 68(4), 99.

McKay, S., & Wong, S.-L. (1996). Multiple discourses, multiple identities: Investment and agency in second language learning among Chinese adolescent immigrant students. *Harvard Educational Review,* 66(3), 577–608.

McLaren, P. (1995). *Critical pedagogy and predatory culture.* London: Routledge.

McNaught, K. (1988). *A penguin history of Canada.* New York: Penguin Books.

McNergney, R. F., & Herbert, J. M. (2001). *Foundations of education: The challenge of professional practice.* Boston: Alyn and Bacon

Mehan, H. (1979). *Learning lessons: Social organization in the classroom.* Cambridge, MA: Harvard University Press.

Merrill, D. (1991). Constructivism and instructional design. *Educational Technology,* 31(5), 45–52.

Merryfield, M. (2003). Like a veil: Cross-cultural experiential learning online. *Contemporary Issues in Technology and Teacher Education,* 3(2), 146–71.

Middle East Online (2004). *UAE population topped four million in 2003.* Retrieved 3 April 2006, from http://195.224.230.11/english/uae/?id=9623

Milem, J. F. (2003). The educational benefits of diversity: Evidence from multiple sectors. In M. Chang. (ed.), *Compelling interest: Examining the evidence on racial dynamics in colleges and universities* (pp. 126–70). Palo Alto, CA: Stanford University Press.

Moll, L. C., Amanti, C., Neff, D., & Gonzalez, N. (1992). Funds of knowledge for teaching: Using a qualitative approach to connect homes and classrooms. *Theory into Practice,* 31(2), 132–41.

Morris, P. (ed.). (1994).*The Bakhtin reader. Selected writings of Bakhtin, Medvedev, Voloshinov.* London: Arnold.

Myers, I. B., & McCaulley, M. H. (1985). *Manual: A guide to the development and use of the Myers-Briggs Type Indicator.* Palo Alto, CA: Consulting Psychologists Press.

Narayan, U. (1988). Working together across difference: Some considerations on emotions and political practice. *Hypatia: A Journal of Feminist Philosophy*, 3(2), 31–48

Nasir, N. S., & Al-Amin, J. (2006). Creating identity-safe spaces on college campuses for Muslim students. *Change*, 38(2), 22–7.

Neisser, U. (ed.) (1986). *The school achievement of minority children: New perspectives*. Hillsdale, NY: Laurence Erlbaum.

Nelson, T. D. (2002). *The psychology of prejudice*. Boston, MA: Allyn & Bacon.

Nesdale, D., Simkin, K., Sang, D., Burke, B., & Frager, S. (1995). *International students and immigration*. Canberra: AGPS.

Ng, I. C. L., (2006). Photoessays in the teaching of marketing. *Journal of Marketing Education*, 28(3), 1–17.

Ng, I. C. L., & Forbes, J. (2006, May–June). *Education as service: The understanding of university experience through the service logic*. Proceedings of the 9th International Research Seminar in Service Management, La Londe: France.

Nicholas, J. L. (1817). *Narrative of a voyage to New Zealand in two volumes*, Auckland, New Zealand: Wilson & Horton.

Nipporica Associates (1997). *Ecotonos: A multicultural problem-solving simulation*. Yarmouth, Maine: Intercultural Press.

Nisbett, R. (2003). *The geography of thought: How Asians and Westerners think differently . . . and why*. New York: Free Press.

Nonaka, I., & Takeuchi, H. (1995). *The knowledge-creating company*. Oxford: Oxford University Press.

Nonaka, I., & Umemoto, K., & Sasaki, K. (1998). Three tales of knowledge-creating companies. In G. von Krogh, J. Roos, & D. Klein (eds), *Knowing in firms: Understanding, managing and measuring knowledge* (pp. 146–72). London: Sage.

Norton, B. (2000). *Identity and language learning: Gender, ethnicity and educational change*. Harlow: Pearson Education.

Norton, B. & Toohey, K. (eds) (2004). *Critical pedagogies and language learning*. Cambridge: Cambridge University Press.

Nystrand, M., & Duffy, J. (2003). *Towards a rhetoric of everyday life: New directions in research on writing, text, and discourse*. Madison, WI: University of Wisconsin Press.

O'Hara-Devereaux, M., & Johansen, R. (1994). *Globalwork: Bridging distance, culture and time*. San Francisco: Jossey-Bass.

Oakes, J., & Lipton, M. (1999). *Teaching to change the world*. Boston, MA: McGraw-Hill.

Ong, A. (1997). Chinese modernities: Narratives of nation and of capitalism. In A. Ong & D. Nonini (eds), *Ungrounded empires: The cultural politics of modern Chinese transnationalism* (pp. 171–201). New York: Routledge.

Ong, A. (1999). *Flexible citizenship: The cultural logics of transnationality*. Durham & London: Duke University Press.

Ormrod, J. E. (2005). *Educational psychology: Developing learners* (5th edn). New Jersey: Prentice-Hall.

Orr, J. (1986). Narratives at work: Story telling as cooperative diagnostic activity. *ACM Conference on Computer Supported Cooperative Work*. Texas, USA.

Ortner, S. (2003, April), East brain, west brain. *The New York Times*. Retrieved 15 August 2006, from http://query.nytimes. com/gst/fullpage.html?res= 9804E5DA163BF933A15757C0A9659C8B63

Ouellett, M. L. (ed., 2005). *Teaching inclusively: Resources for course, department and institutional change in higher education.* Stillwater, OK: New Forums Press.

Palfreyman, D. (2005). Othering in an English language program. *TESOL Quarterly, 39*(2), 211–33.

Pang, N. S. K. (1999). The plain truth is out there. In A. Holbrook, & S. Johnson (eds), *Supervision of postgraduate research in education* (pp. 157–61). Coldstream, Victoria: AARE.

Parekh, B. (1986). The concept of multicultural education. In S. Modgil, G. K. Verma, K. Mallick, & C. Modgil (eds), *Multicultural education: The interminable debate* (pp. 19–31). Philadelphia: Falmer.

Pearson, M., & Brew, A. (2002). Research training and supervision development. *Studies in Higher Education, 27*(2), 135–50.

Pennycook, A. (1995). English in the world/ the world in English. In J. Tollefson (ed.), *Power and inequality in language education* (pp. 34–58). Cambridge: Cambridge University Press.

Peters, J. (1991). Strategies for reflective practice. In R. Brockett (ed.), *Professional development for educators of adults* (pp. 89–96). San Francisco: Jossey-Bass.

Pettigrew, T. F. (1998). Intergroup contact theory. *Annual Review of Psychology, 49*, 65–85.

Pihama, L., & Jenkins, K. (2001). Mātauranga wāhine: Teaching Māori women's knowledge alongside feminism. *Feminism & Psychology, 11*(3), 293–303.

Pinches, M. (1999). Cultural relations, class and the new rich of Asia. In M. Pinches (ed.), *Culture and privilege in capitalist Asia* (pp. 1–55). London & New York: Routledge.

Pintrich, P. R., Smith, D. A. F., Garcia, T., & McKeachie, W. J. (1991). *A manual for the use of motivated strategies for learning questionnaire (MSLQ).* Ann Arbor, MI: National Center for Research to Improve Postsecondary Teaching and Learning, University of Michigan.

Pittaway, E., Ferguson, B., & Breen, C. (1998). Worth more than gold: The unexpected benefits associated with internationalisation of tertiary education. In D. Davis & A. Olsen (eds), *Outcomes of international education: Research findings* (pp. 61–71). Canberra: IDP Education Australia.

Pollock, D., & Van Reken, R. (1999). *Third culture kids: The experience of growing up among worlds.* London: Nicholas Brearley.

Pólya, G. (1945). *How to solve it.* Princeton, NJ: Princeton University Press.

Pratt, M. (1992). *Imperial eyes: Travel writing and transculturation.* London & New York: Routledge.

Price, G. E. (1983). Diagnosing learning styles. In R. M. Smith (ed.), *Helping adults learn how to learn* (pp. 49–55). San Francisco: Jossey-Bass.

Prosser, M., & Trigwell, K. (1999). *Understanding learning and teaching: The experience of higher education.* Buckingham, UK: Open University Press.

Raelin, J. (1997). A model of work-based learning. *Organization Science, 8*(6), 563–78.

Ramsden, P. (1988). Studying learning: Improving teaching. In P. Ramsden (ed.), *Improving learning: New perspectives* (pp. 13–31). London: Kogan.

Reid, A. (1988). *Southeast Asia in the age of commerce, 1450–1680* (Vol.1). New Haven: Yale University Press.

Richards, J. C. (ed.). (2002). *Methodology in language teaching: An anthology of current practice.* Cambridge: Cambridge University Press.

Richardson, J. T. E. (1994). Cultural specificity of approaches to studying in higher education: A literature survey. *Higher Education, 27*, 449–68.

Richlin, L. (2001). Scholarly teaching and the scholarship of teaching. In C. Kreber (ed.) *Scholarship revisited: Perspectives on the scholarship of teaching* (pp. 57–68). San Francisco: Jossey-Bass.

Roman, L. (1993). White is a color! White defensiveness, postmodernism, and antiracist pedagogy. In C. McCarthy, & W. Crichlow (eds), *Race, identity, and representation in education* (pp. 71–88). New York: Routledge.

Roman, L. (1997). Denying (White) racial privilege: Redemption discourses and the uses of fantasy. In M. Fine, L. Weis, L. C. Powell, & L. M. Wong (eds), *Off white: Readings on race, power and society* (pp. 270–82). New York: Routledge.

Rose, N. (1996). Identity, genealogy, history. In S. Hall & P. Du Gay (eds), *Questions of cultural identity* (pp. 128–50). London: Sage.

Roux, J. E. (2002). Effective educators are culturally competent communicators. *Intercultural Education, 13*(1), 37–48.

Ryan, G. W., & Bernard, H. R. (2000). Data management and analysis methods. In N. K. Denzin & Y. S. Lincoln (eds), *Handbook of qualitative research* (2nd edn) (pp. 769–802). Thousand Oaks, CA: Sage.

Ryan, Y., & Zuber-Skerritt, O. (1999). Supervising non-English speaking background students in the globalised university. In Y. Ryan & O. Zuber-Skerritt (eds), *Supervising postgraduates from non-English speaking backgrounds* (pp. 1–11). Buckingham: SRHE & Open University Press.

Salmond, A. (1997). *Between worlds: Early exchanges between Māori and Europeans 1773–1815*. Auckland, New Zealand: Penguin.

Samuelowicz, K., & Bain, J. (2001). Revisiting academics' beliefs about teaching and learning. *Higher Education, 41*, 299–325.

Sanderson, G. (2002). Living with the other: Non-Western international students at Flinders University. Paper presented at the Internationalizing Education in the Asia-Pacific Region: Critical Reflections, Critical Times. *Proceedings of the 30th Annual Conference of the Australian and New Zealand Comparative and International Education Society*.

Saner, R., & Yiu, L. (1994). European and Asian resistance to the use of the American case method in management training: Possible cultural and systemic incongruencies. *International Journal of Human Resource Management, 5*(4), 953–76.

Schön, D. A. (ed.) (1990). *The reflective turn: Case studies in and on educational practice*. New York: Teachers College Press.

Schuetze, U. (2005a). Creativity in second language dialogue. *Proceedings of the Third Annual Hawaii International Conference on Arts and Humanities*. Honolulu, HI.

Schuetze, U. (2005b). Imagine a second language classroom 7,772 kilometres wide. *Proceedings of the Third International Conference on Imagination and Education*. Vancouver, Canada.

Sebeok, T. A., & Danesi, M. (2000). *The forms of meaning*. Berlin: Mouton de Gruyter.

Senge, P. (1990). *The fifth discipline: The art & practice of the learning organization*. New York: Doubleday.

Sikes, P., & Goodson, I. (2003). Living research: Thoughts on educational research as moral practice. In P. Sikes, J. Nixon, & W. Carr (eds), *The moral foundations of educational research: Knowledge, inquiry and values* (pp. 211–33). Maidenhead: Open University Press.

Simmons, L. C., & Munch, J. M. (1996). Is relationship marketing culturally bound: A look at Guanxi in China. *Advances in Consumer Research, 23,* 92–6.

Singh, P. (2004). Offshore Australian higher education: A case study of pedagogic work in Jakarta, Indonesia. In A. Hickling-Hudson, J. Matthews, & A. Woods (eds), *Disrupting preconceptions: Postcolonialism and education* (pp. 211–33). Flaxton: PostPressed.

Singh, P., & Doherty, C. (2004). Global cultural flows and pedagogic dilemmas: Teaching in the global university contact zone. *TESOL Quarterly, 38*(1), 9–42.

Slavin, R. E. (1995). *Cooperative learning: Theory, research and practice* (2nd edn). Boston, MA: Allyn & Bacon.

Smart, D., Volet, E. E., & Ang, G. (2000). *Fostering social cohesion in universities: Bridging the cultural divide.* Canberra: Australian Education International.

Smith, B. (2001). (Re)Framing research higher degree supervision as pedagogy. In A. Bartlett, & G. Mercer (eds), *Postgraduate research supervision: Transforming (R)Elations* (pp. 25–41). New York: Peter Lang.

Smith, L. (2006). Teachers' conceptions of teaching at a Gulf university: A starting point for revising a teacher development program. *Learning and Teaching in Higher Education: Gulf Perspectives, 3*(1) Retrieved 24 April 2006, from www.zu.ac.ae/lthe/vol3no1/lthe03_01_02.html

Smith, R. M. (1982). *Learning how to learn: Applied theory for adults.* Chicago: Follett Publishing.

Smith, R. M. (2001). Approaches to study of three Chinese National Groups. *British Journal of Educational Psychology, 71,* 429–441.

Southern Poverty Law Center (2006a). *Mix it up.* Retrieved 10 October 2006 from http://www.tolerance.org/teens/about.jsp

Southern Poverty Law Center (2006b). *Mix it up online survey.* Retrieved 10 October 2006 from http://www.tolerance.org/pdf/mixitup_online_survey_06.pdf

Spindler, G. (ed.). (1997). *Education and cultural process.* Prospect Heights, IL: Waveland Press.

Spivak, G. C. (1990). *The post-colonial critic: Interviews, strategies, dialogues.* New York: Routledge.

Srivastava, A. (1997). Anti-racism inside and outside the classroom. In L. Roman, & L. Eyre (eds), *Dangerous territories: Struggles for difference and equality in education* (pp. 119–30). New York: Routledge.

Statistics New Zealand (2005). *Demographic trends (2005) reference report.* Wellington, New Zealand: Statistics New Zealand.

Sterman, P. (2005, 21 July). Lean and mean profit machines: UC Irvine extension teaches corporations how to compete, *OC Metro,* p. 1.

Stuart-Fox, M. (2003). *Short history of China and Southeast Asia: Tribute, trade and influence.* Sydney: Allen and Unwin.

Tait, H., Entwistle, N. J., & McCune, V. (1998). Assist: A re-conceptualisation of the approaches to studying inventory. In C. Rust (ed.), *Improving students as learners* (pp. 262–71). Oxford: Oxford Centre for Staff and Learning Development.

Tajfel, H. (1981). *Human groups and social categories.* Cambridge: Cambridge University Press.

Tajfel, H., & Turner, J. C. (1979). An interactive theory of intergroup conflict. In W. G. Austin & S. Worchel (eds), The social psychology of intergroup relations (pp. 33–47). Monterrey, CA: Brooks-Cole.

Tajfel. H. (ed.) (1978). *Differentiation between social groups.* London: Academic Press.

Teasdale, G. R., & Ma Rhea, Z. (eds). 2000. *Local knowledge and wisdom in higher education.* Oxford: Pergamon.

The University of Western Australia. (1999). A management plan for internationalisation. Retrieved 27 August 2003, from http:// www.international.uwa. edu.au/staff/internal/manage.htm

Thrift, N. (1997). The rise of soft capitalism. In A. Herod, S. Roberts & G. Toal (eds), *An unruly world? Globalisation and space* (pp. 25–71). London: Routledge.

Todd, S. (2003). *Learning from the Other: Levinas, psychoanalysis and ethical possibilities in education.* New York: State University of New York Press.

Touraine, A. (1997). *Pourrons-nous vivre ensemble? Egaux et différents.* Paris: Fayard.

Tourism British Columbia (2003). *Video.* Retrieved 8 August 2003, from www. hellobc.com

Tourism Office (2003). *Der Schwarzwald: eine virtuelle Reise.* Freiburg: Tourism Office.

Traill, C. P. (1836). *The backwoods of Canada* [microform]. Vancouver: University of British Columbia.

Triandis, H. C. (1995). *Individualism & collectivism.* Boulder, CO: Westview Press.

Tripp, D. (1993). *Critical incidents in teaching: Developing professional judgment.* New York: Routledge.

Trompenaars, F., & Hampden-Turner, C. (1997). *Riding the waves of culture: Understanding cultural diversity in business.* London: Nicholas Brearley.

Trotman, C. J. (ed.) (2002). *Multiculturalism: Roots and realities.* Indianapolis: Indiana University Press.

Trowler, P., & Cooper, A. (2002). Teaching and learning regimes: Implicit theories and recurrent practices in the enhancement of teaching and learning through educational development programmes. *Higher Education Research and Development, 21*(3), 221–40.

Tsang, E. W. K. (1998). Can Guanxi be a source of sustained competitive advantage for doing business in China? *Academy of Management Executive, 12*(3), 64–73.

Turner, T. (1994). Anthropology and multiculturalism: What is anthropology that multiculturalists should be mindful of it? In D. T. Goldberg (ed.), *Multiculturalism: A critical reader* (pp. 406–25). Oxford: Blackwell.

UAE Ministry for Higher Education and Scientific Research (2006). *The Commission for Academic Accreditation.* Retrieved 5 June 2006, from www.uae.gov.ae/mohe/department_caa.html

UNESCO (2006). *Technology and Learning: Definitions.* Retrieved 2 October 2006, from www.unesco.org/education/educprog/lwf/doc/portfolio/definitions.htm

University Enrolment (2005). *The Daily.* Retrieved 15 August 2006, from www.statcan.ca/Daily/English/051011/d051011b.htm

Urry, J. (2000). *Sociology beyond societies: Mobilities for the twenty-first century.* London: Routledge.

Venables, E., Ahjum, S., & De Reuck, J. (2001). The remembrance of things past: Memory and migration as tropes in the construction of postgraduate subjectivities. In A. Bartlett & G. Mercer (eds), *Postgraduate research supervision: Transforming (R)Elations* (pp. 233–46). New York: Peter Lang.

Vermunt, J. D., & Van Rijswijck, F. A. (1987). *Inventaris leerstijlen voor het Hoger Onderwijs* [Inventory of learning styles for higher education]. Tilburg, The Netherlands: Katholieke Universiteit Brabant.

Volet, S. E., Renshaw, P. D., & Tietzel, K. (1994). A short-term longitudinal investigation of cross-cultural differences using Biggs' SPQ Questionnaire, *British Journal of Educational Psychology, 64*, 301–18.

Vygotsky, L. S. (1962). *Thought and language* (A. Kozulin, Trans.). Cambridge: MIT Press, Massachusetts Institute of Technology.

Vygotsky, L. S. (1978). *Mind in society: The development of higher psychological processes* (M. Cole, Trans.). Cambridge: Harvard University Press.

Wang, J., Wang, G. G., Ruona, W. A., & Rojewski, J. W. (2005). Confucian values and the implications for international HRD. *Human Resource Development International, 8*(3), 311–26.

Watkins, D., & Biggs, J. (2001). *Teaching the Chinese learner: Psychological and pedagogical perspectives*. Melbourne: Australian Council for Educational Research.

Watkins, D. A., & Biggs, J. (eds) (1996). *The Chinese learner: Cultural, psychological and contextual influences*. Hong Kong: Comparative Education Research Centre.

Watkins, D., & Reghi, M. (1991). The Asian-learner-as-a-rote-learner stereotype: Myth or reality, *Educational Psychology, 11*(1), 21–35.

Watzlawick, P. (ed.) (1981). *Die Erfundene Wirklichkeit*. Berlin: R. Piper and Company.

Weber, S. (2003). A framework for teaching and learning 'intercultural competence'. In G. Alred, M. Byram, & M. Fleming (eds), *Intercultural experience and education* (pp. 196–212). Clevedon: Multilingual Matters.

Weinert, A. B. (2004). *Organisations- und personalpsychologie* (5th edn). Weinheim, Basel: Beltz.

Westdeutscher Rundfunk (1995). Waldsterben in Deutschland. Retrieved 8 August 2003, from www.planet-wissen.de

Whitten, P. & Hunter, D. E. K. (1992). *Anthropology: Contemporary Perspectives*. London: Longman.

Williams, R. M., Jr. (1947). *The reduction of intergroup tensions*. New York: Social Science Research Council.

Willis, P. (2001). *The ethnographic imagination*. Malden, MA: Polity.

Wisker, G., Robinson, G., Trafford, V., Warnes, M., & Creighton, E. (2003). From supervisory dialogues to successful Ph.D.s: Strategies supporting and enabling the learning conversations of staff and students at postgraduate level. *Teaching in Higher Education, 8*(3), 383–97.

Wright, S. (ed.) (1994). *Anthropology of organizations*. London: Routledge.

Wu, S. (2002). Filling the pot or lighting the fire? Cultural variations in conceptions of pedagogy. Cultural variations in conceptions of pedagogy. *Teaching in Higher Education, 7*(4), 387–95.

Yang, R. (2002). University internationalisation: Its meanings, rationales and implications. *Intercultural Education, 13*(1), 81–95.

Yau, O. H. M., McFetridge, P. R., Chow, R. M. P., Lee, J. S. Y., Leo, Y. M., Sin, Y., & Tse, A. C. B. (2000). Is relationship marketing for everyone? *European Journal of Marketing*, *34*(9/10), 1111–27.

Ziegahn, L. (2005). Critical reflection on cultural difference in the computer conference. *Adult Education Quarterly, 56* (1), 39–64.

Index